THE
BORDERLINE
PERSONALITY
DISORDER
WORKBOOK

THE BORDERLINE PERSONALITY DISORDER WORKBOOK

Understanding Your Emotions, Managing Your Moods, and Forming Healthy Relationships

Déborah Ducasse, MD
Véronique Brand-Arpon, MA

TRANSLATED BY ALISON DUNCAN

Johns Hopkins University Press
Baltimore

Note to the Reader: This book is not meant to substitute for medical care, and treatment should not be based solely on its contents. Instead, treatment must be developed in a dialogue between the individual and his or her physician. The book has been written to help with that dialogue.

Originally published as *Borderline: cahier pratique de thérapie à domicile*, © Odile Jacob, 2017

Translation copyright © 2021 Johns Hopkins University Press
All rights reserved. Published 2021
Printed in the United States of America on acid-free paper
2 4 6 8 9 7 5 3 1

Johns Hopkins University Press
2715 North Charles Street
Baltimore, Maryland 21218-4363
www.press.jhu.edu

Library of Congress Cataloging-in-Publication Data
Names: Ducasse, Déborah, 1985– author. | Brand-Arpon, Véronique, 1972– author.
Title: The borderline personality disorder workbook : understanding your emotions, managing your moods, and forming healthy relationships /
Déborah Ducasse, MD, Véronique Brand-Arpon, MA ; translated by Alison Duncan.
Description: Baltimore : Johns Hopkins University Press, 2021. | Series: A Johns Hopkins Press health book | "Originally published as Borderline: cahier pratique de thérapie à domicile"—Verso. | Includes bibliographical references.
Identifiers: LCCN 2020023322 | ISBN 9781421440323 (paperback) | ISBN 9781421440330 (ebook)
Subjects: LCSH: Borderline personality disorder. | Borderline personality disorder—Treatment.
Classification: LCC RC569.5.B67 D83 2021 | DDC 616.85/852—dc23
LC record available at https://lccn.loc.gov/2020023322

A catalog record for this book is available from the British Library.

Special discounts are available for bulk purchases of this book.
For more information, please contact Special Sales at specialsales@jh.edu.

Johns Hopkins University Press uses environmentally friendly book materials, including recycled text paper that is composed of at least 30 percent post-consumer waste, whenever possible.

CONTENTS

THE
BORDERLINE PERSONALITY DISORDER
WORKBOOK

PROLOGUE

- Are you hypersensitive? Would you describe yourself as an emotional sponge?
- Does the slightest interaction trigger very intense emotions for you? Do you have trouble regulating your emotions?
- Do you have difficulty channeling your anger?
- Do you feel a deep sense of emptiness?
- Are interpersonal relationships a source of suffering in your life?
- Are you afraid of being abandoned? Do you often believe that the people you're attached to don't love you anymore, are abandoning you, are leaving you, or are pulling away from you?
- Do you look for strong, extremely close relationships? Do you get attached very quickly, intensely, and are often disappointed?
- Are you someone who thinks in absolute terms? Do you think in terms of all or nothing, black or white?
- Are you prone to impulsive behavior, such as episodes of bulimia, compulsive shopping, substance abuse, or cutting?
- Do you tend to act on an impulse and regret it afterward? Do you often speak before you think?
- Do you often think that your life isn't worth living with so much suffering?

Difficulties regulating your emotions, difficulties in interpersonal relationships, impulsivity: these are the main characteristics of borderline personality disorder. Borderline personality disorder, or BPD, is very common. For every one hundred people, it's estimated that four suffer from this disorder in the general population and up to twenty within psychiatric wards. This disorder is associated with considerable existential suffering. In addition, individuals with BPD have an increased risk of suffering from depression, anxiety, addiction, or eating disorders at some point in their lives. This disorder is the one most often associated with the onset of suicidal thoughts and behaviors, which are strategies of last resort to avoid feelings of suffering.

BPD is quite a complex disorder, and every person's experience of it is unique. It's important to remember not to self-diagnose and to work with a professional therapist. A therapist who is qualified to evaluate you can help you come up with an action plan to tackle mood regulation, impulsivity, and forming better personal and professional relationships. Sometimes, your therapist may recommend that you also visit with a physician for medication or other interventions that can help with certain problems you may be experiencing, such as sleeplessness or drinking too much. As part of your overall health, it's important for you to meet regularly with a primary care physician, family physician, or other health care practitioner to discuss your physical and mental health.

Borderline personality disorder is not an easy diagnosis to live with. You need to work with a therapist and others to come up with a plan to help you better understand and manage your moods and make efforts to form relationships with a solid foundation. This book is designed to be used along with therapy to help you answer these two questions:

1. What are the most effective strategies for regulating your emotions, reducing your impulsivity, and being effective in interpersonal relationships?
2. How can you have a life that's meaningful for you?

This workbook represents the first practical guide to integrate the central elements of three validated therapies: dialectical behavior therapy, acceptance and commitment therapy, and positive psychology. Furthermore, the workbook is based on our daily clinical practice at a university hospital.

Using this book, you can follow a step-by-step therapeutic program from home aimed at overcoming the problems that you face on a daily basis. It's not designed to replace conventional care, however. And if you're experiencing significant distress, it's important to remember to reach out to professionals either by calling 911 or by going to the nearest emergency department or clinic.

Are you ready for change? Then let's set off,
together, toward the life you really want to live.

HOW TO USE THIS BOOK

A habit is a behavior that is successively repeated.
Learn new strategies. Put them into practice. Repeat.
And you will end up with new habits that will
literally change your life.

Each chapter teaches specific skills to address the various difficulties encountered when you have a diagnosis of borderline personality disorder. Exercises provided throughout the book are designed to help you completely integrate the new skills that you're learning. If you want significant changes in your life, then take the time to do these exercises.

It's best to follow the order of the chapters: they have been carefully designed so that you progressively and coherently acquire new skills. We recommend that you read a maximum of one chapter per week because the exercises for assimilating the skills in each chapter are designed to be done over the course of one week.

Divided into chapters that progressively teach you specific skills.

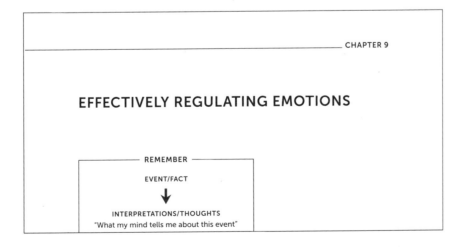

limic episodes. She has even cut herself to relieve the extreme emotional stress. The feeling of shame is often very strong in these situations, followed by anger. Then all the emotions get mixed together. On reflection, Candace believes that her discontent has been with her from a young age.

▷ CANDACE *I've always thought that my sister Jennifer did things better than me. She was a model daughter and a source of so much pride for my parents. I had the feeling that they only had eyes for her. I have to say that Jennifer was very well behaved and quiet, whereas I was rather agitated, full of energy, and loud. Simply put: I bothered them. And all of this made me angry, terribly angry, because as I saw it, my parents didn't hear my problems, didn't understand me and, quite simply, didn't accept me as I was. So, at times, I tried to be as good as Jennifer, but it took such an effort that sometimes it was stronger than me, and I would crack and totally explode without understanding why.*

Candace is your alter ego. This fictional person will be your guide and model throughout the book.

Candace's name in gray introduced by an arrow indicates her commentary.

What are the emotions that bother you the most in your life?

➤ ME _____

Think back to yesterday: what feelings or emotions prevented you from doing what you wanted to do?

Did these feelings change the way you behaved toward yourself or with others?

➤ ME _____

Your Relationships
Now let's talk about relationships—an area that's an equally significant source of suffering for people with borderline personality disorder.

	YES	NO
Are you often afraid that the people you care about will leave you?	☐	☐

Blank lines introduced by an arrow?

It's your turn!

CHAPTER 1

WHICH DIRECTION DO YOU WANT TO GO?

WHAT DO YOU REALLY WANT TO DO WITH YOUR LIFE?

"Happiness is not at the top of the mountain but in how to climb."
—CONFUCIUS

IMAGINE . . .

A person comes toward you, exhausted, full of disappointment, explaining to you that she's been walking for years without successfully finding her way to the place where she'd like to go.

"Where do you want to go?" you ask her.

Much to your surprise, she responds, "I don't know."

A surprising answer? And yet . . .

Most of us are like this person. We're dissatisfied with the life we're living, but we don't know *which* life we want to live or what is *really* important to us. But how can we have the life we want when we don't know what life we want? How can we seize opportunities when we don't know what an opportunity for us is?

Brownie Ware, an Australian nurse, worked in a palliative care unit. She spent several years interviewing people nearing end of life about their biggest regrets. And do you know what came up most often? Ninety-five percent of them said, "I regret not having lived life on my own terms, according to what is really important to me."

By having this book in your hands, you've already taken a step in the direction of a life true to your expectations, to what holds meaning and importance for you. It's the beginning of change. We'll go on this journey toward a new life together: you, us, and Candace.

LET'S INTRODUCE CANDACE

Candace is a 30-year-old young woman of average height with dark hair and big eyes. She's a nurse in the pediatric unit of a hospital, and she's asking for help to learn how to manage her emotions.

"I can't cope anymore. I get worked up about the smallest thing—everything is extreme for me. It's exhausting," she says.

According to Candace, her emotions are always very intense, and they fluctuate often over the course of a day; she feels like she doesn't have any control over her feelings. In the morning, she tends to feel a heightened level of emotional stress that gets worse as the day goes on, especially when she starts interacting with people.

"Relationships have always been difficult for me, and I've been so disappointed by them."

Candace describes herself as someone who thinks in absolute terms—all or nothing, black or white. She often throws herself into relationships quickly and passionately, gives a lot of herself, and expects these relationships to be strong and extremely close.

But unfortunately, after having a wonderful time for a certain period, the other person disappoints Candace for not being as invested in the relationship as she is. Then the relationship usually ends, or continues with many ups and downs. Relationships are a true source of suffering for Candace; she devotes a great deal of time and energy to them (thinking about them often and dwelling on the details). Close relationships are so significant for Candace that the fear that they'll end has become just as significant. Fear of abandonment sometimes leads Candace to do things that she feels ashamed of afterward, that lower her self-esteem.

> "I can't cope anymore. I get worked up about the smallest thing—everything is extreme for me. It's exhausting." —CANDACE

As Candace explains, when she sends a text message to a friend or to her boyfriend, if she doesn't get a quick reply, worst-case scenarios torment her: "What did I do to make them not respond to me? Maybe they don't want me anymore. I care more about them than they do about me . . ." This leads her to send more text messages to make sure of the relationship's continuity. Relief only comes when Candace (finally) receives the long-awaited reply to her text message.

Romantic relationships are characterized by explosive conflicts. Anger can push Candace to punch walls or throw objects on the ground. She explains that she often tends to test the limits of relationships. "I want to see how much he loves me, how confident I can be in the fact that he'll stay with me."

And when her boyfriend is about to leave it all behind, Candace sometimes finds herself begging him not to leave her, even threatening to commit suicide. In that case, the pain is so strong it can feel unbearable.

Candace has regularly had suicidal thoughts during her life, especially in times of distress triggered by relationships. In a crisis, Candace can do impulsive things, such as consume large amounts of alcohol or have bulimic episodes. She has even cut herself to relieve the extreme emotional stress. The feeling of shame is often very strong in these situations, followed by anger. Then all the emotions get mixed together. On reflection, Candace believes that her discontent has been with her from a young age.

▷ CANDACE *I've always thought that my sister Jennifer did things better than me. She was a model daughter and a source of so much pride for my parents. I had the feeling that they only had eyes for her. I have to say that Jennifer was very well behaved and quiet, whereas I was rather agitated, full of energy, and loud. Simply put: I bothered them. And all of this made me angry, terribly angry, because as I saw it, my parents didn't hear my problems, didn't understand me and, quite simply, didn't accept me as I was. So, at times, I tried to be as good as Jennifer, but it took such an effort that sometimes it was stronger than me, and I would crack and totally explode without understanding why.*

I thought that the whole world was against me. My sister first of all. I felt more and more jealous of her because it seemed to me that she monopolized all my parents' love by being so perfect. Then my mother. She sent mixed messages by going from moments when she seemed to understand me and love me sincerely to others when all that mattered to her was her husband's approval and maintaining the appearance of a perfect family. Sometimes my mom demanded perfect behavior from me: a hard-working student, a calm and well-behaved daughter who must not, through my impulsive behavior, disturb the illusion of one big happy family. And above all, I had a strong feeling that my father didn't treat me fairly because it seemed to me that no matter how hard I tried, my efforts were doomed to fail. I was never good enough for him. Even so, I never stopped trying, honestly believing that my worth depended more on my results than on who I was as a person.

That's how I became extremely competitive in soccer. My commitment to this sport relieved the pressure I felt in my family, while also helping me to increase my worth in the eyes of my teammates and coaches, whose admiration felt good. It compensated a bit for my father's demanding and constantly dissatisfied regard. I did as well as I could in school, and my mother, implicitly supporting my father's demands, made me do long hours of homework at night and on weekends. When I made mistakes on school assignments, I was usually punished. I remember that, despite all these efforts, I never felt acknowledged and loved as I would've liked by my father. I remember one day when I came home feeling proud of myself for getting a 90 on an essay, telling myself that this time, maybe, he would finally have that admiring and acknowledging look for which I had waited so long. Unfortunately, his response was to ask me who had gotten a better grade than me! At that moment I realized that however hard I tried, I would never be recognized and loved for who I was. This discovery saddened me as it reinforced the idea that others would probably always be entitled to more attention from my dad—a smart and successful lawyer.

66 I thought that the whole world was against me. 99   —CANDACE

When I was about 13, my uncle on my father's side began to sexually molest me. This went on for several years. And I had no one to talk to about it. I had both an intense fear of my uncle and perhaps an even greater fear of being responsible for my family breaking apart if the abuse came to light. That's when I began restricting calories (interspersed with episodes of bulimia), hoping that if I lost my feminine figure, my uncle would stop molesting me. But it didn't work.

It might have been then that I began to hang out with other kids like me who were struggling to find their place and feel appreciated, recognized, and accepted by those close to them. With them, I felt like I was finally accepted without having to pretend to be what others expected of me. This freedom felt good, and it allowed me to assert myself more. So I started to wear more colorful, "wild" clothes, changed my hair color according to my moods, and got tattoos and piercings that were discreet at first and then a little more visible, including a piercing in my lower lip.

This was the beginning of important friendships for me and the feeling that I'd found an understanding and loving family on my own. While some of these friendships were unstable and resulted in painful breakups, others are still anchors for me today. I know I can count on Mia and Logan, whom I've known since I was 15, at any time for anything. My romantic relationships have been passionate and chaotic, and often very complicated. At home, there were lots of fights and frequent angry outbursts, and it was still hard to find a place to belong in my family.

Smoking and vaping pot helped a bit to distance myself from my life. And I went from using only in social situations, at parties with my friends, to smoking daily. It allowed me to focus on my studies (or so I thought at the time). I started studying to become a nurse, having passed the entrance exam the same year that I graduated from high school. Pot also allowed me to fall asleep and escape the nights when, as soon as I found myself alone, I would have these obsessive thoughts and sometimes gut-wrenching emotions. My behavior was also gradually escalating and becoming high-risk, with one-night stands and sometimes unprotected sex, just to feel alive, as if I existed for someone. I would drink until I passed out or didn't remember how the evening ended.

As you are doing by reading this book, Candace decided to take her life into her own hands and move toward a life that's worth living. And we (Déborah and Véronique) will both guide you, throughout this therapy, in that direction.

To start with, we'll help you *identify* what is *important to you in life.* We'll explore what you really want, who you want to be, what kind of relationships you want to build, and what you want to do in your life to make it richer, more fulfilling, and meaningful.

Life is short; we all have just a limited time on this earth. But during this short time, we have an unlimited choice of ways to spend it. It's these choices that define our lives. So that's what we're going to explore now.

> *The question is: what do I really want to do right now with my life?*

THE DIFFERENCE BETWEEN VALUES AND GOALS

First of all, let's clarify the difference between values and goals.[1]

What Is a Value?
Values represent our deepest desires. They are personal guides that tell us how we want to interact with the world and ourselves. Therefore, this word is not meant in the moral sense of the term but rather as the pos-

sibility of embodying the person we really want to be, of being able to develop strengths or qualities that are meaningful for us.

Values = desired qualities for ongoing actions

A value is something accessible in the present moment. In every moment of our lives, we can choose to embody, or ignore, our values. So, for example, we can develop the value of being a conscientious worker even if we don't currently have a job. This value can be embodied in various areas of life, such as in daily household chores, in school or educational courses, or in seeking personal development that requires skills training.

EXAMPLES OF VALUES

"Do (= action) . . . by being (= value)"
With love, with goodwill, with compassion, with closeness, with friendliness, with curiosity, with beauty, with gratitude, with humor, with perseverance, with humanity

With open-mindedness
In a spirit of cooperation, in celebration, in being passionate, in having self-confidence, being helpful, friendly, dependable, independent, adventurous

Being kind
Being competitive, playful, courageous, being present in the moment, pushing yourself beyond your limits, being nonjudgmental, being elegant, flexible, by encouraging others

Being enthusiastic
Being uninhibited, being resourceful, authentic, warm, connected, creative, interacting, sharing, being moral, empathetic, having integrity, being reliable, generous

Being honest
Being independent, innovative, fair, loyal, nurturing, organized, productive, respectful, sincere, tolerant, helpful

Being willing . . .

What Is a Goal?

A goal is very different from a value. It's something that can be achieved. If we make a comparison with the value of being a "conscientious worker," then an example of a goal could be getting a sought-after job. Once we get the job, we'll cross the goal off the list and probably come up with a new goal. For this reason, people with lives centered exclusively around goals often feel a lot of frustration. Why? Because they're always looking into the future in the illusory hope that achieving the next goal will finally bring them lasting happiness.

From Value to Goal

A life centered around values, however, is not a life without goals. Goals exist, but despite that, the emphasis is first and foremost on values: in other words, in how goals are achieved rather than on the outcome alone. Such an approach is a daily source of fulfillment and satisfaction because these feelings are not as dependent on achieving the goal. I can be deeply satisfied with the way I act regardless of outside events that I can't control.

Therefore, we can't be sure of getting the coveted job, but we can act at any time according to the value of being conscientious and hardworking. A goal always refers to the future—once achieved, it's no longer a goal—whereas a value concerns the present, and this makes it very powerful.

Values are like *directions* that we want to follow throughout our lives, while *goals* are things that we want to accomplish or *achieve*.

The Compass Metaphor

A compass is an instrument that tells the direction and allows you to stay on a defined path. Values do the same for the journey of life. Therefore, when you act according to your values, it's a little like you're orienting yourself toward the east. No matter how far you travel, there will always be more ahead of you. Goals are like the landscapes, mountains, and landmarks that you want to see during your journey to the east.

Therefore, as of this moment, you can choose to act in a way that embodies what is important to you, even if you've neglected that value for years. As the saying goes, today is the first day of the rest of your life.

You have the opportunity to embody the life you really want from now on.

PRACTICAL APPLICATION _____

Complete the tables below, summarizing the significant areas of your life as of this moment. This will allow you to precisely identify what is important to you, in *your* life. Defining those areas that are important to you will allow you to explore how you would like to engage with them (that is, your values). Engaging with these people and activities will then fuel your ability to embody who you are deep down, develop your inner potential, and thus give meaning to your life. Entering the world with a specific kind of intention will become your inner compass, accessible to you at all times, regardless of which inner reality manifests itself. This will contribute to significant inner stability.

Relationships

	CANDACE	ME
Who is important to you in life? *(Write down your name, then the names of the people with whom you have a significant relationship and/or a relationship that takes up space in your life, whether the relationship is an easy or difficult one.)*	– Candace – Dad – Mom – Chris – Logan – Melanie – Jennifer – Mia – Olivia – my dog, Sparkie	

If anything were possible, if you became the person that you really want to be, deep down in your heart, then for each of these relationships:

- What would it look like?
- How would you like to behave in a sustainable way?
- What qualities or strengths would you embody?
- How would you behave toward yourself, to take care of yourself in these relationships?

— Being considerate, attentive

— Being warm

— Being reliable

— Sharing

— Developing intimacy

— Being loving

— Acting with a sense of humor

Personal Development and Health

	CANDACE	ME
· What really matters to you in this area of life? · What do you enjoy doing? · What did you enjoy doing before struggling with suffering?	— Reading about psychology — Art, painting — Sports: dancing — Spirituality — My physical appearance	
· What is meaningful for you in doing these activities? · What qualities or strengths would you like to embody? · How would you like to behave in a sustainable way?	— Pushing myself beyond my limits — Being creative — Being physically active — Being connected to something greater than myself — Improving myself — Taking care of my body — Developing my faith	

Leisure and Entertainment

	CANDACE	ME
• What really matters to you in this area of life? • What do you enjoy doing? • What did you enjoy doing before struggling with suffering?	– Going to the movies – Cooking – Dancing – Playing board games – Reading graphic novels – Going on nature walks – Photography	
• What is meaningful for you in doing this? • What qualities or strengths would you like to embody? • How would you like to behave in a sustainable way?	– Being uninhibited – Living each moment to its fullest – Laughing – Spending time with the people I love – Creating – Having fun	

Learning and Work

	CANDACE	ME
• What really matters to you in this area of life? • What do you enjoy doing? • What did you enjoy doing before struggling with suffering?	– My job: nurse – Watching instructional videos on YouTube – Art history	
• What is meaningful for you in doing this? • What qualities or strengths would you like to embody? • How would you like to behave in a sustainable way?	– Being helpful – Working as a team – Caring for others – Helping – Educating myself – Being inspired	

Other Useful Questions

	CANDACE	ME
What can you spend hours doing without realizing time has passed?	– Dancing – Painting – Reading	
What is meaningful for you in all of this?	– Living each moment to its fullest – Creating – Escaping – Broadening my mind	
What did you get up for this morning? *(Begin your answer to this question with "To . . ." [which orients you toward your motivations] rather than with "Because . . ." [which orients you toward a justification].)*	– To take out my dog, Sparkie – To go to work – To see Chris	
What is meaningful for you in all of this?	– Taking care of Sparkie – Being helpful, helping – Love	

Imagine that tonight, when you go to bed, you'll look back on a great day: how will it have gone? What will have happened?	– I'll have given my time and affection to my patients. – I'll have cuddled with Sparkie. – I'll have spent time with Chris without arguing.
What is meaningful for you in all of this?	– Helping, being loving, warm, helpful – Having self-respect – Being considerate, sharing – Letting go
When you go to bed tonight, how do you want to feel?	– Pride in myself – Rational
How could you behave during the day to feel what you want to feel?	– I could be attentive, cheerful, in the moment, and let things go.
What is so indispensable for you that others must absolutely respect?	– Their word, that they be reliable

What else could you do to respect what is important to you?	– Be reliable

What do you no longer want in your life?	– Recurring arguments with Chris – Being disappointed with friendships – Obsessive worrying – Angry outbursts – Saying yes to everything and feeling overwhelmed

If you don't want that anymore, then what do you want? What I really want is:	– Stable and harmonious relationships – To stop waiting for people – To better manage my emotions – To be able to say no, to assert myself

For what cause are you ready to push yourself beyond your limits?	– Not isolating myself from others – The fight against animal cruelty

What do you like giving to others? *(If you could give anything, what would like to give? It's not about helping for the sake of it but helping because you deeply love doing this.)*	– Love – Emotional connection

What would you be willing to do for free or even pay to do?	– Painting
If you were a billionaire, what would you want to keep doing?	
What would you do today if it was your last day on Earth?	– I would spend as much time as possible with my parents and Chris.
What would you do if you knew you only had one year left to live?	
What is really important to you in that?	– Family – Love – Sharing moments together

Sometimes we think more in terms of goals than of direction. We want to meet that partner, get that job, enjoy things like love, friendship, or recognition. Or we want to achieve an emotional goal, like being happy or having more self-confidence. Or even goals to stop doing things, such as no longer using cocaine, no longer having panic attacks, no longer losing our cool, or no longer being shy.

To identify the values adjacent to a goal, we can ask ourselves some or all of the following questions.[2] (In answering, start with the phrase: "If I achieved this goal . . . ")

· What would I do differently?

· How would I behave?

· What different behaviors would I implement in my relationships, my professional life, my social life, or my family life?

- What personal qualities or strengths would I want to have?
- What would show that I represent my values?
- What would it allow me to do that's both meaningful to me and significant in general?

For example, if you had high self-esteem, or were happy, or felt like you belonged, or if you had a big car/perfect body/fantastic job, what would you change in the way you behave? What would you do differently? How would your behavior be different?

THE STORY OF THE OLD PROFESSOR AND THE ROCKS

One day, an elderly professor was hired to give a lecture on effective time management to a group of fifteen managers of large companies. This course was one of five workshops that made up their day of training, and so the professor had only an hour to teach the material.

Standing in front of this elite group, all of whom were ready to take note of everything this expert was about to teach them, the professor looked at each of them slowly and finally said, "We're going to do an experiment." From under the table that separated him from his students, the professor pulled out a large clear jar that he delicately placed in front of him. Next, he pulled out approximately a dozen rocks about the size of tennis balls and placed them one by one in the large jar. When the jar was filled to the top and it was impossible to add another rock, he slowly lifted his gaze to his students and asked them, "Is the jar full?"

They all replied, "Yes."

He waited a few seconds and added, "Really?"

Then he bent over again and from under the table pulled out a container filled with pebbles. Carefully, he poured the pebbles on top of the large rocks then lightly shook the jar. The pebbles filtered between the rocks to the bottom.

Again, the professor lifted his gaze to his audience and asked his question: "Is the jar full?"

This time, his brilliant students began to understand his little game. One of them replied, "Apparently not!"

"Good!" replied the professor.

He bent over again and, this time, pulled out from under the table a bag of sand. With care, he poured the sand into the jar. The sand filled in the spaces between the large rocks and the pebbles.

Once again, he asked, "Is the jar full?"

This time, without hesitation and in unison, the brilliant students replied, "No!"

"Good!" replied the professor.

And as his prestigious students expected, he took the water pitcher that was on the table and filled the jar to the brim.

The professor looked up at his group and asked, "What great truth does this experiment show us?"

Quite clever, the boldest of the students, thinking about the lecture's topic, answered, "It shows that even when we believe that our schedule is completely full, if we really want it, we can add more appointments, more things to do."

"No," replied the professor. "That's not it. The great truth that this experiment shows us is the following: if we don't put the large rocks in the jar first, we can never make them all fit later."

There was a long silence, each student processing the truth of these words.

The professor then asked them, "What are the large rocks in your life? Your health? Your family? Your friends? Learning? Fighting for a cause? Or something else entirely? And more importantly, how might you behave in a sustainable way in all of these important areas of your life?"

"What you have to remember is the importance of putting your large rocks first in your life, otherwise you risk missing out on life. If you give priority to the small things, you'll fill your life with pebbles and sand and you won't have enough precious time left to devote to the important parts of your life.

"So, don't forget to ask yourself the question: 'What are the *large rocks* in my life?' Then, put them in your jar—life—first."

With a friendly wave of the hand, the professor said goodbye to his audience and slowly left the room.

PRACTICAL APPLICATION

Exercise for the Coming Week

Every night, identify what was important to you during your day. This trains us to be grateful, which helps us focus on everything we're constantly receiving. This practice counteracts our attention's usual way of spontaneously focusing on everything that's wrong, everything that we don't have, increasing our feeling of dissatisfaction and estrangement from the rest of the world. In this way, bringing our attention to everything we have increases our feeling of contentment and connection to count-less people and things around us.

Day	When did I feel rational/open/alive?	What was I doing in those moments?	What is really important to me?
1			
2			
3			
4			
5			
6			
7			

CHAPTER 2

WHAT IS BORDERLINE PERSONALITY DISORDER?

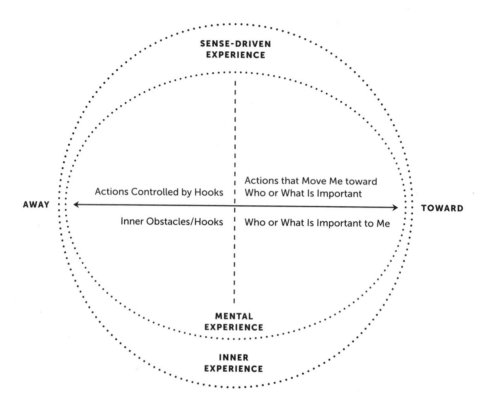

SENSE-DRIVEN EXPERIENCE

AWAY

Actions Controlled by Hooks

Inner Obstacles/Hooks

Actions that Move Me toward Who or What Is Important

Who or What Is Important to Me

TOWARD

MENTAL EXPERIENCE

INNER EXPERIENCE

BASIC TOOL: THE MATRIX

We're going to show you a model, a point of view, that many people have found useful for doing the things that are important to them when they're faced with obstacles. It's called a *matrix*.[1]

According to this model, when we see a living thing, we can see that it's either moving toward something or moving away from it. For example, if we see a rabbit in a field, we can see that it's either moving toward the neighbor's carrot patch or away from the neighbor's dog.

As human beings, we try to move either toward or away from things we *experience with the five senses* (meaning things external to us), or away from things that we don't want to think about or don't want to feel, or even toward things that are important to us in life.

HOW TO FILL IN THE MATRIX

Fill in the Lower Right Quadrant of the Matrix

In the lower right quadrant of the matrix we write down what is *important to us*: the life we really want to live, the *direction* we want to go. This is what we worked on in chapter 1.

Now Fill in the Lower Left Quadrant of the Matrix

We have a question to ask you: do you always do things that move you toward who or what is important to you in life? In the way that matters to you? Or not always?

▷ CANDACE *Not always*

▶ ME _____

If we don't always act in a way that brings us closer to who or what is important to us in life, it's because there must be obstacles.

There are two types of obstacles:

1. First are what we call *external obstacles*. For example: a friend of ours moved from France to the United States, and his parents stayed in France. He can't come to family dinners on Saturdays anymore since he's too far away. This is an external obstacle.

2. Another kind is what we'll call *inner obstacles*. For example: before moving, this friend would see his parents once a week; now he only calls them on Skype once a week. The outcome is guilt, apathy, "I'll do it later," and so much back and forth that he ends up not calling them at all.

These inner obstacles are like hooks: when the bait appears, we tend to bite, and that leads us to do something other than what we would've done if we hadn't let ourselves be "hooked."

PRACTICAL APPLICATION

Are there any inner obstacles that prevent you from moving toward what is important to you in life? If so, what are they? *(Write down the first things that immediately come to mind.)*

> CANDACE Here is what the lower right quadrant of Candace's matrix looks like:

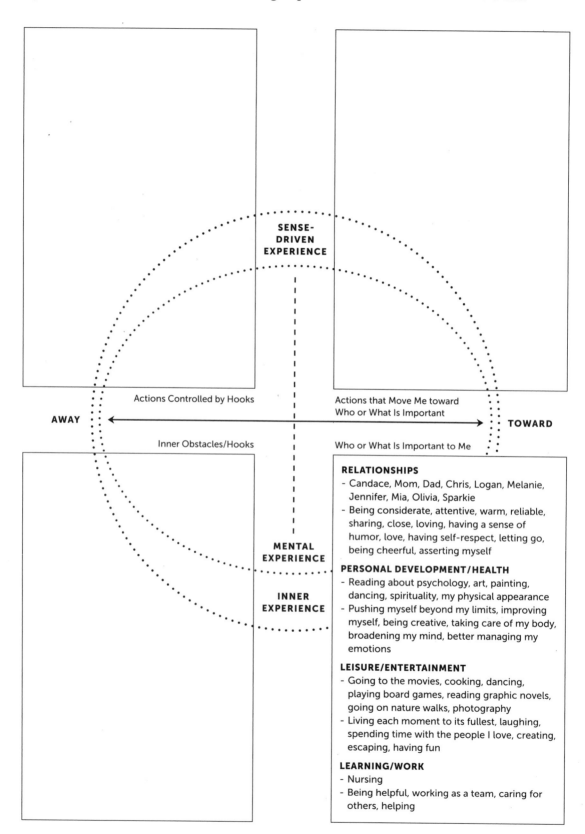

SENSE-DRIVEN EXPERIENCE

Actions Controlled by Hooks

Actions that Move Me toward Who or What Is Important

AWAY ← → TOWARD

Inner Obstacles/Hooks

Who or What Is Important to Me

MENTAL EXPERIENCE

INNER EXPERIENCE

RELATIONSHIPS
- Candace, Mom, Dad, Chris, Logan, Melanie, Jennifer, Mia, Olivia, Sparkie
- Being considerate, attentive, warm, reliable, sharing, close, loving, having a sense of humor, love, having self-respect, letting go, being cheerful, asserting myself

PERSONAL DEVELOPMENT/HEALTH
- Reading about psychology, art, painting, dancing, spirituality, my physical appearance
- Pushing myself beyond my limits, improving myself, being creative, taking care of my body, broadening my mind, better managing my emotions

LEISURE/ENTERTAINMENT
- Going to the movies, cooking, dancing, playing board games, reading graphic novels, going on nature walks, photography
- Living each moment to its fullest, laughing, spending time with the people I love, creating, escaping, having fun

LEARNING/WORK
- Nursing
- Being helpful, working as a team, caring for others, helping

ME It's your turn. Fill in the lower right quadrant of your matrix with this information.

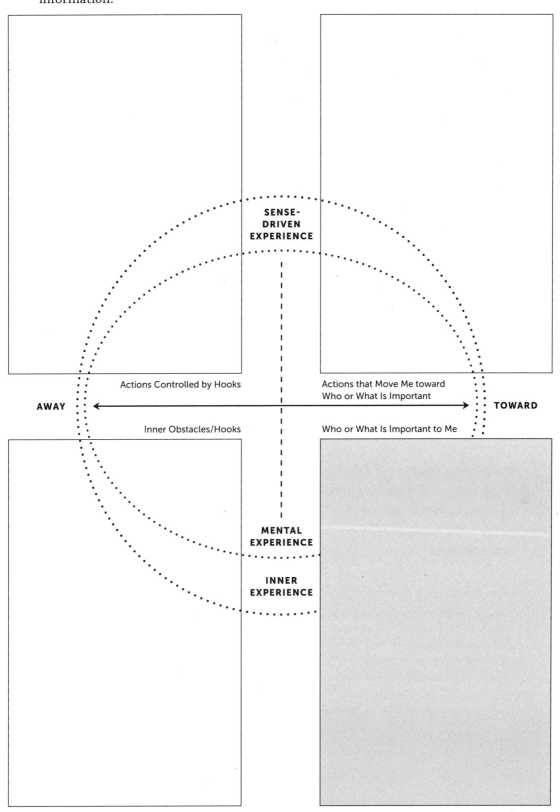

SENSE-
DRIVEN
EXPERIENCE

Actions Controlled by Hooks

Actions that Move Me toward
Who or What Is Important

AWAY ←——————————————→ TOWARD

Inner Obstacles/Hooks

Who or What Is Important to Me

MENTAL
EXPERIENCE

INNER
EXPERIENCE

CANDACE	ME
– Anger – Fear that Chris will break up with me – I'll look like an idiot. – They must think I'm weird. – I'm not interesting. – Fear of being a disappointment – Fear of being disappointed – Sadness – Hypersensitivity: intense emotions that change a lot – Shame – Emptiness – She uses me – Fear of abandonment – I'm pathetic. – Idealization/devaluation – Paranoid thoughts ("he's trying to hurt me") – Fear of failure – Fear of rejection	

If you've had the thought "I'll do it later" or "What's the point?" and if it's a thought that you often have and that prevents you from moving forward, then write it down!

Identifying Your Inner Obstacles

Below are several questions to help you identify your inner obstacles and complete the previous table. Check YES or NO and, if YES, write your answer in the table:

Your Emotions

	YES	NO
What are your emotions like over the course of a single day? Do they vary a lot? Are you very sensitive to the slightest thing happening around you or inside you (like a memory that suddenly comes back to you)?	☐	☐
Are you hypersensitive, like an emotional sponge?	☐	☐

	YES	NO
Are your emotions often intense?	☐	☐
Do the smallest things trigger anger for you?	☐	☐
Is anger problematic in your life?	☐	☐
Do you often feel ashamed of who you are, of what characterizes you?	☐	☐
Do you have trouble acknowledging and naming what you feel?	☐	☐
Do you feel empty most of the time?	☐	☐

What are the emotions that bother you the most in your life?

➤ ME _____

Think back to yesterday: what feelings or emotions prevented you from doing what you wanted to do? Did these feelings change the way you behaved toward yourself or with others?

➤ ME _____

Your Relationships
Now let's talk about relationships—an area that's an equally significant source of suffering for people with borderline personality disorder.

	YES	NO
Are you often afraid that the people you care about will leave you?	☐	☐
Are you someone who thinks in absolute terms? Do you tend to see people and relationships as black or white, all or nothing?	☐	☐
Do you tend to idealize the other person and the relationship, then totally devalue them/it once they don't/it doesn't fit the image you had?	☐	☐

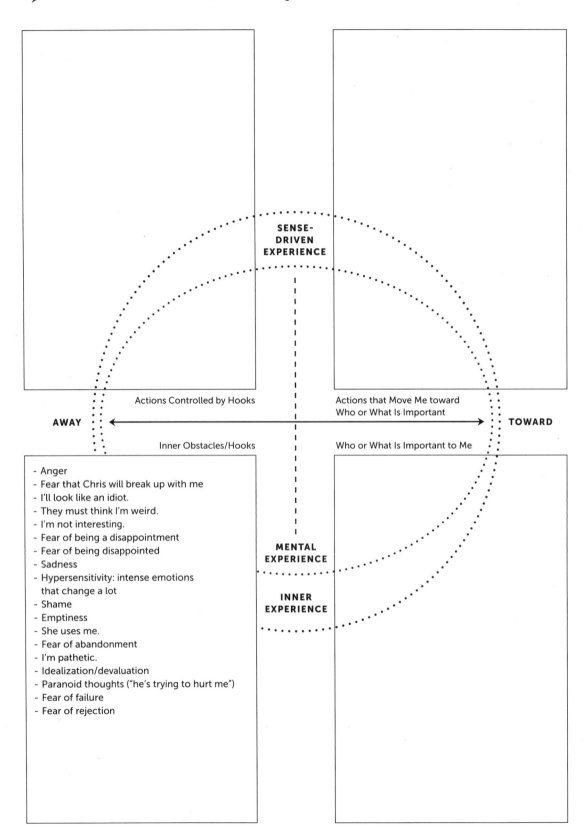

CANDACE Here is what the lower left quadrant of Candace's matrix looks like:

SENSE-DRIVEN EXPERIENCE

Actions Controlled by Hooks

Actions that Move Me toward Who or What Is Important

AWAY ← → **TOWARD**

Inner Obstacles/Hooks

Who or What Is Important to Me

- Anger
- Fear that Chris will break up with me
- I'll look like an idiot.
- They must think I'm weird.
- I'm not interesting.
- Fear of being a disappointment
- Fear of being disappointed
- Sadness
- Hypersensitivity: intense emotions that change a lot
- Shame
- Emptiness
- She uses me.
- Fear of abandonment
- I'm pathetic.
- Idealization/devaluation
- Paranoid thoughts ("he's trying to hurt me")
- Fear of failure
- Fear of rejection

MENTAL EXPERIENCE

INNER EXPERIENCE

ME It's your turn. Fill in the lower left quadrant of your matrix with this information.

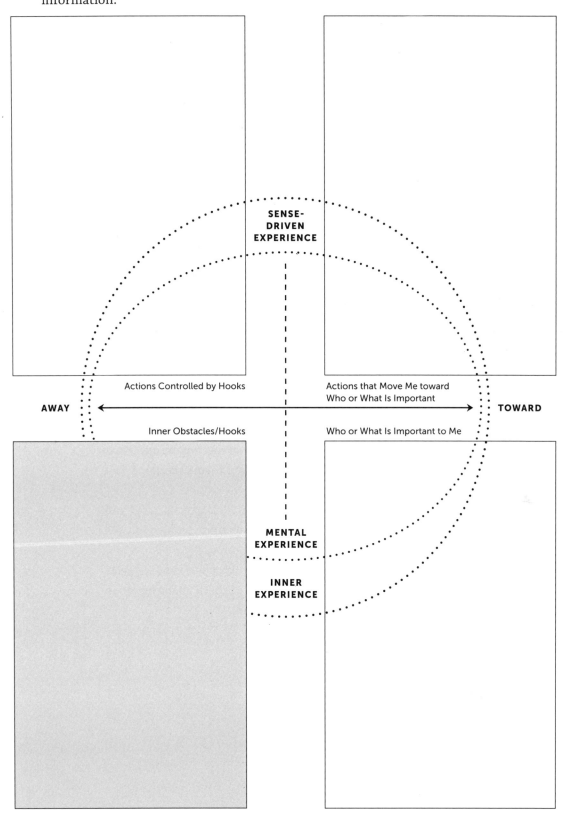

SENSE-
DRIVEN
EXPERIENCE

Actions Controlled by Hooks

Actions that Move Me toward
Who or What Is Important

AWAY ◄─────────────────────────────► TOWARD

Inner Obstacles/Hooks

Who or What Is Important to Me

MENTAL
EXPERIENCE

INNER
EXPERIENCE

What thoughts do you regularly have in relationships that cause you pain? For example: "They don't care about me," "I'm not interesting enough," "I don't know what to say," "I seem ridiculous," "They must think I'm pathetic," "If I disappoint them, they'll leave me," "I'm not lovable for who I am." *(Write down the thoughts that your mind is telling you.)*

➤ ME _____

_____

Think of a friend or companion, past or present, with whom you have or had a difficult significant relationship (or one that took up space in your life).

Write down that person's name: _____

What obstacles (thoughts, emotions) often presented themselves to you in the context of this relationship that cause you pain? Are or were these obstacles rare in your life, or do these same obstacles often arise for you?

➤ ME _____

_____

Fill in the Upper Left Quadrant of the Matrix

When your hooks present themselves to you, what do you do other than acting in a way that moves you toward what is important to you?

If we filmed you with a camera, what would we see you doing? What would you try to do to avoid or get rid of these difficult thoughts and emotions?

Are there people, places, situations, or activities that you avoid and steer clear of when your hooks make you suffer or that you avoid in the first place so they don't even present themselves to you?

These are things that you do more for the purpose of moving away from these obstacles (or while under the control of these obstacles) than for moving toward what is important to you in life.

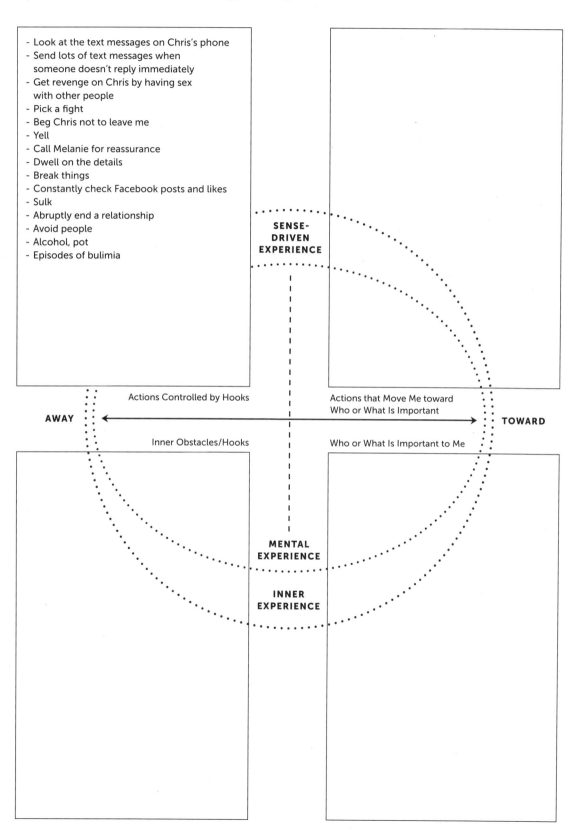

CANDACE Here is what the upper left quadrant of Candace's matrix looks like:

- Look at the text messages on Chris's phone
- Send lots of text messages when someone doesn't reply immediately
- Get revenge on Chris by having sex with other people
- Pick a fight
- Beg Chris not to leave me
- Yell
- Call Melanie for reassurance
- Dwell on the details
- Break things
- Constantly check Facebook posts and likes
- Sulk
- Abruptly end a relationship
- Avoid people
- Alcohol, pot
- Episodes of bulimia

SENSE-DRIVEN EXPERIENCE

Actions Controlled by Hooks

Actions that Move Me toward Who or What Is Important

AWAY

TOWARD

Inner Obstacles/Hooks

Who or What Is Important to Me

MENTAL EXPERIENCE

INNER EXPERIENCE

ME It's your turn. Fill in the upper left quadrant of your matrix with this information.

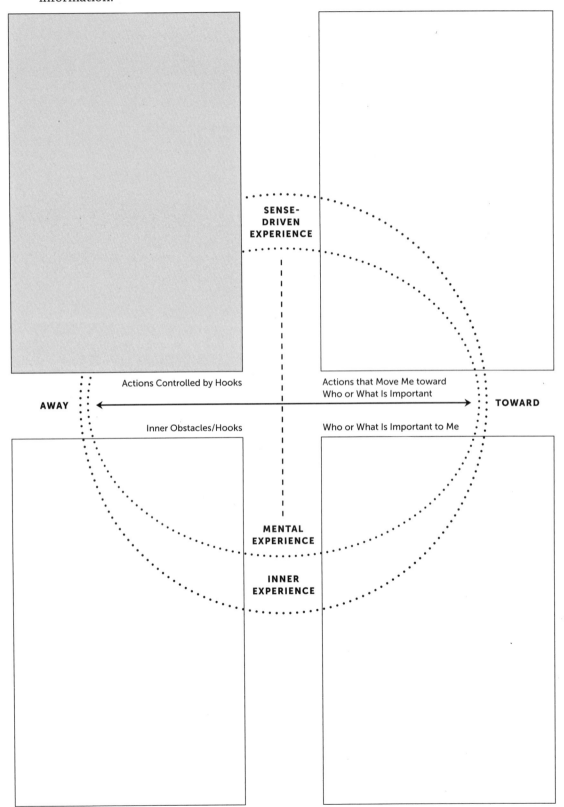

SENSE-DRIVEN EXPERIENCE

Actions Controlled by Hooks

Actions that Move Me toward Who or What Is Important

AWAY ←——————————————→ TOWARD

Inner Obstacles/Hooks

Who or What Is Important to Me

MENTAL EXPERIENCE

INNER EXPERIENCE

PRACTICAL APPLICATION

Take another look at each *obstacle/hook* that you identified in the lower left part of your matrix. What does each one lead you to do when you let yourself be hooked?

CANDACE	ME
– Look at the text messages on Chris's phone	
– Send lots of text messages when someone doesn't reply immediately	
– Get revenge on Chris by having sex with other people	
– Pick a fight	
– Beg Chris not to leave me	
– Yell	
– Call Melanie for reassurance	
– Dwell on the details	
– Break things	
– Constantly check Facebook posts and likes	
– Sulk	
– Abruptly end a relationship	
– Avoid people	
– Drink alcohol, smoke or vape pot	
– Have bulimic episodes	

If you're having a hard time clearly identifying what you're doing when you let yourself be hooked, follow the steps below:

What would you name the hook?

▷ **CANDACE** *Anger*

▶ **ME** _____

When was the last time this hook appeared for you? Describe the circumstances (where? when? with whom?).

▷ **CANDACE** *Last night, I was at Chris's; he was looking at his text messages while I was talking to him.*

▶ **ME** _____

_____

_____

What did you tell yourself in that moment? What did you feel? Where and how did you feel it in your body?

▷ **CANDACE** *He doesn't care about me. He doesn't respect me. Who was it who texted him? Anger. Lump in my throat, tension in my muscles, flushed face.*

▶ ME _____

_____

What did you do next?

▷ **CANDACE** *I yelled, I snatched the phone from his hands and threw it across the room.*

▶ ME _____

_____

Is this what you would have done deliberately? Would you have done this even if this hook hadn't presented itself to you? *(Answer yes or no.)*

▷ **CANDACE** *No.*

▶ ME _____

If you answered NO, you've bitten this hook.

If you answered YES, you haven't bitten this hook.

Sometimes we go in the same direction as expected, but we no longer do it in the same way, and that's what makes all the difference. For example: the rabbit can run to escape the dog and still go in the direction of the carrots, but it no longer does this to get closer to the carrots. Ostensibly nothing has changed, but fundamentally and in terms of the feeling and meaning, it's not the same thing anymore.

Once you've bitten the hook, notice what you do next and how you struggle.

Fill in the Upper Right Quadrant of the Matrix

What things can or could we see you do in order to move toward the things or people who are important to you in life?

If these hooks weren't there, what would you do more often? What would you do if these hooks weren't there? What actions would you take that are likely to enrich your life?

When you do everything written in the upper left part of the matrix, does that prevent you from doing things you would like to do?

> CANDACE Here is what the upper right quadrant of Candace's matrix looks like:

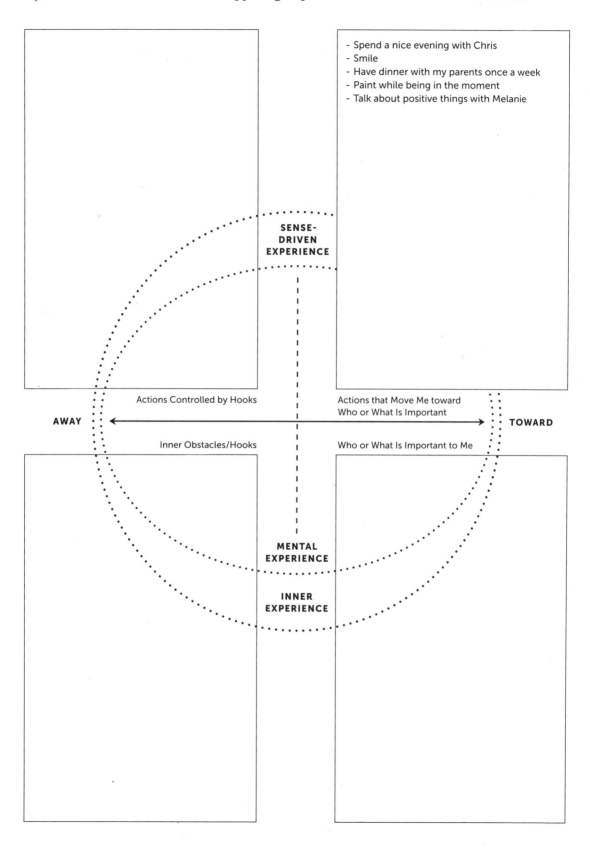

- Spend a nice evening with Chris
- Smile
- Have dinner with my parents once a week
- Paint while being in the moment
- Talk about positive things with Melanie

SENSE-
DRIVEN
EXPERIENCE

Actions Controlled by Hooks

Actions that Move Me toward
Who or What Is Important

AWAY

TOWARD

Inner Obstacles/Hooks

Who or What Is Important to Me

MENTAL
EXPERIENCE

INNER
EXPERIENCE

ME It's your turn. Fill in the upper right quadrant of your matrix with this information.

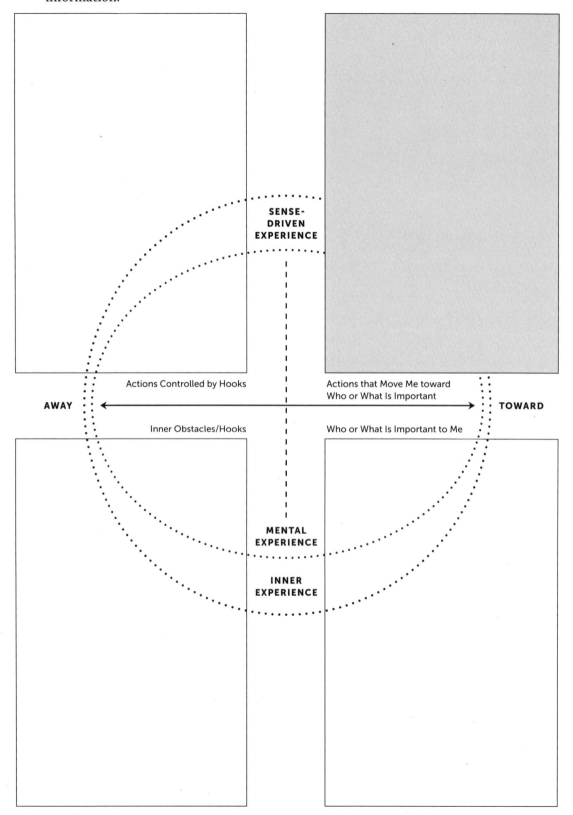

SENSE-
DRIVEN
EXPERIENCE

Actions Controlled by Hooks

Actions that Move Me toward
Who or What Is Important

AWAY

TOWARD

Inner Obstacles/Hooks

Who or What Is Important to Me

MENTAL
EXPERIENCE

INNER
EXPERIENCE

PRACTICAL APPLICATION

Write down just a few examples of things that would move you toward the things and people who are important to you. You'll discover that the possibilities are, in fact, endless.

CANDACE	ME
– Spend a nice evening with Chris	
– Smile	
– Have dinner with my parents once a week	
– Paint while being in the moment	
– Talk about positive things with Melanie	

UNDERSTANDING THE MATRIX

Do the actions written in the upper left part of your matrix work?

Reread the things you do to move away from what you don't want to think or feel. Do you think they're effective in the short term? Do they work in the short term to reduce hooks? *(The "short term" ranges from a few milliseconds to a few minutes.)*

▷ **CANDACE** *Yes, they give me relief in general, but really only in the very short term, because it's even worse right after. I tell myself that I've lost it again, I feel guilty, I tell myself that I'll never be able to cope.*

How about you? Is what you do (the upper left) effective in the short term?

➤ ME _____

_____

_____

_____

▷ **CANDACE** *When I argue with Chris and slam the door when I leave the room, I feel better, I feel a huge relief for a few milliseconds after. But a few seconds later, I feel ashamed, guilty, and even angrier. And it's true that if I didn't pay attention to the first milliseconds, I'd say it just makes things worse.*

What you're doing does make sense. You do it because it *reduces* the intensity of hooks in the short term.

Now, let's ask if what we're doing (the upper left) is working in the long run, that is if *the hooks never came back, or came back less intensely or less frequently.*

> **CANDACE** *No! It doesn't work! I'm going in circles . . . They constantly come back, and then I do the same thing again.*

How about you? Is what you do (the upper left) effective in the long run?

> **ME** _____

_____

_____

_____

_____

Therefore, quite often what you're doing works in the short term, but in the long run either has no effect or makes things worse. No wonder you feel stuck!

The emergency exit (the upper left) gets us out of a situation, but it rarely brings us where we want to go.

What happens is that the hooks appear, so you do something from the upper left part of your matrix, and the hooks come back, and you do the same thing again. And then your range of behavior becomes narrower. It's a really hard way to live.

Now that your matrix is complete (p. 40), do you see the same *endless loop* as on Candace's matrix (on the next page)?

Now let's look at whether what you're doing (the upper left) moves you toward the people and things that are important to you in life (in other words, the right-hand side of the matrix).

> **CANDACE** *It isn't effective! It still moves me away!*

> **ME** _____

_____

_____

_____

_____

CANDACE Here is what Candace's fully completed matrix looks like:

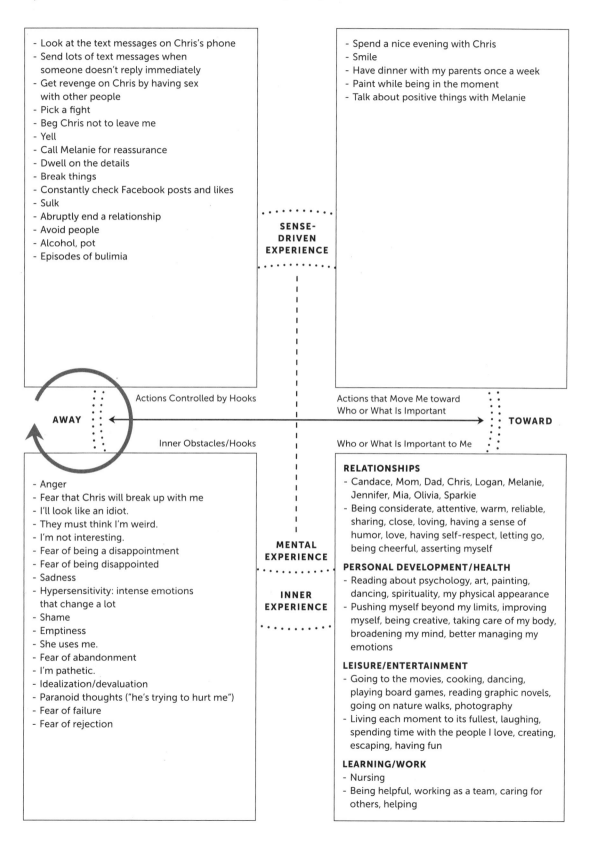

- Look at the text messages on Chris's phone
- Send lots of text messages when someone doesn't reply immediately
- Get revenge on Chris by having sex with other people
- Pick a fight
- Beg Chris not to leave me
- Yell
- Call Melanie for reassurance
- Dwell on the details
- Break things
- Constantly check Facebook posts and likes
- Sulk
- Abruptly end a relationship
- Avoid people
- Alcohol, pot
- Episodes of bulimia

- Spend a nice evening with Chris
- Smile
- Have dinner with my parents once a week
- Paint while being in the moment
- Talk about positive things with Melanie

SENSE-DRIVEN EXPERIENCE

Actions Controlled by Hooks

Actions that Move Me toward Who or What Is Important

AWAY

TOWARD

Inner Obstacles/Hooks

Who or What Is Important to Me

- Anger
- Fear that Chris will break up with me
- I'll look like an idiot.
- They must think I'm weird.
- I'm not interesting.
- Fear of being a disappointment
- Fear of being disappointed
- Sadness
- Hypersensitivity: intense emotions that change a lot
- Shame
- Emptiness
- She uses me.
- Fear of abandonment
- I'm pathetic.
- Idealization/devaluation
- Paranoid thoughts ("he's trying to hurt me")
- Fear of failure
- Fear of rejection

MENTAL EXPERIENCE

INNER EXPERIENCE

RELATIONSHIPS
- Candace, Mom, Dad, Chris, Logan, Melanie, Jennifer, Mia, Olivia, Sparkie
- Being considerate, attentive, warm, reliable, sharing, close, loving, having a sense of humor, love, having self-respect, letting go, being cheerful, asserting myself

PERSONAL DEVELOPMENT/HEALTH
- Reading about psychology, art, painting, dancing, spirituality, my physical appearance
- Pushing myself beyond my limits, improving myself, being creative, taking care of my body, broadening my mind, better managing my emotions

LEISURE/ENTERTAINMENT
- Going to the movies, cooking, dancing, playing board games, reading graphic novels, going on nature walks, photography
- Living each moment to its fullest, laughing, spending time with the people I love, creating, escaping, having fun

LEARNING/WORK
- Nursing
- Being helpful, working as a team, caring for others, helping

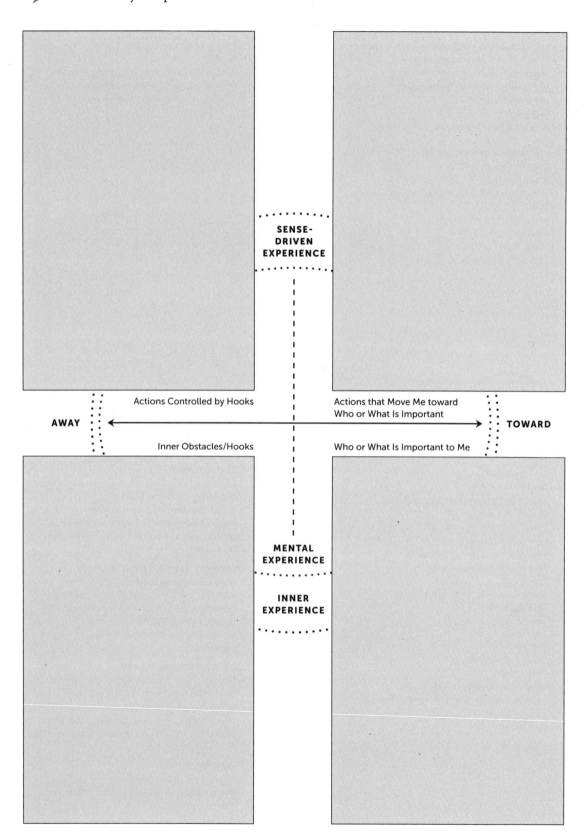

SENSE-
DRIVEN
EXPERIENCE

Actions Controlled by Hooks

Actions that Move Me toward
Who or What Is Important

AWAY ← → **TOWARD**

Inner Obstacles/Hooks

Who or What Is Important to Me

MENTAL
EXPERIENCE

INNER
EXPERIENCE

WHAT IS BORDERLINE PERSONALITY DISORDER? _____

Borderline personality disorder can be defined as the coexistence of

- *specific hooks* that frequently appear for you (the lower left part of the matrix)
- *what you do* when you let yourself be hooked (the upper left part of the matrix)
- *the distance* from what is important to you (the right-hand side of the matrix)

Psychiatrists worldwide use the same classification to diagnose borderline personality disorder: the *Diagnostic and Statistical Manual of Mental Disorders (DSM)*.[2] The *DSM* defines nine criteria linked to borderline personality disorder, organized into four domains. In order to diagnose borderline personality disorder, five of the nine criteria in the following table must be met.

Let's look at Candace's matrix on p. 39 and see which borderline personality disorder criteria she appears to present.

It's important to remember not to self-diagnose and to work with a professional and qualified therapist. If you're experiencing significant distress, it's important to remember to reach out to professionals either by calling 911 or by going to the nearest emergency department or clinic.

> **ME** How about you? In taking another look at your matrix, what borderline personality disorder criteria can you find?

THE START OF A NEW LIFE _____

Taking Stock
Before starting this program in the direction of the life you really want to live, complete this self-assessment to determine, as of today, the intensity of each of this disorder's domains for you. Take the time to answer thoughtfully and honestly. You will measure your progress at the end of the book.

Self-Assessment
For each question, write down to what extent the statement corresponds to your usual way of operating—in other words: how much has the described behavior been present over the course of your life? How we usually operate is in keeping with a repeated pattern of behavior that persists independently of periods of depression.

The Nine *DSM* Criteria

CANDACE

(see the matrix on the following page)

		CANDACE
EMOTIONAL DYSREGULATION	1. Affective instability due to a marked reactivity of mood	− Hypersensitivity: intense emotions that change a lot
	2. Identity disturbance: markedly and persistently unstable self-image or sense of self	
	3. Chronic feelings of emptiness	− Emptiness
	4. Inappropriate, intense anger or difficulty controlling anger	− Yelling − Breaking things − Anger
IMPULSIVITY	5. Impulsivity in at least two areas that are potentially self-damaging (spending, sex, substance abuse, etc.)	− Getting revenge on Chris by sleeping with other people − Alcohol, pot − Episodes of bulimia
	6. Recurrent suicidal behavior, gestures, or threats, or self-mutilating behavior	
DIFFICULTY IN INTERPERSONAL RELATIONSHIPS	7. Frantic efforts to avoid real or imagined abandonment	− Look at the text messages on Chris's phone − Send lots of text messages when someone doesn't reply immediately − Pick a fight − Beg Chris not to leave me − Constantly check Facebook posts and likes − Fear that Chris will break up with me − Fear of abandonment
	8. A pattern of unstable and intense interpersonal relationships	− Sulk − Abruptly end a relationship − Idealization/devaluation
DISSOCIATIVE SYMPTOMS	9. Transient, stress-related paranoid ideation or severe dissociative symptoms	− Paranoid thoughts ("he's trying to hurt me")

CANDACE Here is Candace's matrix with the borderline personality disorder criteria (in bold) that she appears to present:

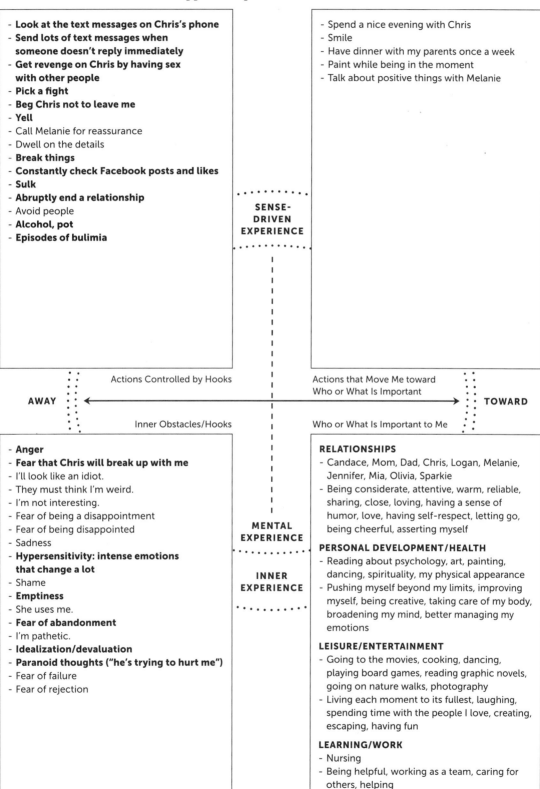

Away — Sense-Driven Experience (Actions Controlled by Hooks)
- **Look at the text messages on Chris's phone**
- **Send lots of text messages when someone doesn't reply immediately**
- **Get revenge on Chris by having sex with other people**
- **Pick a fight**
- **Beg Chris not to leave me**
- **Yell**
- Call Melanie for reassurance
- Dwell on the details
- **Break things**
- **Constantly check Facebook posts and likes**
- **Sulk**
- **Abruptly end a relationship**
- Avoid people
- **Alcohol, pot**
- **Episodes of bulimia**

Toward — Sense-Driven Experience (Actions that Move Me toward Who or What Is Important)
- Spend a nice evening with Chris
- Smile
- Have dinner with my parents once a week
- Paint while being in the moment
- Talk about positive things with Melanie

AWAY ←——————————→ TOWARD

Inner Obstacles/Hooks

Who or What Is Important to Me

Away — Inner Experience (Inner Obstacles/Hooks)
- **Anger**
- **Fear that Chris will break up with me**
- I'll look like an idiot.
- They must think I'm weird.
- I'm not interesting.
- Fear of being a disappointment
- Fear of being disappointed
- Sadness
- **Hypersensitivity: intense emotions that change a lot**
- Shame
- **Emptiness**
- She uses me.
- **Fear of abandonment**
- I'm pathetic.
- **Idealization/devaluation**
- **Paranoid thoughts ("he's trying to hurt me")**
- Fear of failure
- Fear of rejection

Toward — Inner Experience (Who or What Is Important to Me)

RELATIONSHIPS
- Candace, Mom, Dad, Chris, Logan, Melanie, Jennifer, Mia, Olivia, Sparkie
- Being considerate, attentive, warm, reliable, sharing, close, loving, having a sense of humor, love, having self-respect, letting go, being cheerful, asserting myself

PERSONAL DEVELOPMENT/HEALTH
- Reading about psychology, art, painting, dancing, spirituality, my physical appearance
- Pushing myself beyond my limits, improving myself, being creative, taking care of my body, broadening my mind, better managing my emotions

LEISURE/ENTERTAINMENT
- Going to the movies, cooking, dancing, playing board games, reading graphic novels, going on nature walks, photography
- Living each moment to its fullest, laughing, spending time with the people I love, creating, escaping, having fun

LEARNING/WORK
- Nursing
- Being helpful, working as a team, caring for others, helping

In order to judge whether a type of behavior is habitual, you must be able to cite several examples to prove it.

Rate yourself between 0 = not at all characteristic of me and 10 = completely characteristic of me. No calculations are necessary for this test. Just circle the number that corresponds to you.

1. In recent years, has the idea that a person who's very important to you might leave you often made you angry? Is fear of abandonment very present in your life?

0	1	2	3	4	5	6	7	8	9	10

2. Do your relationships with the people who are very important to you regularly have lots of ups and downs? Are you a person who is "too absolute," who quickly gives 100% of yourself in a relationship, who idealizes the other person, and then ultimately feels disappointed when that other person doesn't measure up to your expectations?

0	1	2	3	4	5	6	7	8	9	10

Do you frequently tend to have intense relationships?

0	1	2	3	4	5	6	7	8	9	10

3. In recent years, have you, on several occasions, suddenly changed how you think of yourself? In other words, does the image you have of yourself often change radically? Are you different depending on who you're with so much so that sometimes you don't know who you really are?

0	1	2	3	4	5	6	7	8	9	10

In recent years, have there been many sudden changes in your goals, career plans, religious beliefs, or lifestyle? Has what you love or what you believe varied a lot over time?

0	1	2	3	4	5	6	7	8	9	10

4. In recent years have you *often* done things impulsively? For example:

- buying things you can't afford
- having sex with people you barely know or having unprotected sex
- drinking too much or taking drugs
- driving recklessly

- eating uncontrollably
- making decisions on a whim that you regret afterward

0	1	2	3	4	5	6	7	8	9	10

5. In recent years, have you tried to harm yourself (cutting, burning, hitting the wall with your fists or head) or attempted or threatened to commit suicide?

0	1	2	3	4	5	6	7	8	9	10

6. Are you regularly someone who is very sensitive to everything happening around you, so much so that your emotions change a lot in the same day and are more intense than those of most other people? Would you define yourself as an "emotional sponge"?

0	1	2	3	4	5	6	7	8	9	10

7. Do you often feel empty inside?

0	1	2	3	4	5	6	7	8	9	10

8. In general, are you prone to anger? In other words, do even small things make you feel intense anger?

0	1	2	3	4	5	6	7	8	9	10

9. Do you often have angry outbursts or get so angry that you lose control of yourself?

0	1	2	3	4	5	6	7	8	9	10

10. When you're very stressed, do you become suspicious of others ("people are mad at me" or "people want to hurt me"), or do you feel especially disconnected (the feeling of not being yourself anymore or like being in a daydream)?

0	1	2	3	4	5	6	7	8	9	10

The Foundations of a New Personal Identity

Who can see that you're doing what you're doing in order to move away from what you don't want to think or feel, or to move toward what is important to you in life?

▷ **CANDACE** *I can.*

▶ **ME** *I see. I can see what is important to me in life, I can see my inner obstacles or what I don't want to think or feel (hooks), and then I can see if what I'm doing is to move toward what is important to me in life or to move away from what I don't want to think or feel.*

We've Now Presented Our Model

Imagine that you can choose between *two possible lives*: in one life most of what you do is done to move you away from what you don't want to think or feel, and in the other life most of what you do is done to move you toward what is important to you in life. If you could choose or vote for one of these two lives, which one would you choose or vote for?

For us, the choice is made, and the work you'll do in this book will help you move toward life #2. Therefore, we'll work together toward what is important to you. Our philosophy won't be to put all our energy into fighting hooks. In fact, that's probably what you've been doing for years, and it doesn't have the expected results to improve your life. On the other hand, our philosophy will be to teach you to more easily choose to *move toward what is important to you*, even when faced with hooks.

Scientific studies and our experience have taught us that acting consistent with the person that we would like to be and in the direction of what is important to us in spite of existing hooks:

1. is more effective in creating a life that corresponds to how we want to live;
2. reduces the frequency and intensity of hooks better than when we try to reduce them.

This is simply because we spend more time on the right side than on the left side of the matrix. Therefore, even if the hook is always there, it's functionally less significant in our life.

It's like a radio in the room: if it bothers us, it's the only thing we hear. But if a conversation grabs our interest, we don't hear the radio anymore, even though it's still on the same station with the same nonsense being broadcast.

> **"We choose the second life: to do the utmost to move ourselves toward what is important to us in life."** —CANDACE, VÉRONIQUE & DÉBORAH

The Bus Metaphor

You're driving a bus, and the passengers are all of your unpleasant thoughts and emotions (the lower left part of the matrix).[3] There are also pleasant thoughts and emotions on the bus, but sometimes the difficult passengers are very intrusive.

The passengers are shouting really loudly in your ear, asking you to turn the bus one way or the other. But there's only one person who has the power to choose the bus's direction: *you, the driver*. As the driver, you can *choose to steer the bus* in the direction you want, in the direction that corresponds to what is important to you, despite the presence of the passengers shouting in your ear. And then, as you go along the route, if you head toward the places you want to see, the things that are important to you, you'll hear the passengers shouting less and less. It'll be a bit like the sound of the radio on in the background.

And for that to happen, you of course have to define what is important to you in life: where the driver wants to go.

Two Key Skills for Using the Matrix

Skill One: Sorting

This is the ability to train ourselves to sort between the left and the right side of the matrix. By doing this, actions that fall on the right side increase. In fact, the more attention we give to the actions on the right, the more they start developing, because they're positively reinforced by the knowledge that we're acting in a way that leads us toward what is important to us. To do this, we're going to learn to feel "what makes me 'move toward'" as opposed to "what makes me 'move away.'"

Do you know how to ride a bike? When you lose your balance on a bike and it starts to lean to one side, you feel it somewhere in your body, and you make an adjustment to make the bike upright again. It isn't your brain that starts calculating the bike's angle of incline and the angle you need to correct it, right? It's a feeling in your gut that tells you.

Similarly, moving away from what we don't want to think or feel, and moving toward what is important to us, is something we can do by feeling. We're going to develop this ability together over the course of this program.

Careful, though, because this is different from "feeling good" or "feeling bad."

▷ **CANDACE** When Candace drinks alcohol to escape what she doesn't want to think or feel, she feels good in the moment. In contrast, when she apologizes to her boyfriend after insulting him, she feels bad at the time because it's an uncomfortable thing to do. However, when she apologizes, she moves closer to the person she'd like to be.

The feeling on the right side of the matrix we're talking about has to do with being in harmony with ourselves.

❝ If you want something you have never had, you must be willing to do something you have never done. If you do what you have always done, you will get what you have always gotten. ❞ —THOMAS JEFFERSON

Skill Two: Small Steps

This is a method that involves moving forward by taking small steps out of our comfort zone while still staying in a zone that allows us to take care of ourselves.

What's our comfort zone? It's everything that's familiar: our habits and our routines. Comfort doesn't necessarily mean pleasant, but rather safe. We can find pleasure in our comfort zone because it gives us a feeling of security, but it isn't fulfilling. We can think of our comfort zone as a zone of stagnation.

Leaving our comfort zone requires effort and requires us to tolerate some discomfort so that we can keep moving forward in the direction of what is important to us. In fact, there are hooks around the comfort zone, such as "fear of failure," "fear of the unknown," "I'm not good enough," and "what's the point?"

But you can't expect to have different experiences by staying in your comfort zone. By leaving your comfort zone, you'll find new opportunities, and your life—and you—will evolve in a direction that is meaningful for you. Leaving your comfort zone lets you move forward in the direction of the zone where the magic

SMALL STEPS

Comfort Zone

Self-Care Zone

Zone Where the Magic Happens

GROW   IMPROVE   CHANGE   LEARN

happens. Every time you do a new thing, you enlarge your field of possibilities . . . and your comfort zone gets bigger.

What we'd like to do is help you more easily choose to act outside of your comfort zone, while staying within your self-care zone. The step must be at the boundary between what's comfortable and what challenges you. If you have to make a choice between two different steps, we encourage you to choose the one that will best let you take care of yourself.

Choose small things you can do regularly rather than big things from time to time.

Throughout this book you'll discover the keys for living the life that suits YOU, a life tailored to the person you really want to be. One clarification, however: it isn't what you know that determines your life, it's what you do.

Therefore, putting each of these key skills into practice will be the essential ingredient in creating this life that's worth living.

> ❝It looks impossible until you do it, and then you find it is possible.❞
> —EVELYN UNDERHILL

PRACTICAL APPLICATION

Exercise for the Coming Week
Set an alarm on your phone to go off every two hours during the day. When the alarm goes off, observe: am I acting under the control of my hooks or am I acting in the direction of what is important to me?

CHAPTER 3

HOW DOES BORDERLINE PERSONALITY DISORDER DEVELOP?

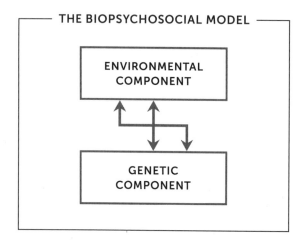

THE BIOPSYCHOSOCIAL MODEL

ENVIRONMENTAL COMPONENT

GENETIC COMPONENT

At this time, the biopsychosocial model is well validated for explaining the development of borderline personality disorder.

There are two main components that interact with one another: a genetic component and an environmental component.

THE GENETIC COMPONENT

Studies on the domains of borderline personality disorder such as impulsivity have documented that the children of impulsive parents will themselves be impulsive, even if these children aren't raised by their biological parents. Therefore, for some domains, such as impulsivity, there's a genetic inheritance.

Additionally, people presenting with borderline personality disorder will have a heightened genetic sensitivity to emotions. Even so, this genetic component isn't enough for a disorder to develop. Some people will use this emotional sensitivity for art and creativity, demonstrating that this isn't the only thing that will make the disorder develop.

THE ENVIRONMENTAL COMPONENT

For borderline personality disorder to develop, an environmental component intervenes. This is called a disabling environment. This is an environment that isn't going to help a child acknowledge his emotions, name them, and give them meaning. Therefore, this environment will not encourage the validation of what the child experiences emotionally.

For example, when a baby is crying, his mother will usually try to understand what the baby's emotional expression means. She'll try to make sense of what her child is experiencing. For example, she'll ask him, "There, there, you're crying . . . Are you hungry? Is your diaper wet?" She'll make sense of the child's crying. Or else, when the child is laughing, the mother will try to find the underlying cause of this emotion. She may realize that he's laughing because something is moving in front of his eyes. So she'll grab the object, shake it, and play with him. An exchange is created between the mother and her child, and a meaning is given to what he's experiencing.

Some families won't encourage this integration of meaning with what the child is experiencing. There are three main types of disabling environments.

Families That Don't Encourage Emotional Expression

These are families that will tend to create a climate in which a child's emotional expression isn't welcome. Such emotional expression won't be encouraged or recognized when it occurs. This can happen in families in which there's discomfort with the expression of emotions, which is passed on from generation to generation. This nonrecognition of a child's emotions can also be found when one of the parents suffers from a psychological disorder (particularly depression), making it difficult to be available for the child's emotional education.

Sometimes emotional expression will be repressed. The message will be: "You don't have to feel what you feel." There's no place for emotional expression. For example, when a child is crying, he might hear: "Stop whining" or "Go to your room and calm down." In the end, the child's feelings won't be validated by the parents.

The child's feelings won't be validated by the parents.

It can go as far as abuse. In fact, we find physical abuse (beating, physical contusions), sexual abuse, or emotional abuse (insults, devaluation of the child) more often in the life stories of people with borderline personality disorder. Abuse is often more severe and recurrent than in other mental illnesses, and it's also more often not acknowledged by the family. The underlying theory is that it's not necessarily the abuse itself that gives rise to borderline personality disorder; rather, it's the fact of being abused by someone close to you and not having support or validation from those who are supposed to be protecting you. In fact, it has been suggested that children who have been abused but who are emotionally validated by those close to them develop borderline personality disorder less often.

We must be particularly careful with regard to the family's role in the development of borderline personality disorder. This disorder results from the interaction between a genetic vulnerability and repetitive environmental stressors. Lack of validation alone is not enough to cause someone to develop borderline personality disorder. Virtually any child, as they are growing up, might occasionally feel they are not being validated by their parents. The problem is when lack of validation becomes pervasive and consistent, affecting most of the relationships experienced by the patient as he is growing up. The goal of this section is not to assign blame for the patient's current problems, but to help him understand the relationship patterns involved in the development of this disorder and how some of those patterns might even persist in the patient's current relationships as an adult.

Families That Recognize Emotions Only When They're Overexpressed

This kind of environment only hears emotion when it's at its peak. Let's consider this analogy: A little boy in the checkout line at a supermarket wants some candy. His mother doesn't want to buy him any. "We're eating in an hour," she says. At first the child whines, and the mother replies, "No, no, you're not having any candy!" Then, after a minute, the child starts screaming. The mother is going to punish him, but he starts rolling on the floor, and the mother realizes that she's the focal point of the entire store. That's when she buys the candy. Because the child's emotion was overexpressed, it was recognized by his mother.

Thus, some families will hear the child's emotion only when it's overexpressed, which will cause an overexpression of emotions by the child, who wants to be heard by those close to him.

Families with High Expectations

Another type of disabling environment may be found in families described as elitist, that have high expectations of their child and that oversimplify the goals to be achieved and the ability to resolve problems. This type of family operates with the oversimplified thinking "all you need to do is . . ." An example is a school-age child who is feeling down. His grades drop because he's anxious. Finally his parents oversimplify the problem by saying to him, "If you worked more, you'd get better grades." Only, in the evening, he can't work because he feels down.

A Word of Caution: The disabling environment is not necessarily ill intentioned. For that matter, it rarely is. It does what it can.

This type of environment is also found in families in which social appearance is very important. Parents want an excellent socio-professional situation for their child and adopt high achievement standards. The child might feel that his parents' love is conditioned on their dream of social success (good grades in school, a respectable profession, success in competitive sports). The environment has such high expectations that by adopting this high standard the child stifles his own feelings.

INTERACTION BETWEEN THE GENETIC AND ENVIRONMENTAL COMPONENTS

Genetic vulnerability and the disabling environment interact. Gradually, the child will have less and less confidence in what he feels ("After all, others must know better than I do what I should feel in this situation"). That child progressively loses touch with what he feels and with his body. He has difficulty regulating emotions, impulsive behaviors, and problems in interpersonal relationships.

PRACTICAL APPLICATION

Take another look at your matrix from chapter 2, p. 40, and review the hooks that you wrote down in the lower left section of the matrix. These hooks didn't emerge by accident. They're the result of your past experiences, some of which were particularly traumatic.

- Look at the text messages on Chris's phone
- Send lots of text messages when someone doesn't reply immediately
- Get revenge on Chris by having sex with other people
- Pick a fight
- Beg Chris not to leave me
- Yell
- Call Melanie for reassurance
- Dwell on the details
- Break things
- Constantly check Facebook posts and likes
- Sulk
- Abruptly end a relationship
- Avoid people
- Alcohol, pot
- Episodes of bulimia

- Spend a nice evening with Chris
- Smile
- Have dinner with my parents once a week
- Paint while being in the moment
- Talk about positive things with Melanie

SENSE-DRIVEN EXPERIENCE

Actions Controlled by Hooks

Actions that Move Me toward Who or What Is Important

AWAY ←——————————————————→ **TOWARD**

Inner Obstacles/Hooks

Who or What Is Important to Me

- Anger
- **Fear that Chris will break up with me**
- **I'll look like an idiot.**
- **They must think I'm weird.**
- **I'm not interesting.**
- **Fear of being a disappointment**
- **Fear of being disappointed**
- Sadness
- Hypersensitivity: intense emotions that change a lot
- **Shame**
- Emptiness
- She uses me
- **Fear of abandonment**
- **I'm pathetic.**
- Idealization/devaluation
- Paranoid thoughts ("he's trying to hurt me")
- Fear of failure
- Fear of rejection

MENTAL EXPERIENCE

INNER EXPERIENCE

RELATIONSHIPS
- Candace, Mom, Dad, Chris, Logan, Melanie, Jennifer, Mia, Olivia, Sparkie
- Being considerate, attentive, warm, reliable, sharing, close, loving, having a sense of humor, love, having self-respect, letting go, being cheerful, asserting myself

PERSONAL DEVELOPMENT/HEALTH
- Reading about psychology, art, painting, dancing, spirituality, my physical appearance
- Pushing myself beyond my limits, improving myself, being creative, taking care of my body, broadening my mind, better managing my emotions

LEISURE/ENTERTAINMENT
- Going to the movies, cooking, dancing, playing board games, reading graphic novels, going on nature walks, photography
- Living each moment to its fullest, laughing, spending time with the people I love, creating, escaping, having fun

LEARNING/WORK
- Nursing
- Being helpful, working as a team, caring for others, helping

What are the hooks that bother you the most these days?

▷ CANDACE *The hooks that bother me the most are:*

- *shame ("They must think I'm weird" / "I'll look like an idiot" / "I'm pathetic")*
- *fear of abandonment*

➤ ME _____

_____

In what memorable situations did these hooks appear for you in the past? In the presence of what?

▷ CANDACE

- Shame: *"They must think I'm weird," "I'll look like an idiot," "I'm pathetic." I remember when my father would punish me by publicly humiliating me (in the supermarket, in front of my classmates). I also remember that in middle school some of the kids in my class would make fun of me, push and shove me in the hallways, and steal my things. I felt incredibly ashamed and humiliated.*

- Fear of abandonment: *"Fear that Chris will break up with me," "I'm not interesting," "Fear of being a disappointment." As a child, I felt that my father didn't love me for who I was. He only showed signs of affection or paid attention to me when I was the best at something (like at school or soccer). That's when I started thinking that I wasn't interesting enough to be loved for who I was. Even my mother seemed to pay much more attention to making my father happy than to spending time with me. So I often felt abandoned, even though I lived with my mom and dad.*

➤ ME _____

_____

_____

_____

What were you doing at the time when you felt that? Was anyone close to you struggling with the same thing? How did they react in these situations?

▷ CANDACE

- Shame: *"They must think I'm weird," "I'll look like an idiot," "I'm pathetic." I would hide. I would try to make myself as small as possible. I would beg my father to stop. I would see my father in control during social interactions with friends or family, and trying to maintain the appearance of a "normal" family.*

– Fear of abandonment: *I always tried to be the best so that my father would love me. When my parents would leave for an evening out or a weekend away, I would call them over and over again. I would keep a notebook with the phone numbers of other relatives in case my parents abandoned me somewhere.*

➤ ME _____

_____

_____

_____

_____

It's likely that your current behaviors (the upper left part of the matrix) are the same as your behaviors at the time when these problems started appearing for you. Perhaps these are the same behaviors you observed someone close to you doing.

In reality, the hooks that appear for you today have become deeply embedded because of painful past experiences. Those experiences are a thing of the past, but your mind continues to present you with the same hooks over and over again. Your mind is telling you there's still an emergency situation, even though that's no longer the case.

You aren't that other person, or even the same person you were a few years ago. Hooks are always there, but you have the opportunity to manage them differently and to act differently.

You have a choice in what you do, even if you don't have a choice in what goes on inside you. It isn't what you *think* that shapes your life, it's what you *do*.

Over the course of this book, we'll accompany you in managing the things that arise for you differently—more effectively—so that when you can choose what you do, you'll be consistent with the person you really want to be, with the person you really are deep down.

CHAPTER 4

THE THREE STATES OF MIND

WHAT IS THE MIND?

The mind is the part of us that experiences life. Underlying this experience is:

— what we perceive of the world around us through the five senses

— what is produced by our mind (our brain):

- *Thoughts*, what I say to myself, the sentences that my mind produces. These thoughts may appear to me as sounds (in my own voice or in the voice of another person who tends to say this phrase) or as images (still or animated scenes, reenacting a memory, or anticipating the future).
- *Emotions*, what I feel. These are emotional states, both pleasant and unpleasant. We have several chapters on emotions later on in the book. You'll become an expert on emotions!

The psychologist Marsha Linehan postulated three different states of mind: reasonable mind, emotion mind, and wise mind.[1]

Reasonable Mind

This is a state of mind in which current life experience is rational and logical. In reasonable mind, we're in a process of *Cartesian rationalism*.

Reasonable mind allows you to plan, organize, and evaluate. It's used in everyday life to make a shopping list, follow instructions, or solve a math problem.

Reasonable mind also provides access to what we know about ourselves. This knowledge about ourselves concerns:

- Our objective life conditions (current or past).

▷ **CANDACE** In reasonable mind, Candace knows, for example, that her classmates made fun of her when she was in middle school (past life conditions). Candace also knows that she's a nurse, that she knows how to paint, that Logan is one of her friends, and so on (current life conditions).

- What we know about the mind's propensity to produce certain hooks (the lower left part of the matrix) and the way we usually react to them (the upper left part of the matrix).

▷ **CANDACE** In reasonable mind, Candace knows that her mind often tends to offer her the "fear of abandonment" hook and that she usually reacts by sending lots of text messages or testing the other person's boundaries.

- What we know about what is important to us (the lower right part of the matrix).

In this state of mind, we're dealing with intellectual knowledge. We're not connected to our emotions. It's not that emotions don't exist; we're just not taking them into account.

What's the risk of being only in a state of reasonable mind? Erasing emotion. Consider that, rationally, I should feel a certain way (without taking into account how I actually feel). For example, feeling sadness but not listening to what that tells me because "I have no reason to be sad."

The problem in not taking emotion into account is that it will keep trying to get our attention until we *do* take it into account. We'll see all this in detail in the chapters dedicated to emotions.

Emotion Mind

This is a state of mind in which current life experience is emotional. In emotion mind, we're guided by our emotions. We see life through *the filter of our emotions*.

Emotion mind allows you to be creative, to have the energy to push yourself beyond your limits for what is important to you.

What's the risk of being only in a state of emotion mind?

Having a biased, restricted vision of reality. Everything is colored by our emotional state. In this state of mind, our emotions are overflowing, and they control our behavior. In emotion mind, I feel as if emotion is everything and everywhere, and I'm unable to focus on anything else. I lose my freedom of choice.

▷ **CANDACE** For example, when Candace feels extremely angry, she sees red (everything is colored by this emotion), and she'll release her pent-up feelings by punching walls.

The behavior driven by emotion mind is like taking an emergency exit. The problem with emergency exits is that they rarely lead us where we would have chosen to go. We're just looking for a short-term solution to lower our inner tension, without taking a step back or considering its long-term effectiveness for our life.

Wise Mind or Mindfulness

Wise mind is "that which perceives," as distinct from that which is perceived. It is the integration of reasonable mind and emotion mind—and a little more than that too! It's also an intense feeling of being in the right, *of being consistent with what matters to you.*

In wise mind, I have access to

– the thoughts and emotions that the situation brings up for me

– what I usually do in this situation

– what I know to be important to me

You're seeing the most complete and integrated view of the picture.

" Mindfulness means paying attention, on purpose, in the present moment and non-judgmentally, to the experience unfolding moment by moment. "   —JON KABAT-ZINN

What Exactly Is Wise Mind?

▷ **CANDACE** Let's take an example from Candace.

Situation: Candace is having a meal with her parents, during which she tells a story. Her father interrupts her to ask her an unrelated question. Candace gives a short reply and continues her story. Her father reprimands her for being rude.

What Happened: Here, the situation triggered the emotion of anger for Candace, which relates to *emotion mind.* In a situation like this, Candace knows that she usually yells, gets up from the table, and slams the door as she leaves. She also knows that her relationship with her parents is important to her, and she knows that she would like to have a sharing

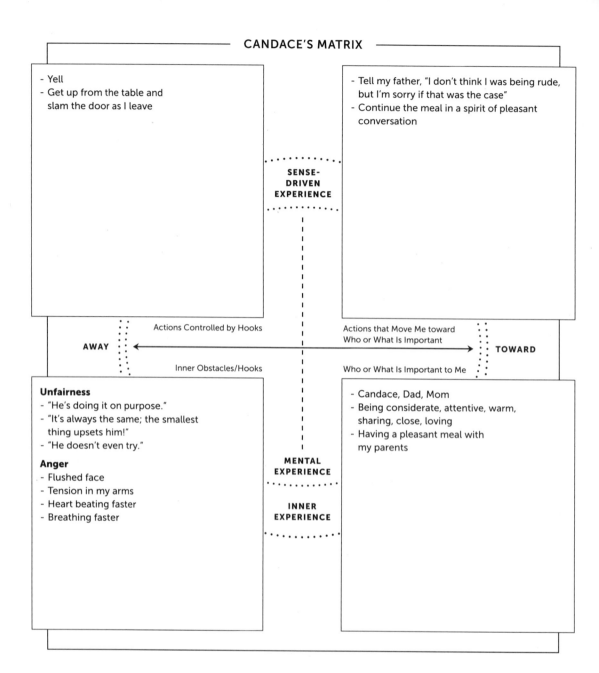

Sense-Driven Experience (upper left):
- Yell
- Get up from the table and slam the door as I leave

Sense-Driven Experience (upper right):
- Tell my father, "I don't think I was being rude, but I'm sorry if that was the case"
- Continue the meal in a spirit of pleasant conversation

AWAY — Actions Controlled by Hooks / Inner Obstacles/Hooks ← → **TOWARD** — Actions that Move Me toward Who or What Is Important / Who or What Is Important to Me

SENSE-DRIVEN EXPERIENCE

MENTAL EXPERIENCE

INNER EXPERIENCE

Inner Experience (lower left):

Unfairness
- "He's doing it on purpose."
- "It's always the same; the smallest thing upsets him!"
- "He doesn't even try."

Anger
- Flushed face
- Tension in my arms
- Heart beating faster
- Breathing faster

Inner Experience (lower right):
- Candace, Dad, Mom
- Being considerate, attentive, warm, sharing, close, loving
- Having a pleasant meal with my parents

and close relationship with them; what is important to her is to have a pleasant meal with her parents. This line of thinking relates to *reasonable mind*. So Candace tells her father, "I don't think I was being rude, but I'm sorry if that was the case," and continues the conversation in a state of *wise mind*.

To be more precise, it isn't so much the situation itself that triggered the emotion of anger for Candace but Candace's interpretation of the situation (or the thoughts that sprung to mind in that situation and that

Candace latched onto): "He's doing it on purpose," "It's always the same; the smallest thing upsets him," "He doesn't even try."

Mindfulness is central in taking control of your life. It involves controlling your attention, with flexibility and kindness, moment by moment.

Mindfulness allows you to:

– make your emotions your allies and improve their regulation

– be truly present in what you do, moment by moment

– make effective choices for your life

In the end, it will significantly improve your quality of life!

PRACTICAL APPLICATION

Exercise for the Coming Week

Every day, *identify* times when you are in *different states of mind*. Becoming aware of what is happening within us is the first step. This allows us to get out of autopilot mode, come back to the present moment, and make informed choices for our lives. Learning to be aware of what is going on in our minds is fundamental.

Day	Situations When I Was in Reasonable Mind	Situations When I Was in Emotion Mind	Situations When I Was in Wise Mind
1			
2			
3			
4			

5			
6			
7			

CHAPTER 5

THE THREE "WHAT" SKILLS FOR PRACTICING MINDFULNESS

"The primary cause of unhappiness is never the situation but your thoughts about it." —ECKHART TOLLE

There are three skills for practicing mindfulness: observing, describing, and participating.

OBSERVING

Observing means to notice something. We can observe:

– what happens outside of ourselves, through *our five senses*

– what happens *within ourselves*

In order to observe what's happening within ourselves, we need to be aware of changes taking place within us. What changes within ourselves can we observe?

– *changes in our feelings* (emotions are expressed by changes in the body). For example, flushed cheeks, tightening in the throat, an accelerating heartbeat

– *changes in our thoughts* in the form of mental images or sounds

This first step simply entails developing our level of alertness and being aware of what's happening within us, moment by moment. Observing involves announcing to ourselves, "Something interesting is happening here" (without labeling or describing what it is).

DESCRIBING

After observing that something is happening, we can express this experience in words. What does that mean?

It means accurately describing what's happening. Much like a curious scientist, we try to describe what's happening within us or outside of us with as much objectivity and precision as possible, without interpreting it.

▷ **CANDACE** Let's take another look at one of Candace's examples from the previous chapter.

Situation: Candace is having a meal with her parents, during which she tells a story. Her father interrupts her to ask her an unrelated question. Candace gives a short reply and continues her story. Her father reprimands her for being rude. In this situation, Candace can describe:

— the situation or facts

▷ **CANDACE** *I'm having a meal with my parents. I'm telling a story. My father asks me an unrelated question. I reply with a few words and continue my story. My father says to me: "Unbelievable! You're being snippy with me again!"*

— her thoughts

▷ **CANDACE** *"He's doing it on purpose," "It's always the same, the smallest thing upsets him," "He doesn't even try."*

— her feelings

▷ **CANDACE** *Flushed face, tension in my arms, heart beating faster, breathing faster.*

Can you see the difference between "facts" and "thoughts"? Is there a difference between perceiving "he's doing it on purpose" as a fact or as a mere thought?

A thought is not necessarily the truth. It's not because Candace has the thought "he's doing it on purpose" that her father really is doing it on purpose.

How do we put some distance between ourselves and our thoughts? How can we perceive that thoughts are not facts? There are two methods to do this.

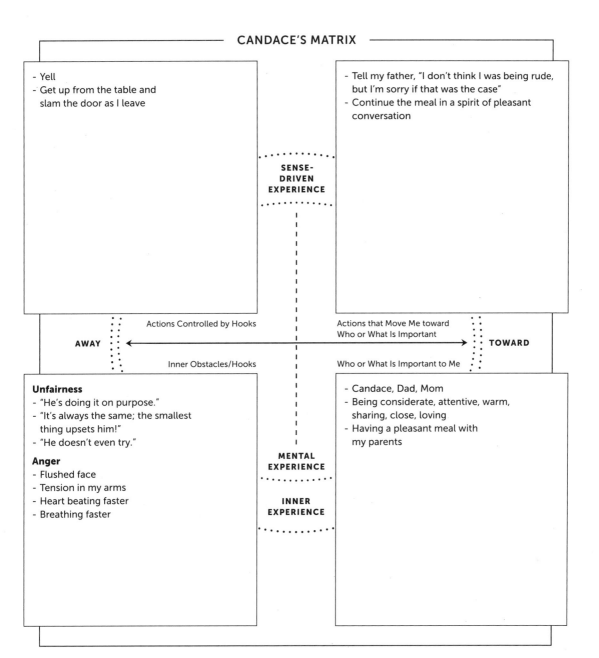

CANDACE'S MATRIX

(Upper left — Actions Controlled by Hooks, Away)
- Yell
- Get up from the table and slam the door as I leave

(Upper right — Sense-Driven Experience, Toward)
- Tell my father, "I don't think I was being rude, but I'm sorry if that was the case"
- Continue the meal in a spirit of pleasant conversation

SENSE-DRIVEN EXPERIENCE

AWAY ← → **TOWARD**

Actions Controlled by Hooks

Actions that Move Me toward Who or What Is Important

Inner Obstacles/Hooks

Who or What Is Important to Me

(Lower left — Inner Obstacles/Hooks, Away)

Unfairness
- "He's doing it on purpose."
- "It's always the same; the smallest thing upsets him!"
- "He doesn't even try."

Anger
- Flushed face
- Tension in my arms
- Heart beating faster
- Breathing faster

(Lower right — Who or What Is Important to Me, Toward)
- Candace, Dad, Mom
- Being considerate, attentive, warm, sharing, close, loving
- Having a pleasant meal with my parents

MENTAL EXPERIENCE

INNER EXPERIENCE

How to Differentiate Thoughts from Facts
First Method: Boxes, or How to Distinguish between Facts, Thoughts, and Feelings

Let's do an experiment . . . Before we introduce this method, let's do a little experiment together. Complete the table on the next page. Fill in each line from left to right:

- Read the statement on each line.
- First fill in the "thoughts/interpretations" box: What are you saying to yourself? What's your head telling you at this moment?
- Then fill in the "emotions" box: If you entirely believe what your thoughts are telling you, how does that make you feel?

To help you, we've put some examples of answers in this table.

FACTS	Describe the different possible thoughts/ interpretations	Emotions associated with the thought/ interpretation
1. I send a text to a friend to ask her to spend the evening together. One hour later, no response.	– I'm not interesting enough for her. – She's not a true friend. – She hasn't seen my text yet. – _____ – _____ – _____	– Sadness, shame – Sadness, anger – Waiting, rather calm – _____ – _____ – _____
2. Two hours later, still no response.	– She's definitely not a friend. She's good for nothing. – Something bad happened to her. – She's still not available. – _____ – _____ – _____	– Sadness, anger – Fear – Irritation – _____ – _____ – _____

What do your thoughts and emotions make you want to do? Answer honestly before reading on.

➤ ME _____

_____

_____

• _____

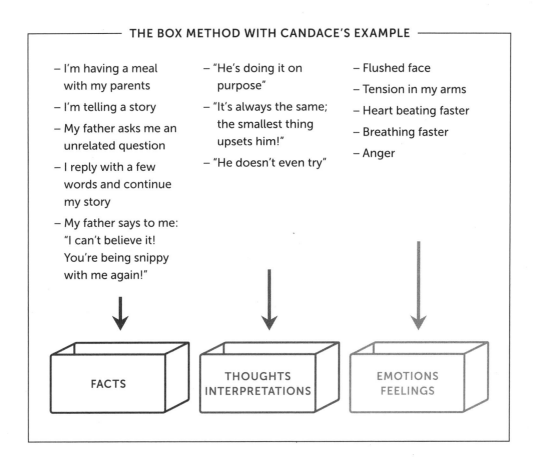

THE BOX METHOD WITH CANDACE'S EXAMPLE

- I'm having a meal with my parents
- I'm telling a story
- My father asks me an unrelated question
- I reply with a few words and continue my story
- My father says to me: "I can't believe it! You're being snippy with me again!"

- "He's doing it on purpose"
- "It's always the same; the smallest thing upsets him!"
- "He doesn't even try"

- Flushed face
- Tension in my arms
- Heart beating faster
- Breathing faster
- Anger

FACTS

THOUGHTS INTERPRETATIONS

EMOTIONS FEELINGS

▷ **CANDACE** *Badger my friend with texts; leave a message on her voice-mail saying that I know she doesn't want to spend the evening with me anyway; turn off my phone declaring that now it's too late; delete her from my contacts.*

Ten minutes later, my friend replies to my text: "Yes, ok for tonight, looking forward to it!"

What does this experiment show us?   When we stick to our thoughts as if they were facts, we adopt behaviors that we regret later.

In practical terms, when a situation arises, think of *three boxes* (on paper or in your head!):

- a "Facts" box
- a "Thoughts/Interpretations" box
- an "Emotions/Feelings" box

These boxes can be colored to distinguish between them. Then fill the three boxes with the elements of the situation.

Second Method: "I have the thought that . . ."

Let's do an experiment . . . Make the following negative thought come to you: "She doesn't want to spend time with me."

Play along—do it before reading more!

Now, repeat this thought silently to yourself while adding to the beginning: "I have the thought that . . ." Now it reads: "*I have the thought that* she doesn't want to spend time with me."

Now, repeat it to yourself one more time, but this time add this phrase: "I noticed that I had the thought that . . ." Now it reads: "*I noticed that I had the thought that* she doesn't want to spend time with me."

What did you observe through this experiment?

For most of us, this experiment lets us distance ourselves from the thought. We can observe the thought as a mere mental phenomenon and not as an absolute truth.

CHOOSING WHAT I DO AMOUNTS TO

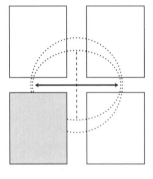

1. Taking into account what is presented to me (without reacting to it impulsively), observing then describing = hooks

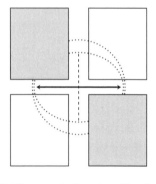

2. Putting me in touch with what I know about myself:

    – my usual way of reacting in this situation

    – what is important to me in life

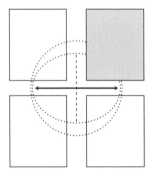

3. Adopting a behavior while being aware of all of this, being fully present in what I do = PARTICIPATING

PARTICIPATING

Participating means fully engaging in the action we've chosen in the way we've decided (that is, based on our values). This comes after having taken the time to observe and describe. Therefore, it's *choosing what I do* and being fully present in it. One of the key ideas to fully understand is that *our automatic thoughts do not control our actions.* Thoughts have a great influence on our actions when we become attached to them—that is, when we take what they tell us as absolute truths! But our thoughts have much less influence when we take a step back from them.

Let's do an experiment . . . Put down everything you have in your hands. Now, bring to mind the thought "I can't lift my right arm." Are you thinking it? If so, try raising your right arm.

What's happening? You're thinking, "I can't lift my right arm," but your right arm is lifted, right? You see, you can have a thought and do something other than what this thought is telling you.

You can do what is important to you, even though your thoughts are telling you that you can't or are making you do something else.

PRACTICAL APPLICATION:
LET'S TAKE A LOOK AT A MOMENT IN YOUR LIFE _____

Identify a situation that led you to behave impulsively and that had negative consequences for you, or identify someone who didn't take care of you or who made the original situation worse. Describe the situation you were in then.

Answer the following nine questions, and then transfer your answers into the matrix on p. 71 where specified by each question number.

1. Write down the impulsive behavior you've identified as behavior that doesn't take care of you. *(This is how you've behaved when very much under the control of what you didn't want to think or feel [when the emotional stress was high] instead of moving toward what is important to you or what would take care of you in the long run.)*

> ME _____

2. Can you identify the emotion that caused such unpleasant stress? What thoughts were associated with it? *(These are likely thoughts that you tend to have and that regularly cause this kind of emotional stress.)*

> ME _____

3. When you were in touch with these thoughts and emotions, it was unpleasant. Where did you feel this in your body? How would you describe this sensation? *(It's important to describe it precisely so that when we experience this unpleasant sensation, we can recognize that we're reacting physically to these particular thoughts and emotions.)*

➤ ME _____

4. Identify what would be really important to you in this situation now. What would allow you to really take care of yourself? Fundamentally, when you experience this type of unpleasant stress, how would you like to behave? What are the values that you identified in the matrix in chapter 2, p. 25, that would be truly important for you to embody? What would be important to you in that? *(These are things that are meaningful to you.)*

➤ ME _____

5. Write down what you could do to move in the direction of those values identified in the lower right part of your matrix. Specifically, the next time you experience similar emotional stress, what could you do that both takes care of you and allows you to be the person you really want to be and at the same time is a little different from what you usually do? What would the person you'd really like to be do?

➤ ME _____

6. If the step is too big or too difficult to do as it is, what can you do to make it easier?

➤ ME _____

7. Why would it be important for you to do what you just wrote down in the upper right part of your matrix (questions 5 and 6)? *(If it's already sufficiently complete and clear, it's not necessary to write more.)*

➤ ME _____

Reread what you wrote in the right-hand side of the matrix.

8. What does that make you feel in your body? Where? How would you describe it?

➤ ME _____

Does this make more sense than what is written on the left-hand side of the matrix?

9. If YES, can you find a word that describes what a life like this would be like? What intense feeling do you have in your core when you imagine this?

➤ ME _____

MY MATRIX

Fill in the matrix below with the answer that corresponds to each question number.

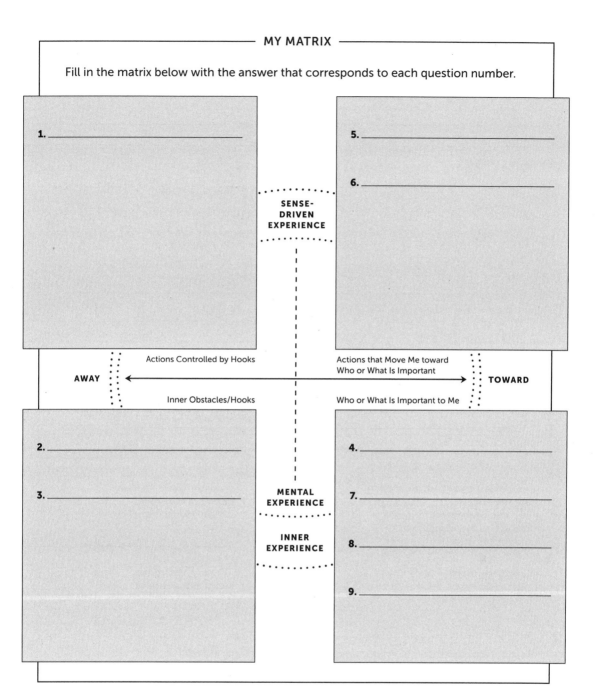

1. _____

5. _____

6. _____

SENSE-
DRIVEN
EXPERIENCE

Actions Controlled by Hooks | Actions that Move Me toward
Who or What Is Important

AWAY ◄─────────────────────► TOWARD

Inner Obstacles/Hooks | Who or What Is Important to Me

2. _____

3. _____

MENTAL
EXPERIENCE

INNER
EXPERIENCE

4. _____

7. _____

8. _____

9. _____

If YES, would you agree to leaving a little room for inner obstacles (written in the lower left part of the matrix) should they arise for you, quit fighting them, and take the small step that you've identified in the upper right of your matrix, because it allows you to move forward toward a life that has meaning for you?

> **CANDACE** *I sent Chris a text message so we could spend the evening together. He didn't reply right away. So I sent three more text messages, and then I called three times (including once from a blocked number). He still hasn't replied.*

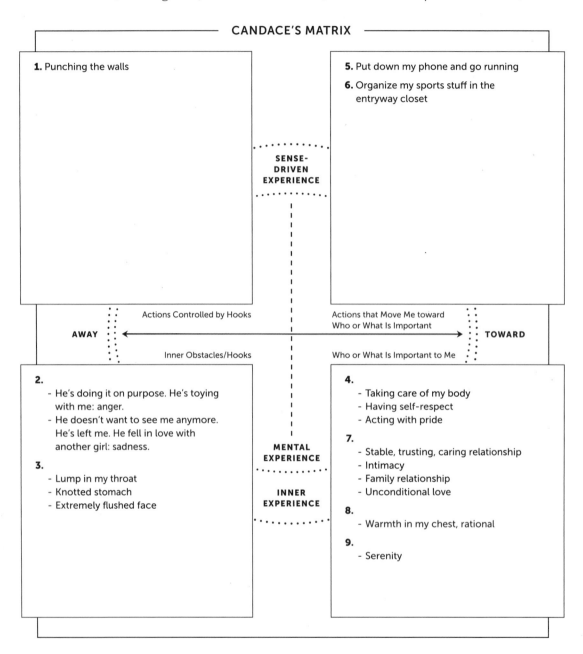

CANDACE'S MATRIX

1. Punching the walls

5. Put down my phone and go running

6. Organize my sports stuff in the entryway closet

SENSE-DRIVEN EXPERIENCE

AWAY

Actions Controlled by Hooks

Actions that Move Me toward Who or What Is Important

TOWARD

Inner Obstacles/Hooks

Who or What Is Important to Me

2.
- He's doing it on purpose. He's toying with me: anger.
- He doesn't want to see me anymore. He's left me. He fell in love with another girl: sadness.

3.
- Lump in my throat
- Knotted stomach
- Extremely flushed face

MENTAL EXPERIENCE

INNER EXPERIENCE

4.
- Taking care of my body
- Having self-respect
- Acting with pride

7.
- Stable, trusting, caring relationship
- Intimacy
- Family relationship
- Unconditional love

8.
- Warmth in my chest, rational

9.
- Serenity

For the hours and days ahead, watch what happens. If you aren't able to take the small step, the simple act of having written it down in the matrix is already a way you're moving forward in the direction you want for your life. This progress will happen later or in some other way.

And if you did take the small step, great! In that case, observe the difference in your feelings. It's probably related to pushing yourself beyond your limits, pride, and consistency with your values.

Exercise for the Coming Week

Every day, identify times when you are in different states of mind.

Identify times when you have made decisions in a state of *wise mind* (specify the new behaviors and if they caused a difference in terms of your deepest feelings—consistency with your values, feeling fulfilled, and so on).

Day	Situations When I Was in Reasonable Mind	Situations When I Was in Emotion Mind	Situations When I Was in Wise Mind
1			
2			
3			
4			
5			
6			
7			

CHAPTER 6

THE THREE "HOW" SKILLS FOR LIVING MINDFULLY

One thing at a time + taking a nonjudgmental approach
+ acting effectively = living mindfully.

Having learned about the three tools for practicing mindfulness (observing, describing, and participating), next we'll take a look at the three skills for how to live it. These three skills are:

— one thing at a time

— taking a nonjudgmental approach

— acting effectively

FOCUSING ON ONE THING AT A TIME

In life, we're often not fully present in what we do. Indeed, there's a part of us that takes ourselves elsewhere: this can be our thoughts, our emotions, or what we experience with our five senses that trigger these mental phenomena.

▷ **CANDACE** *Quite often, I do many things at the same time. I eat while watching TV, and at the same time I feed my dog. I can even call a friend at the same time! I tell myself that it saves me time. In retrospect, it's true that I'm not really present in what I'm doing. I often even forget what my friend told me on the phone.*

At the end of the day, it makes me feel scattered, which makes me feel even emptier. I don't feel like I'm living fully.

We're going to learn to do only one thing at a time. This doesn't mean rigid control of our attention but rather a movement of coming and going.

In fact, when we're focused on an activity, our attention is regularly being grabbed by other things. That's normal; it's how the human mind usually works. What we're going to practice doing differently is returning to our current activity.

To do this, whenever you notice your attention has moved away from what you were doing, you'll choose to return to it with kindness. This "coming and going" of your attention will probably take place dozens and dozens of times during a single activity.

Being present in one thing at a time involves:

- noticing when my attention is moving away from the present moment
- making a conscious choice to bring my attention back, with kindness, to the current activity

Most of us think that if we do many things at once, we'll accomplish more. That's not true!

It's not effective to try to do many things at the same time. This doesn't mean you can't switch from one thing to another and then go back to the first. The important thing is that you concentrate as best as you can on what you're doing in that moment. This applies as much to physical activities as mental activities. It's about voluntarily paying attention to what you're doing without letting yourself get caught up in your mind's wanderings.

Whenever you realize you're elsewhere, return as best as you can, and with kindness, and invest fully in what you're doing.

Tip: Write It Down!

Sometimes, while we're doing an activity, our minds are bombarded with orders ("You have to do that") and even threats ("Do it now or else you'll forget").

When you do something, give it your full attention. When your thoughts remind you of something you have to do, instead of dividing your attention, write it down on a piece of paper and then return to what you were doing.

Be aware that your mind will always suggest doing something better or more urgent than what you're doing in the present moment! The mind of every human being works this way. You can't control the thoughts that your mind suggests to you; that's just how it is. On the other hand, you can choose what you do in the moment.

TAKING A NONJUDGMENTAL APPROACH

Mindfulness requires being nonjudgmental toward ourselves and others. It's about not labeling things as good or bad. It's not possible to practice mindfulness when we're being judgmental. Why not?

Because when we're being judgmental, we're not being fully present in reality. We're simplifying; we're seeing through the filter of our interpretation. We're seeing things from a very narrow point of view.

For example: you tell yourself that a particular person is perfect. The problem is that when she does or says something that you don't like or that doesn't meet your expectations, you'll be disappointed. Why? Because, colored by judgment, your expectations are unrealistic.

In any situation, just as for any person,
black and white coexist at all times.

One of the risks of judging is generalizing, or seeing things from only one angle. As a result, the decisions you make take into account only this one perspective.

Imagine . . .

You meet someone for the first time. She exhibits explosive behavior, guided by anger. You say to yourself: "This is an angry person."

Why is this judgment risky for future encounters you'll have with this person?

You'll tend to interpret all of her actions based on this judgment. Your attention will be drawn to any sign of an angry outburst on her part—which will validate your original judgment.

Judgment sets a situation in stone.

Let's consider an example . . . You try to repair your washing machine, but you don't succeed the first time. If you say to yourself, "I'm no good at this, I'll never be able to do it," what will you be inclined to do? Probably give up.

Now imagine that you stepped away from this judgment, and you tried to simply describe the situation. That could result in: "I tried to repair the washing machine by unplugging it. That didn't work."

What's the difference between this thought and the judgmental thought? With this thought, there seem to be alternative strategies that could help you overcome this situation. How can I then adapt my behavior to the situation?

The fact remains that we don't choose the thoughts we have.

> *The problem isn't having judgmental thoughts, everyone has them! The problem is latching onto these thoughts and considering them to be absolute truths.*

When a judgmental thought comes to you, you can use the box method or the "I have the thought that" method (see chapter 5).

ACTING EFFECTIVELY

This is about moving toward what is important to you in any given situation. It's also about avoiding creating even bigger problems by wanting to react to an initial problem.

For example: you're at the counter of a public service office. You just came to pick up a document that's important to you. The clerk is talking with her colleague. This makes you feel angry; you tell yourself she's wasting your time. If you get angry at her or leave the room and slam the door behind you, you jeopardize your chances of getting the document you came for. By doing this, you're not being effective. You won't fulfill your goal since you won't get your document.

How could you practice mindfulness in this situation?

> *It's about moving toward what is important to you in any given situation.*

PRACTICAL APPLICATION _____

Here's a strategy for practicing mindfulness in the situation we've just described:

1. Observe with your five senses what you see and hear at the counter.

2. Describe the situation: the facts! For example: "I'm the fourth person in line for counter no. 2. The clerk is chatting with her colleague."

▶ ME _____

3. Observe and name the thoughts that come to you. For example: "I have the thought that she really couldn't care less about people," "I have the thought that she's wasting my time."

> ME _____

4. Observe and name the emotions that these thoughts evoke for you and what this makes you feel in your body. For example: "I feel angry," "I have a lump in my throat, my face is flushed, and my heart is beating faster."

> ME _____

5. Identify the urgent need, what it makes you feel like doing in the moment. For example: "I feel like punching her in the face and slamming the door as I walk out."

> ME _____

6. Identify what is important to you in this situation. If you weren't feeling uncomfortable, what would really matter in this situation? For example, in this case: getting my document.

> ME _____

7. Are you ready to make space for these unpleasant emotions and feelings (in this case, it's about making room for the lump in your throat, flushed face, and faster heartbeat), so you can move toward what is really important to you in this situation?

> ME _____

8. What emotion would you feel deeply tomorrow if you had achieved what is important to you despite the obstacle that arose for you? (In this case, you'd probably feel proud.)

> ME _____

We can also show this process in our usual tool: the matrix. Fill in the matrix with the answer that corresponds to each question number as shown.

Acting effectively requires recognizing the situation and acting consciously. It's not about reacting to what you think the situation should be (for example: "The clerk should prioritize the customers over her conversation with her colleague. That's what she's being paid for!"). Acting effectively means choosing how to act based on reality as it really is. Therefore, we must observe and describe the situation and what it produces within us. Accept reality as it is, even if it doesn't meet our expectations. Then act accordingly.

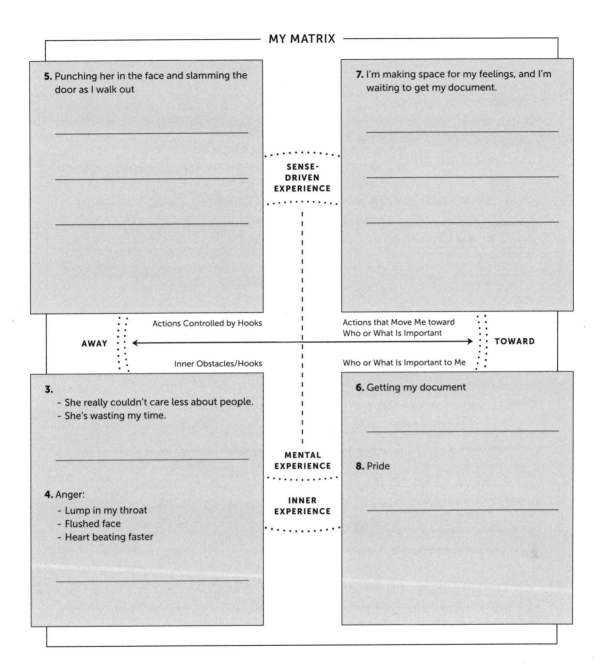

MY MATRIX

5. Punching her in the face and slamming the door as I walk out

7. I'm making space for my feelings, and I'm waiting to get my document.

SENSE-DRIVEN EXPERIENCE

Actions Controlled by Hooks

AWAY ← → **TOWARD**

Actions that Move Me toward Who or What Is Important

Inner Obstacles/Hooks

Who or What Is Important to Me

3.
- She really couldn't care less about people.
- She's wasting my time.

6. Getting my document

MENTAL EXPERIENCE

8. Pride

4. Anger:
- Lump in my throat
- Flushed face
- Heart beating faster

INNER EXPERIENCE

Exercise for the Coming Week

Every day, identify times when you are in different states of mind.

When you're confronted with something that causes emotional stress, fill in the table on the next page, and try to take a small step back so you can choose to participate mindfully (making a decision that's effective for your life).

SITUATION 1

Describe what you observed
(thoughts, feelings, and emotions)

Write down the small step chosen
in mindfulness

Identify your deepest feelings
when you fully engage with this
small step (participation)

SITUATION 2

Describe what you observed
(thoughts, feelings, and emotions)

Write down the small step chosen
in mindfulness

Identify your deepest feelings
when you fully engage with this
small step (participation)

SITUATION 3

Describe what you observed
(thoughts, feelings, and emotions)

Write down the small step chosen
in mindfulness

Identify your deepest feelings
when you fully engage with this
small step (participation)

REGULATING EMOTIONS

If you're reading this book, then just like Candace, how you experience your emotions is often intense or even overwhelming. They take up a lot of space in your life. So much space that sometimes you feel like they take up all the space, to the point of controlling some of your behaviors.

These behaviors are considered to be emergency actions (the upper left part of the matrix). We do them automatically—we're being controlled by our unpleasant emotions and feelings. Their sole purpose is to tamp down these unpleasant emotions and feelings as quickly as possible. We shouldn't judge these behaviors because they do have a function: they try to relieve the discomfort in the short term (when Candace is angry with Chris and slams the door, it gives her instant relief).

However, these impulsive behaviors aren't effective for your life in the long run. Not only do they not take care of you, but they also make you move away from what is important to you.

But if there are emotions there, it's because these things are important to you.

In the next chapters, we suggest a totally different approach regarding the unpleasant and/or overwhelming emotions that you experience. It's not a matter of running away from them or avoiding them at all costs anymore. As a matter of fact, you've been using this strategy for years, and it doesn't have the desired results. Not only does it not work in the long run, but it also moves you away from what is important to you.

So we'll change strategy!

You'll integrate new skills that have been scientifically proven to be effective in regulating emotions. We'll guide you toward acceptance, which means experiencing things as they are without trying to change them, even if it's painful. Yes, you read that correctly! One thing is certain: if you follow the process described in this book step by step, you'll gain infinite freedom when it comes to your emotions.

> 66 The definition of insanity is doing the same thing over and over again and expecting different results. 99 —ALBERT EINSTEIN

To do this, allow yourself to be guided toward the possibility of bringing your awareness, gently, amiably, and kindly, in the direction of: "How do difficult things show up in my body? Where precisely? Can I stay with it for a while since it's the current reality? What I feel tells me that something important is going on for me in this moment. Can I notice the meaning behind it? Is it possible to live the experience, to just be with it, because I know precisely what it is and that it doesn't take up all the space anymore?"

It's about being able to say to yourself: "That's just how things are right now. I know it'll pass; I have this assurance. I can then continue to implement behaviors that take care of me and that make sense for my life." The next chapters will guide you in this direction.

CHAPTER 7

EVERYTHING YOU'VE ALWAYS WANTED TO KNOW ABOUT EMOTIONS

"You can't stop the waves, but you can learn to surf.**"**
—JOSEPH GOLDSTEIN

In order to regulate something, you first have to have observed and described it. When you notice that you feel the sensation of hunger (growling stomach, tiredness), you can respond to it by eating. It's the same for emotions.

WHAT ARE EMOTIONS? WHERE DO THEY COME FROM?

An emotion is a state with sensations of pleasure or distress. Emotions are produced by the brain and are manifested in the body. When we feel an emotion, changes occur in our bodies: muscles tense or relax, heart and respiratory rates accelerate or slow down. These physical sensations vary depending on the type of emotion. Being alert to these changes in the body as soon as they appear is the first step in effectively regulating emotions.

An emotion appears in a situation or context. It's triggered by an outside event (perceived by sensory organs: what you see, hear, and so forth) or by an internal event (a memory, a mental image, a sensation).

Emotions send us a message about our inner balance. There are many emotions because our bodies transmit many types of information. Every human being comes into the world with the ability to feel these various emotions. Therefore, they're useful for our survival.

Some emotions—anger, sadness, curiosity, fear, surprise, disgust, and joy—are innate (present from birth).

Two other emotions are acquired through socialization. These are guilt and shame.

HOW CAN YOU RECOGNIZE EMOTIONS?
WHAT'S THEIR PURPOSE?

Emotions inform me about my state of mind here and now.

Emotions are the physical manifestations of your thoughts, that is, of how you interpret the impact of the external reality on your conditions for happiness—which does not mean that these are real external conditions that need to be fulfilled in order to be happy! However, because of our personal and socio-cultural history, we have constructed a representation of ourselves that requires specific conditions to feel good and/or to have value. An emotion signals to you that there is a gap (for unpleasant emotions) or a correspondence (for pleasant emotions) between "the expectations you had for the current moment of life" and "what appears to you as an external reality."

Whether pleasant or unpleasant, emotions are always useful. They give us valuable information about our inner state. Most people fight unpleasant emotions and don't want to feel them at any cost. Big mistake!

An emotion is like a warning light on a car's dashboard. When a red light pops up on your car's dashboard, what do you do? Answer honestly. Do you put a sheet over it so you can't see it anymore? Or do you try to identify what this warning light is telling you?

The second solution, right? The same goes for emotions. Your body produces an emotion to send you a message. Not wanting to be in touch with this emotion is like putting a sheet over your dashboard. You might encounter problems later on down the road that are bigger than the initial discomfort that this warning light is causing you.

So, an emotion, even if unpleasant, is never dangerous. It's the strategies we put in place to not feel an emotion that can be. It's not the dashboard's warning light that's dangerous but doing everything possible not to see it that is!

> *When it comes to emotions,*
> *control is the problem, not the solution.*

The more you try to fight an emotion, the more intense it becomes. Effective regulation of emotions requires that you agree to feel them as soon as they appear.

The nine emotions presented here are like the primary colors. All the various shades are possible. Thus, anger can range from irritation to rage; fear, from apprehension to terror; and joy, from serenity to a feeling of fullness (see the table on the following pages for all of these nuanced variations).

Careful: an emotion does not express the reality of a situation; it's the reflection of our interpretation of the situation (what we think of this situation). Feeling fear in a situation (for example, public speaking) doesn't necessarily mean that the situation is dangerous.

Let's do an experiment . . . Pick up a pen. For each emotion in the table:

— reread its description

— recall a situation that triggered this emotion. Imagine this situation as if you were reliving it. What do you observe in your body?

— circle the signs in the table that you feel in your body frequently, especially when you experience this emotion

ANGER

Body Language: How do I recognize this emotion in my body?	Chest: A disk-shaped sensation, ranging from a small part of the chest up to the chest's entirety. Anger can feel like an outward thrust from the body's core; a sensation of heat, tightness, or weight. "I feel like I have a weight on my chest," "My shirt feels too tight," "My chest feels compressed, as if it wants to expand and can't," "My lungs feel stuck, my breathing isn't full," "It's as if I have a metal band around my chest."
	Throat: A sensation along the length of the throat sometimes extending all the way down to the stomach. Anger is manifested as increased energy, most often felt as energy moving upward in the body (sometimes it also ascends and descends or moves back and forth). "There's a column of fire in my chest," "My whole chest is on fire."
	Upper back: A triangular area within the neck and shoulder blades. Anger is expressed through muscle tension, which can extend down the arms to clenched fists. "My upper back feels rigid and tense."
	Shoulders: Rigidness, covering the entire width of the back (from one shoulder to the other), which can extend down the arms to clenched fists. "My shoulders feel like a metal bar."
	Facial traits: Tight jaw, clenched teeth, tight or pinched lips, flared nostrils, furrowed brow, frowning eyebrows, pressure behind the eyes, frozen gaze
	Increased heart and respiratory rates
	Posture: Shaking hands and feet

Function: What's the purpose of this emotion?	It signals to me that there is a gap between *my expectations* and *reality*: "It shouldn't be happening like that! It's unfair!"
	Anger is experienced toward someone (others or oneself) or something (a situation, behavior, or idea).
	Be careful not to confuse "feeling angry" (experiencing the emotion of anger) with "acting angrily" (aggressive or violent behavior).
Urge to Act: What does this emotion push me to do in the heat of the moment or under its control?	– Struggle to change external reality – Seek to harm, get revenge – Unload energy (scream, throw, hit, insult others)
Nuances of this emotion	Annoyance, irritation, bitterness, frustration, animosity, hostility, aversion, exasperation, fury, hatred, rage, outrage

SADNESS

Body Language: How do I recognize this emotion in my body?	Upper back and chest: A weight on the upper body, shoulders are hunched forward. Decreased energy, muscles feel weak. Sadness is expressed as a diminished level of energy. "I feel a heaviness, a weight on my shoulders," "I feel tired, empty," "I have no energy," "I feel cold."
	Throat: A spasm. "I have a lump in my throat."
	Facial traits: Slack face, the corners of the lips pull down, the inner parts of the eyebrows rise slightly, drooping eyelids, unfocused stare, misty-eyed, tears
	Slower heart and respiratory rates, often accompanied by deep sighs
	Posture: Weak muscle tone, body rather motionless and caved in on itself
Function: What's the purpose of this emotion?	It signals to me that there is a gap between *my expectations* and *reality*: I must mourn the loss of this person, or situation, or material possession that made my life more pleasant. My life will be worse without it. In this new external reality, this person or thing will be missed and create unhappiness. Experience of loss, something lacking.
Urge to Act: What does this emotion push me to do in the heat of the moment or under its control?	– Fall asleep – Fold in on myself – Give up
Nuances of this emotion	Grief, disappointment, dejection, despondency, sorrow, discouragement, despair, desolation, melancholy, nostalgia

GUILT

Body Language: How do I recognize this emotion in my body?	Chest: A hollowness, a sensation of slow suction inward toward the core. "There's a hollow feeling the size of a coin in my core," "I have a sinking feeling in my stomach."
Function: What's the purpose of this emotion?	It signals to me that there is a gap between *my expectations* and *reality*: "I shouldn't have done that." It signals that we consider one of our actions to be wrong or inappropriate.
Urge to Act: What does this emotion push me to do in the heat of the moment or under its control?	– Undo or make up for what I have or haven't done – Seek reassurance that whatever I have or haven't done isn't a big deal
Nuances of this emotion	Unworthiness, remorse, torment

SHAME

Body Language: How do I recognize this emotion in my body?	Face: A sensation of heat. "I feel as if my face is on fire," "I feel small, like when I was scolded as a child." Facial traits: Lips disappear inside the mouth, slightly frowning eyebrows, eyes lowered toward the ground Posture: Head down, bent over
Function: What's the purpose of this emotion?	It signals to me that there is a gap between *my expectations* and *reality*: "I have less value than other people. When others think of me, they reject, pity, or are disgusted by me." Shame signals that we consider ourselves to be deviant in relation to a social norm. We believe we do not fulfill all the conditions needed to have value. Individuals with borderline personality disorder often feel shame. We'll study this emotion in detail in chapter 18.
Urge to Act: What does this emotion push me to do in the heat of the moment or under its control?	Hide or disappear
Nuances of this emotion	Disgrace, devaluation, discomfort, embarrassment, unworthiness, inferiority, underestimation, humiliation

CURIOSITY

Body Language: How do I recognize this emotion in my body?	Chest: The entire chest thrusts forward, increased energy. "I feel attracted, magnetized."
	Facial traits: Eyes wide open
	Posture: Head straight or leaning forward, open posture
Function: What's the purpose of this emotion?	It signals to me that there is a gap between *my expectations* and *reality*: It's an opportunity in my life to explore and immerse myself in something that interests me.
Urge to Act: What does this emotion push me to do in the heat of the moment or under its control?	Go explore, spend time engaged with whatever created this emotion
Nuances of this emotion	Attraction, desire, enthusiasm, drive, longing

FEAR

Body Language: How do I recognize this emotion in my body?	Abdomen: A hard lump, ranging in size from small to covering the entire abdomen. The abdomen feels contracted, as if something is stuck. "I have a knot in the pit of my stomach."
	Legs and arms: Trembling, flailing, clamminess, sweating, weakness. People often describe it as: "I feel weak in the knees," "My arms have no strength," "I'm sweating."
	Throat: Tightness, contraction, feels obstructed by a lump, spasms. "I feel like I'm choking, my throat is closing," "I'm running out of air, I'm suffocating."
	Facial traits: The mouth opens and extends outward from the face, the upper eyelids rise, the lower eyelids tend toward the inner corner of the eye, the eyebrows rise, eyes opened wide, pale skin
	Accelerated heart rate, diarrhea, an urge to urinate
	Posture: The body retracts and stops moving, frozen stance, arms move forward in a shield position
Function: What's the purpose of this emotion?	It signals to me that there is a gap between *my expectations* and *reality*: Danger! Things will probably go wrong!
Urge to Act: What does this emotion push me to do in the heat of the moment or under its control?	Freeze, stop, don't go there

Nuances of this emotion	Apprehension, nervousness, mistrust, torment, dread, concern, fright, anguish, anxiety, worry, alarm, panic, phobia, bewilderment, terror

SURPRISE

Body Language: How do I recognize this emotion in my body?	Posture: Frozen, open, increased tension. "I feel as if time has stopped for a moment."
	Facial traits: Staring wide-eyed, raised eyebrows, mouth half-open
	Breathing briefly stops
Function: What's the purpose of this emotion?	It signals to me that there is a gap between *my expectations* and *reality*: This situation is unexpected, I need to evaluate as soon as possible whether this is favorable or unfavorable for me.
Urge to Act: What does this emotion push me to do in the heat of the moment or under its control?	It makes me stop and evaluate
Nuances of this emotion	Astonishment, amazement

DISGUST

Body Language: How do I recognize this emotion in my body?	Abdomen and throat: A wave of nausea, digestive reflux reaching to the mouth, digestive spasms, salivation. "My stomach is spasming," "I'm nauseated, I want to vomit."
	Facial traits: The chin is contracted, the upper lip rises revealing the upper teeth, the nose wrinkles, the nostrils rise and dilate, the eyebrows frown, eyes are half closed
	Posture: Palms turned outward, showing an attitude of rejection
Function: What's the purpose of this emotion?	It signals to me that there is a gap between *my expectations* and *reality*: It's not good for me. This is toxic for me.
	We can experience disgust for a food, a situation, or a person.
Urge to Act: What does this emotion push me to do in the heat of the moment or under its control?	Distance myself from it, reject it

Nuances of this emotion	Sourness, bitterness, aversion, disdain, nausea, repugnance

JOY

Body Language: How do I recognize this emotion in my body?	Chest: Soft warmth, lightness, feeling of openness radiating out, which begins in the core and ascends out toward the shoulders. "I have butterflies in my stomach, I feel sparks." "My chest is inflated, filled with a soft warmth."
	Facial traits: Lips drawn toward the ears (smile), the cheeks go up, exposing the teeth of the upper jaw, crow's feet around the outer corners of the eyes
	Posture: Open
Function: What's the purpose of this emotion?	It signals to me that there is a gap between *my expectations* and *reality*: This is good for me here and now.
Urge to Act: What does this emotion push me to do in the heat of the moment or under its control?	– Enjoy – Share – Perpetuate the emotion – Jump, sing, scream, and so on
Nuances of this emotion	Serenity, plenitude, relief, bliss, contentment, pleasure, delight, hope, ecstasy, cheerfulness

MANY TYPES OF EMOTIONS

Emotions are fleeting. They can last from a few seconds to a few minutes. Emotions, when not sustained, come and go. They're like the waves on the surface of the ocean.

It's impossible to be drowned by the wave of an emotion. Even when unpleasant, emotions have a beginning, a middle, and an end.

Mood

When an emotion is sustained by behaviors, whether they are visible from the outside (listening to sad music on repeat) or not (obsessive thoughts), our affective tone will take hold for several days. We're talking about mood. Your days will then be affected by the same feeling. It's a bit like putting on glasses with lenses that are the same color as your emotion: you then see everything around you through this filter.

Secondary Emotions

Refusing to accept an emotion can lead to a vicious cascade of new emotions, called secondary emotions. These emotions occur when a primary emotion wasn't accepted. For example, I have a secondary emotion when I feel ashamed of feeling sad, or when I feel angry for feeling sad, and so on.

A few weeks ago, Chris told Candace that he was going to go skydiving with his friends. She felt extremely angry ("He has no consideration for me, it's disrespectful!"). On closer inspection, anger was actually a secondary emotion. Candace's primary emotion was fear ("It's dangerous, he could have a fatal accident, I could lose him").

Be alert in acknowledging primary emotions. They are what informs you about your inner state here and now, and they inform you about the content of the message being delivered to you. They also inform you about what you believe you need to be true (that is, your mental construct of your needs) in order to feel comfortable.

PRACTICAL APPLICATION _____

Exercise for the Coming Week

Implementation: Essential for moving forward!

- Practice recognizing the first signs of each of these emotions for you.
- Be aware of changes to the sensations in your body: observe and describe these changes as soon as they appear.
- Practice naming emotions: What emotion do these changes in your body seem to correspond to? What does this emotion tell me here and now?

THE FEELING OF EMPTINESS

The feeling of emptiness is one of the criteria for borderline personality disorder. Like every criterion, it isn't required to make the diagnosis. As a reminder, the diagnosis of borderline personality disorder is conditioned on meeting at least five out of the list of nine criteria (see p. 42).

However, people suffering from this disorder frequently experience emptiness. Apathy or loneliness produces a feeling of emptiness, which reflects fears of abandonment or annihilation. This feeling of emptiness can be extremely painful.

Some people compare it to an empty shell or to a sweater forgotten at the back of a closet; in order to exist, they need to be filled by a human presence. Individuals with borderline personality disorder often tend to seek out strong personal relationships to fill this emptiness.

▷ **CANDACE** Candace has never really been single; as soon as a romantic relationship ends, she moves on to a new relationship so she won't be alone . . . to fill this emptiness. In addition, when Candace finds herself alone at home, episodes of bulimia have the same function as a personal relationship: they fill the emptiness and make her stop feeling this excruciating discomfort. Finally, Candace sometimes feels this emptiness even when she's around people ("alone in the middle of everyone"). In these situations, she describes a lack of a strong emotional connection with the person or people around her, which produces an intense feeling of emptiness.

In fact, individuals with borderline personality disorder tend to use various strategies to avoid feeling this emptiness and to keep it at bay. These strategies can be effective in the short term (by lessening unpleasant feelings), but they are often harmful in the long run. They move us away from creating a life that has meaning, a life we can be proud of.

These strategies are attempts to fill the emptiness (bulimic episodes) or to seek thrills (drugs, intense personal relationships).

WHAT IS EMPTINESS FOR ME?

In order to develop effective strategies when facing problems, the first step is to identify precisely what the problem is. Let's start by exploring together how emptiness manifests in you.

PRACTICAL APPLICATION

Identify a time when you felt empty. (Describe the situation you were in at the time.)

➤ ME _____

Answer the following ten questions and put your answers in the matrix on the next page where specified by each question number.

1. Describe what this situation brought up for you. What thoughts? What emotions?

➤ ME _____

2. When you're in touch with these thoughts and emotions, it's unpleasant. Where do you feel this in your body? How would you describe this sensation? (It's important to describe it precisely so that when we experience this unpleasant sensation, we can recognize that we're reacting physically to these particular thoughts and emotions.)

➤ ME _____

Get in touch with these feelings for a few moments.

3. When you were in touch with these feelings, what did they make you want to do in the moment? It could be things that you did in this situation or that you did not do (but that you strongly felt like doing in the moment). These are things you did (or wanted to do) under the control of hooks, rather than moving toward what is important to you and would take care of you in the long run.

➤ ME _____

4. This situation is a difficult one because it interferes with an area of life that's important to you. What area does it affect? Which of your important relationships is affected? *(In fact, several things that are important to you might be affected.)*

➤ ME _____

5. In this area (or with this person), what is *really* important to you? Deep things that are important to you underlie it. That's why it's painful. Why is this area important to

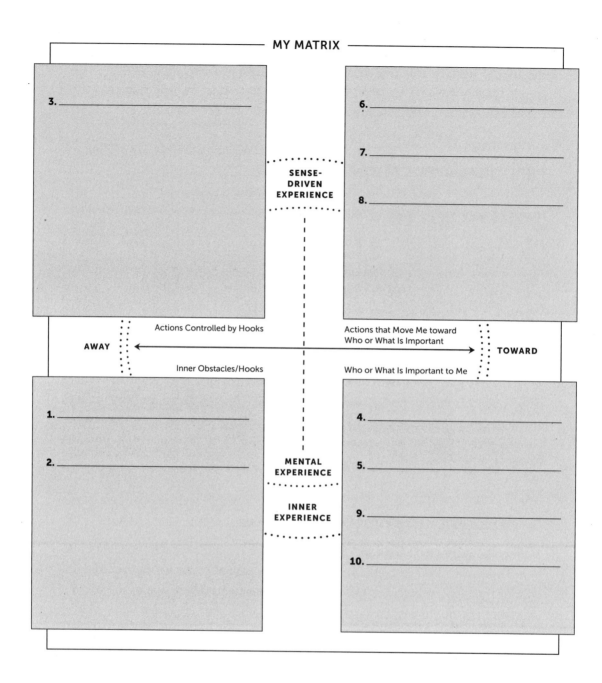

MY MATRIX

3. _____

6. _____

7. _____

8. _____

SENSE-
DRIVEN
EXPERIENCE

Actions Controlled by Hooks

Actions that Move Me toward
Who or What Is Important

AWAY ←————————————————→ TOWARD

Inner Obstacles/Hooks

Who or What Is Important to Me

1. _____

2. _____

4. _____

5. _____

MENTAL
EXPERIENCE

INNER
EXPERIENCE

9. _____

10. _____

you? What deep meaning does this area of life have for you? If anything were possible, if there weren't all the stuff that's written in the lower left part of your matrix, what kind of person would you want to be in this area? How would you want to behave while taking care of yourself?

➤ ME _____

6. Can you identify a behavior to move toward that area (or toward that person) that we just identified? This behavior should be a little different from what you usually do and should still take care of you. *(Notice what you could do to go in the direction of embodying the value(s) identified at the bottom right of your matrix.)*

Specifically, the next time you experience the feeling of emptiness, what could you do that allows you both to take care of yourself and to be the person you really want to be and at the same time is a little different from what you usually do? What would the person you'd really like to be do?

➤ ME _____

7. If the step is too big or too difficult to do as it is, what can you do to make it easier to achieve? What other life areas can you develop that take care of you and that in the bigger picture enable you to take this step later on?

➤ ME _____

8. In the hours and days ahead, what might we see you do specifically to move in this direction?

➤ ME _____

Reread the right-hand side of your matrix.

9. What does that make you feel in your body? Where? How would you describe it?

➤ ME _____

Are the things written on the right-hand side of the matrix more meaningful than those written on the left-hand side?

10. If YES, can you find a word that describes what a life like this would be like? What intense feeling do you have in your core when you imagine this?

➤ ME _____

If YES, would you agree to leaving a little room for inner obstacles (written in the lower left part of the matrix) should they arise for you? Would you agree to quit fighting them and take the small step that you've identified in the upper right part of the matrix, because it allows you to move forward toward a life that has meaning for you?

For the hours and days ahead, watch what happens. If you aren't able to take the small step, just the simple act of having written it down in the matrix is already a way you're moving forward in that direction.

CANDACE'S MATRIX

Situation: *Sunday night, I was home alone; Chris was with his friends*

3.
- Drink alcohol
- Smoke pot
- Send Chris texts threatening to leave him, telling him that our relationship means nothing
- Bulimic episode
- Go out to a club and have sex with the first guy who shows interest
- Constantly check Facebook posts and likes

6. Next time I'm alone, organize an evening for myself: reading, painting

7.
- Schedule the next date with Chris
- Meditate every day in order to better manage unpleasant feelings in stressful situations
- Delete my Facebook account

8.
- Make a list of the activities that are good for me
- Meditation: 10 minutes every night

SENSE-DRIVEN EXPERIENCE

Actions Controlled by Hooks

AWAY ←——————————————————→ **TOWARD**

Actions that Move Me toward Who or What Is Important

Inner Obstacles/Hooks

Who or What Is Important to Me

1.
- I'm alone in the world, I'm abandoned
- A feeling of emptiness
- No one loves me, I'm no good, sadness
- Chris is going to meet some other girl, fear

2.
- Hollow feeling in my stomach
- Lump in my throat

MENTAL EXPERIENCE

INNER EXPERIENCE

4. My relationship with myself

5.
- Develop myself personally, grow, be independent
- Freedom

9. The tension in my chest eases

10. Confidence, pride, independence

And if you did take the small step, great! In that case, observe the difference in your feelings. Could it be related to pushing yourself beyond your limits, pride, and consistency with your values?

WHAT DO I DO ABOUT THIS EMPTINESS WHEN I'M EXPERIENCING IT?

Step One: Acceptance

Accept this feeling. Every human being experiences apathy or emptiness. This feeling is sending us a message to return to the true self—who we really are in our core rather than who our ideas about ourselves mistakenly make us believe we are. As a matter of fact, wanting to avoid feeling this feeling at all costs:

- *intensifies the unpleasant experience*. As you know now, fighting an emotion or feeling increases its intensity. This painful experience then takes up all the space;

- leads you to implement *avoidance strategies that are harmful* to you and move you away from creating a life that you would be truly proud of.

In the next chapter you'll find a detailed guide for accepting this feeling when you're experiencing it.

Step Two: Recharge Your Batteries

Experiencing emptiness invites me to return to myself, to who I really am deep down. How do I take care of myself? How can I develop myself personally? How can I revitalize myself completely?

List your revitalizing activities (that make you feel whole and increase your internal energy) that do not require the presence of a third party:

CANDACE'S LIST	MY LIST
– Take a bath	
– Meditate	
– Read a good detective novel	
– Read inspirational biographies	
– Watch personal development videos on YouTube	
– Listen to music	
– Paint	

A Word of Caution

- Each of these activities is only meaningful when done in a state of mindfulness: being fully present in what you're doing. We want to come back to our true nature of full, peaceful joy and contentment.

- This isn't about doing lots of activities to avoid feeling empty. After agreeing to make room for this emptiness, I can choose to act in a way that's meaningful for taking care of myself holistically. I can choose an activity that connects me to myself, to the person I truly am. It's about getting out of the "doing" mode (being on autopilot, being physically present but mentally absent) in order to be in the "being" mode (being fully present in what I'm doing in the present moment). During this activity, I can be mentally connected to others but in a different way than usual. Others are not here to fill my emptiness anymore. By being connected to my true nature of full, peaceful joy and contentment, others become the support through which I express my values. For example, while painting, I can be fully present in the present moment and deeply connected to the intention of giving to others.

CHAPTER 9

EFFECTIVELY REGULATING EMOTIONS

```
┌─────────── REMEMBER ───────────┐
│                                 │
│           EVENT/FACT            │
```

```
│                                 │
│    INTERPRETATIONS/THOUGHTS     │
│ "What my mind tells me about this event" │
```

```
│                                 │
│            EMOTION              │
│      "How it makes me feel"     │
│                                 │
└─────────────────────────────────┘
```

BEFORE WE BEGIN

In previous chapters we've seen that it's not effective (and even danger-ous) to try to fight an emotion. An emotion is like a warning light on a car's dashboard. It's a messenger sent by our brain. This messenger ex-presses itself through bodily signals; an emotion always gives us useful information about our inner state. Effective regulation of emotions al-ways involves accepting those emotions.

Sometimes the events of everyday life can't be changed, but our rela-tionship to them can change. We generally suffer more than we should—not so much because of the events that occur but because of how we *interpret* these events and *become attached* to our interpretations.

Depending on how we interpret a situation, our emotion will be dif-ferent. Recall the box experiment (chapter 5).

Therefore, it's about detaching from our interpretations and recog-nizing reality for what it is and not for what our mind tells us it is. Reality is sometimes painful; it's unavoidable.

By latching on to our interpretations, our mind often tends to make reality more painful than it really is. Pain is transformed into suffering when we try at all costs not to feel our emotions. Fighting it turns pain into suffering.

The cure is acceptance.

What I Need to Know about Reality

- Sometimes I can change it, after accepting that it is what it is at this moment.

  For example: First I need to accept that I have a drinking problem if I want to be able to change things. If I stubbornly refuse to see that I have a problem—if I don't accept it—I won't be able to take the steps to change it.

- Sometimes I can't change it, and I just have to accept it as it is.

  For example: I can't change the death of a loved one. I have to accept this fact as part of reality.

What I Need to Know about Emotion

Emotion is always something to accept, and never something to avoid or resolve.

" Grant me the *serenity* to accept the things I cannot change, the *courage* to change the things I can, and the *wisdom* to know the difference. "
                                                        —MARCUS AURELIUS

HOW CAN YOU ACCEPT YOUR EMOTIONS IN PRACTICE?

Next you'll find a detailed guide to take you step by step toward accepting an emotion. This guide is the high road to effectively regulating emotions. If you take it, it will allow you to:

- take *a step back* from events. This will give you the opportunity to not be overwhelmed by an emotion but simply be aware of the sensations that the emotion triggers during that moment;

- *give emotions the space* to which they're entitled, without giving them more space than they need. This means making room for emotions so that they don't take up all the space;

- *free yourself from painful extremes* and hope for greater emotional stability;

— become the master of what you do and gain some space so as not to respond in "action/reaction" mode. In fact, you'll gain the ability to be with these feelings, thoughts, and emotions even if they're difficult, without letting them control your actions.

This guide can be used as is. Its framework represents the different steps of emotional acceptance. Feel free to customize this tool, both in the way it's worded and in the time that you devote to each step of this process.

PRACTICAL APPLICATION: SELF-GUIDED ACCEPTANCE OF AN EMOTION _____

You'll probably need to read the guide the first few times, but gradually, you'll take it over completely on your own.

Let yourself be guided by the suggestions below. Each one serves a purpose, and the order is important. Take as much time as you need at each step; if necessary, some steps can be repeated several times in succession.

Regarding intention during this exercise:

– don't try to change the state of things; instead, try to get in touch with what already exists during this moment;

– don't try to distract the mind, even with breathing. Breathing is only an anchor, a safe place.

Choose a rather quiet place and settle into a seated position, if possible, with your feet flat on the floor. Keep your back straight, either supported by the back of the chair or not, but relaxed. It's a position of awakening, of engaged openness toward the experience of the moment.

Now, if you feel comfortable in your position, close your eyes so as to be as attentive as possible to your inner experience. With practice, you'll be able to keep your eyes open when doing this exercise in your daily life. The goal is not to change or resolve anything, but rather to let be what is.

1. I'm making contact with the present moment. What's going on in me in this moment?

2. I'm aware of the points of contact between my body and my support: my feet against the floor, my pelvis against the seat of the chair, and my hands on my thighs.

3. What are my thoughts in this moment?

4. What are the sensations in my body?

5. Where in my body are the most noticeable sensations? How are they expressed (feeling of tightness, tension, knots, heat, tingling, intensity, and so forth)? I name them as precisely as possible, noticing their nuances.

6. What are my feelings and emotions in this moment? I give them words; I label them. These words are my words, and they must be those that best represent, for me, the experience of this moment.

7. I choose, with gentleness and kindness, to let this experience be, without fighting it, regardless of how pleasant or unpleasant it is. I let go since there is nothing to judge about the state of things; it's just the current reality. It's too risky to not let this state be, because it will come back later, stronger, and the pain will also be even stronger. This experience informs me of what I need to know about reality in this moment, of what important message it has for me.

8. When I decide, I identify an area where I can best feel my breathing moment by moment, exhaling followed by inhaling. It could be:

- either the abdomen that expands and contracts;
- or the upper lip beneath the nostrils, which cools with each inhale and warms with each exhale.

9. I observe and feel my breath as best as I can in the area I've chosen.

10. If, at a certain moment, I notice that my mind is wandering or that my thoughts are taking me elsewhere, I choose gently, with kindness and without judgment, to bring my awareness back to my breathing.

11. As best as I can, I try to feel fully anchored in my breathing, fully reassured by this breathing that is always accessible and available.

12. Then, when I feel ready, on an inhale, I explore the uncomfortable area I initially identified. On the inhale, I target the area as best as I can, and I bring my breath there as best as I can. On the exhale, I put space, flexibility, and gentleness there.

13. I know that other human beings sometimes feel the same things I do. It's painful. I allow myself to bring all the attention that I'm capable of in this moment to this area. It's a bit like having a cut on my fingertip that I'd put a bandage on after carefully cleaning the wound.

14. I inhale and exhale into this area as best as I can, without trying to resolve anything, without trying to change or remove the discomfort. I simply bring a little compassion and space there.

15. Now, when I feel ready, on an exhale, I turn the spotlight of my attention on my body as a whole.

16. And even if part of my body is still uncomfortable, my body is whole. I can feel a kind of completeness. The feeling in this area in my body is no longer unbearable; it doesn't scare me anymore because I know it well now. It's perfectly defined and described. It has the right to be what it is, because in any case it's the current reality. It's neither good nor bad, neither too much nor not enough. It's how it is in this moment. It's just a temporary experience in one limited area of my body, like a wave on the surface of the ocean.

17. If I don't yet feel sufficiently in touch with my feelings, or if the wave of emotion still takes up all the space, or is still too invasive or overwhelming, I can start the exercise again from no. 3 and do it as many times as necessary.

18. Maybe I notice that primary feelings have been replaced by other feelings. In fact, the first wave of emotion can happen, be validated and accepted, but then give way to a secondary wave. Then that becomes the current reality. In this case, I can also start the exercise again from no. 3. Maybe I notice that my thoughts, sensations in my body, and emotions are no longer the same, and that I have access to new perspectives.

19. I now make space for all my inner experience of this moment and I choose, on an exhale, to expand the field of my attention beyond my breath and to observe my body as a whole. Perhaps I can feel my stable and complete body, my body that breathes from head to toe.

20. Then I observe my posture and my facial features, right in this moment.

21. I open my eyes.

You'll probably notice that it's now possible to "stay with" the experience of the present moment and that you no longer need to change it or reduce its unpleasantness immediately and at any cost. It's at this moment that you'll become aware of the ephemeral nature of an emotion: it passes like a wave if it's not sustained by resistance or mental distraction. In fact, it's when we stop trying to resolve this state that it resolves itself.

- *It's all about intention:* don't apply this skill in order to make an emotion go away; it'll have the opposite effect! Choose to accept this emotion in order to recognize and validate it.

- *Be forgiving, kind, and full of compassion for yourself.* Your emotional state is already unpleasant enough, so don't aggravate it. If you cut your finger, you wouldn't put dirt on the wound, would you? You'd clean and bandage it; you'd take care of yourself. Do the same with your emotions.

- *Take care of yourself* as you'd take care of the most important person in your life.

Practice

Do you know how to ride a bike? The first time you got on a bike, what happened? You fell after a few seconds, didn't you? If you rode a bike immediately without difficulty, sign up for the Guinness World Records!

It was the same way when you learned to walk, or to do any other activity that you now do naturally.

A habit is a succession of *repeated behaviors.* To create a new habit, change your behavior and repeat it.

To create the new habit of effectively regulating your emotions, you're going to have to practice. Repeat this new strategy again and again.

Just as when you learned to ride a bike, at the beginning you won't see the results of practicing until you've repeated it often enough to feel comfortable with this new way of operating and it becomes one of your habits.

How Can You Practice the Skill of Accepting Emotions?

To begin, we recommend that you experiment with this acceptance process on a regular/formal basis. You can do this exercise at your own pace by following the instructions in the self-guided acceptance exercise.

Decide in advance *three times* during the day when you'll choose to get in touch with your inner experience by following the self-guided exercise.

▷ CANDACE Her choice: in the morning at 8:30, midday before lunch, and in the evening after doing the dishes.

➤ ME _____

These times will probably be less emotionally charged, and that's good! When you began learning to ride a bike, did you start on a steep mountain path? Certainly not!

Be in the same practicing mindset when it comes to developing the skill of accepting emotions. At first practice in rather neutral emotional conditions, and then choose an area in your body where there's physical discomfort rather than an area where there's strong emotion. When the exercise becomes easier, choose slightly more emotionally charged areas, but not ones that are too strong. Choose irritation

SELF-GUIDED ACCEPTANCE OF EMOTIONS

*Acceptance of the inner experience, in its entirety,
beginning at the moment of awareness of a change in the body.*

1. Get in touch with the reality of the experience in the present moment.
   - What are my thoughts?
   - What are the sensations in my body?
   - What are my emotions?
   - Answer with detail, noticing nuances in this moment.
2. Anchor yourself to your breathing, as best as you can, without trying to change anything.
3. Let go, using the breath as a vehicle for compassion and space.

   In the case of persistent thoughts, feelings, and emotions still left to explore, start again from no. 1.

4. Expand awareness to the body as a whole.

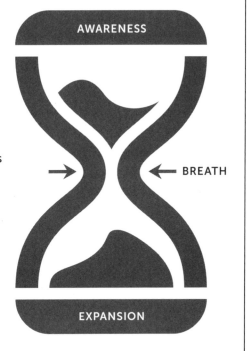

AWARENESS

← BREATH

EXPANSION

rather than rage, worry rather than terror, and so on. Finally, when you feel really familiar with this approach, you'll be able to practice it in any circumstances. Do it as soon as possible after the appearance of internal changes—as soon as the emotion appears. The more an emotion is heard and taken into consideration early on, the easier it will be to regulate it.

▷ **CANDACE** *Initially, I was doubtful about this exercise. It scared me. I thought, "What if it triggers things in me I can't control? And then, I'll be all alone managing it afterward!"*

But finally, I understood that meditation doesn't trigger anything that isn't already there; it's just that I wasn't aware of it. I was trying to distract myself so I wouldn't feel it . . . but eventually it overflows and takes up all the space inside me!

Since I began practicing regularly, I notice changes in myself more often and more easily right when they appear, and I'm able to better regulate them. I find myself less often in extreme situations where I feel overwhelmed. These overwhelming waves have turned into "baby waves"!

KNOWING HOW TO ANALYZE EMOTIONS

Now you've learned that an emotion is linked to a thought or to an interpretation of a situation (event/fact). Knowing how to distinguish each stage in this process (see box on p. 99) is crucial.

We suggest you practice this as follows:

- *Think back* to a time earlier today that you experienced an emotion.
- *Return* to that moment.
- Then, *answer* the questions below.

PRACTICAL APPLICATION _____

1. What was the triggering event? Was it internal or external? What triggered the emotion?

An emotion is a reaction to a triggering event. But it's not always easy to identify the cause. In fact, sometimes you might say, "I was just having a quiet time at home, nothing even happened!" In this case, consider investigating:

- When precisely did you start feeling a change?
- This change can be associated with a stimulus that comes to you through your five senses (an image, smell, sound, and so on) or an internal stimulus (a memory or a thought).

If possible, note the date and time it occurred (the specific time, not an approximate one).

Triggering event: _____

2. What changes and sensations did you feel in your body?

An emotion is felt in the body. It's something that can't be prevented and that exists even if you're not aware of it. See how it manifests itself in your body.

- Even if the change in your body wasn't significant, where in your body did you feel it? Where was this change expressed in your body? *(Example: in your chest, in your stomach, in your throat, and so on)*

Site of the physical change: _____

- How was this change expressed inside my body? *(Example: hollowness, feeling of inner emptiness, muscle weakness, tightness, spasms, palpitations, tension, tingling, hot or cold, and so on)*

Description of the physical change: _____

3. How did you interpret this event? What did you say to yourself in this situation? What did your mind tell you about yourself or about the situation?

Thoughts/interpretations: _____

4. What is the emotion?

Based on your analysis above, you can now name the emotion. Refer to the descriptive list of the nine primary emotions (chapter 7): anger, sadness, guilt, shame, curiosity, fear, surprise, disgust, and joy. Can you name this emotion even more precisely by noticing its nuances?

Name of the emotion: _____

5. Urge to act: What did you want to do in the heat of the moment or under the control of the emotion?

Urge to act: _____

6. Valued action: What would the person you'd really like to be do? What behavior would allow you to move toward what is important to you in this situation? What behavior would take care of you in this situation?

Valued action: _____

7. Values: What is fundamentally important to you in doing this valued action? What values does it embody? Who does it take care of and how?

Values and/or what is important: _____

8. Actual behavior: What was your actual behavior?

Actual behavior: _____

9. Function of the emotion: What did this emotion signal to you? What was its purpose?

Function of the emotion: _____

This is a description "after the fact" of what happened when you experienced an emotion. Gradually, you'll learn to complete this analysis promptly after an emotion appears or in the moment it first emerges. The goal is for you to have a choice in what you do and for your actual behavior to match your valued action.

An important note: Explore pleasant emotions just as much as unpleasant emotions! As a matter of fact, if not properly regulated, a pleasant emotion can lead to impulsive behavior—an urge to act—that moves you away from what is important.

Let's connect this with the matrix through a little game.
Where on your matrix would you place the different steps (1 to 9) of this analysis? Which box of the matrix does each step correspond to? *It's up to you!*

Upper left: _____

Upper right: _____

Lower left: _____

Lower right: _____

See the answer on the following page.

Exercise for the Coming Week
Every evening, analyze an emotion that you experienced during the day.

The goal of this exercise is to train you to make conscious choices that are aligned with who you truly are. We are usually unaware of the automatic psychological processes that occur in our consciousness but that nevertheless are making us act. As soon as we feel bad, we immediately try to escape the discomfort. As soon as we feel good, we try to make it last at all costs. We act on the basis of our emotions, which are the result of the idea we've constructed about ourselves (and, depending on our personal and socio-cultural history, about what we believe we absolutely need to experience and what we especially do not need to experience in order to feel comfortable or to have value). Without learning to identify the inner process (thought, emotion, urge to act) that is spontaneously occurring, we repeat the same patterns over and over again. We experience exactly the same situations (though

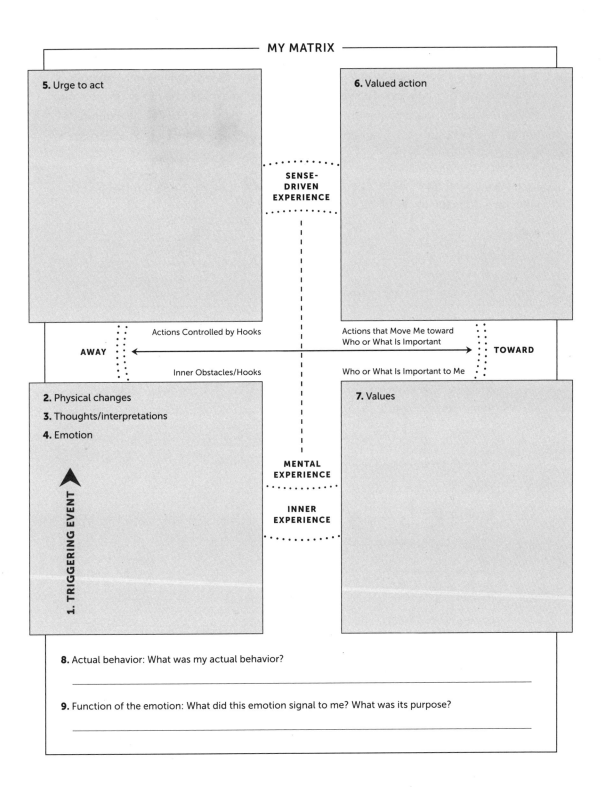

5. Urge to act

6. Valued action

SENSE-DRIVEN EXPERIENCE

Actions Controlled by Hooks

Actions that Move Me toward
Who or What Is Important

AWAY ←————————————————————→ **TOWARD**

Inner Obstacles/Hooks

Who or What Is Important to Me

2. Physical changes
3. Thoughts/interpretations
4. Emotion

1. TRIGGERING EVENT

MENTAL EXPERIENCE

INNER EXPERIENCE

7. Values

8. Actual behavior: What was my actual behavior?

_____

9. Function of the emotion: What did this emotion signal to me? What was its purpose?

_____

they might seem different), and we react in the same way, getting ourselves stuck in a circle of suffering and losing our inner freedom. By becoming aware of what is happening within us, we understand our emotions' message about our relationship to external reality; we become the observer who is no longer confused by our experience, and we thus gain freedom of action. We become free to act in accordance with who we really are deep down.

➤ **CANDACE** Candace chose to do this in the evening after doing the dishes, when she does the acceptance exercise (chapter 9).

➤ ME _____

Day	Process for Analyzing an Emotion
1	Triggering event: _____ Site and description of the physical changes in my body: _____ Thoughts/interpretations of the triggering event: _____ Name of the emotion: _____ Urge to act: _____ Valued action: _____ Values: _____ Actual behavior: _____ Function of the emotion: _____
2	Triggering event: _____ Site and description of the physical changes in my body: _____ Thoughts/interpretations of the triggering event: _____ Name of the emotion: _____ Urge to act: _____ Valued action: _____ Values: _____ Actual behavior: _____ Function of the emotion: _____

3

Triggering event: _____

Site and description of the physical changes in my body: _____

Thoughts/interpretations of the triggering event: _____

Name of the emotion: _____

Urge to act: _____

Valued action: _____

Values: _____

Actual behavior: _____

Function of the emotion: _____

4

Triggering event: _____

Site and description of the physical changes in my body: _____

Thoughts/interpretations of the triggering event: _____

Name of the emotion: _____

Urge to act: _____

Valued action: _____

Values: _____

Actual behavior: _____

Function of the emotion: _____

5

Triggering event: _____

Site and description of the physical changes in my body: _____

Thoughts/interpretations of the triggering event: _____

Name of the emotion: _____

Urge to act: _____

Valued action: _____

Values: _____

Actual behavior: _____

Function of the emotion: _____

6

Triggering event: _____

Site and description of the physical changes in my body: _____

Thoughts/interpretations of the triggering event: _____

Name of the emotion: _____

Urge to act: _____

Valued action: _____

Values: _____

Actual behavior: _____

Function of the emotion: _____

7

Triggering event: _____

Site and description of the physical changes in my body: _____

Thoughts/interpretations of the triggering event: _____

Name of the emotion: _____

Urge to act: _____

Valued action: _____

Values: _____

Actual behavior: _____

Function of the emotion: _____

CHAPTER 11

BECOMING LESS HYPERSENSITIVE TO EMOTIONS

EMOTIONAL VULNERABILITY FACTORS

Have you ever noticed that some days you're more vulnerable, or sensitive, to emotions? On some days do things affect you much more than usual?

▷ CANDACE *When I slept badly the night before, or when I have a lot of things to do at work, or during my period, the smallest thing someone says to me gets blown out of proportion! Everything around me (and especially interactions with other people) affects me much more than normal. The slightest thing upsets me!*

Are you like Candace? What contributes to making you more vulnerable to emotions?

➤ ME _____

_____

Here's a *list of factors* that contribute to *increased vulnerability to emotions* in most individuals with borderline personality disorder:

 — situations of extreme stress and multiple priorities

 — fatigue

 — lack or excess of sleep

 — consumption of alcohol or drugs

 — stimulants, such as coffee

 — windows of time before and during menstruation

- poor compliance with medication regimens
- physical pain
- somatic illness (flu, bronchitis, and so on)

You have *control* over these factors! Improving your *lifestyle* and taking care of *your body's health* can reduce your sensitivity to emotions.

HOW TO BE LESS EMOTIONALLY VULNERABLE

Sleep
Optimal bedroom setup

- *Noise.* Avoid windows that face the street or opt for double-paned windows. Use ear plugs. Sounds can disrupt your sleep even if they aren't loud enough to wake you up.
- *Temperature.* Make sure your room doesn't exceed 68°F. In the summer, air-condition or air out the room before going to bed.
- *Light.* We sleep better in the dark:
    - turn off all the lights
    - close the curtains so you won't be bothered by outside lights or the sunrise
    - avoid stray light, such as from a digital alarm clock
- *Cell Phone/Smartphone.* Your phone emits waves that disturb sleep. Avoid putting your phone on your nightstand, or set it on airplane mode.
- *Animals.* Avoid sleeping with your pet. It can be a source of interrupted sleep. Make a comfortable place in the living room for pets so they too can feel like they're in their own bed.
- *Bed Quality.* Choosing a mattress and base for your bed is essential. Better comfort guarantees less restlessness, and therefore less waking up in the middle of the night. The *size counts* too: a big bed provides more space per person and better sleeping conditions for two people. The ideal width is 76 inches and the ideal length is at least 8 inches longer than your height.

Getting ready for bed
Dim the lights at least one hour before going to bed. Turn off all screens (or opt for white text on a black background for e-readers). Choose sub-

dued lighting. To end the day on a good note, make your gratitude journal the last thing you do before falling asleep.

Sleep duration

The average amount of sleep for an adult is eight hours, but some "short sleepers" are happy with six hours of sleep, while "long sleepers" need nine to ten hours of sleep to feel rested.

The ideal duration of a night's sleep is one that allows you to feel rested and function well during the day. When you're on vacation, it's easy to assess your sleeping needs.

Sleeping too much or too little in relation to your sleeping needs reduces cognitive performance and increases emotional vulnerability.[1]

Exercise

What's the minimum for beginners?

Over the course of a week, it's recommended to do (choose one):

- at least 150 minutes of a moderate-intensity endurance activity

- at least 75 minutes of a sustained-intensity endurance activity

- an equivalent combination of a moderate- and sustained-intensity activity

- every day: the equivalent of at least 30 minutes of brisk walking

What's optimum?

Over the course of a week, do (choose one):

- at least 300 minutes (five hours) of a moderate-intensity endurance activity

- at least 150 minutes of a sustained-intensity endurance activity

- an equivalent combination of a moderate- and sustained-intensity activity

---

WHAT IS AN ENDURANCE ACTIVITY?

It's a physical activity that improves cardio-respiratory function. For example: brisk walking, running, cycling, jumping rope, swimming . . . or even Zumba (which combines cardio-respiratory exercise with energizing music!).

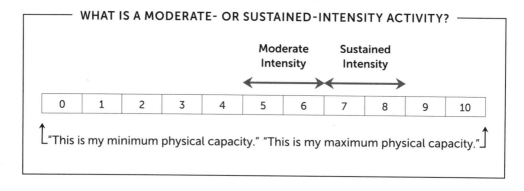

Muscle-strengthening exercises

These must involve the major muscle groups and should be performed at least two days a week. For muscle strengthening, nothing beats core-building exercises. It's recommended to do *5 sets of 5, holding each for 30 seconds to 1 minute*, with a recovery period of 30 seconds.[2]

Diet

Balance caloric intake to maintain a normal weight

- *Determine if your weight is normal.* To do this, calculate your BMI (body mass index: weight (in pounds) divided by height (in inches) squared then multiplied by 703 (703 x weight/height^2). For example, a height of 65 inches and a weight of 130 pounds equals a BMI of 21.6.[3]

BMI (703 × [lbs/in^2])	Interpretation
Below 16.5	Malnutrition
16.5 to 18.5	Underweight
18.5 to 25	Normal weight
25 to 30	Pre-obesity
30 to 35	Obesity class I
35 to 40	Obesity class II
Above 40	Obesity class III

A Word of Caution: BMI is an indicator, not an absolute fact. It doesn't take into account gender, age, or the distribution of fat in the body (fat located in the abdomen has the greatest impact on an individual's health and fitness).

- *Estimate the amount of fat in the abdomen.* This is indicated by waist size or circumference which should measure less than 35 inches for women and 40 inches for men.

- *Limit salt consumption* (sodium) from all sources, and make sure to consume iodized salt.
- *Hydrate.* Consume 1.5 to 2 liters of water a day.[4]

What kinds of foods should I choose?

- *Foods that are low in carbohydrates.* Choose green vegetables, onions, turnips, avocados, tomatoes, squashes, eggplants, sunflower seeds, and proteins (eggs, wild fish, shellfish, poultry, beef, and duck). Avoid refined grains and other foods with a high glycemic index.[5]
- *Foods that are rich in healthy fats.* Choose extra virgin olive oil, sesame oil, coconut oil, clarified butter, almond milk, olives, and cheeses (with the exception of blue cheese).[6]
- *Foods that are rich in omega-3.* Choose fatty fish (such as salmon, sardines, mackerel, or tuna), olive oil, flaxseed oil, walnut oil, cod liver oil, chia seeds, and walnuts.[7]
- *Foods that are rich in antioxidants.* Choose vegetables, berries, fruits with hulls, turmeric, and foods rich in vitamins A, C, and E.[8]
- *Probiotic foods* or those containing beneficial bacteria. These are fermented foods, mainly cabbage and dairy products, that contain bifidobacteria or lactobacilli from natural sources.
- *Foods that are rich in prebiotics* (which ensure the preservation of the natural intestinal flora). Choose garlic, onions, Jerusalem artichokes, asparagus, and leeks.
- In cases of recurrent digestive problems, it's important to screen for gluten intolerance. A gluten-free diet will prevent damage to the brain by reducing inflammation.[9]

All of these foods help reduce intestinal permeability, strengthen the immune system, and reduce inflammation. This optimizes healthy brain function.[10]

A healthy diet optimizes healthy brain function.

Meditation (or *Mindfulness*)

According to Jon Kabat-Zinn, meditation is a psychological practice that aims to:

- guide our attention
- in the present moment
- without value judgment

This is the core competency that we refer to throughout this book. If what we're offering you is the tree of effective skills for living a life that's in full bloom, then *mindfulness* is its trunk![11]

Guided meditations are formal practices; all the skills taught in this book are meant to be done in a state of mindfulness as informal practices. Let's distinguish between these two modes:

- *Formal practice* is similar to a tennis player practicing his backhand with a ball machine.

- *Informal practice* is similar to the same tennis player playing a match.

Formal meditation is practice, while informal meditation is embodied daily in the game of life. In everyday life, the word "meditation" refers to completely different meanings from what the psychological practice is in reality.

WHAT MEDITATION IS AND WHAT IT IS NOT

Meditation is not:	Meditation is:
☒ Deep reflection	☑ *Bringing attention to the experience of the present moment:* − the five senses − feelings − thoughts
☒ Emptying the mind	☑ *The lack of engagement with thoughts* Observing one's thoughts as passing events in the mind and not seeking an absence of thoughts
☒ A religious or spiritual approach	☑ *A psychological technique:* − for regulating emotions − for optimizing attentional control
☒ Relaxation or sophrology	☑ *Acceptance of emotions* and not the achievement of a state of relaxation

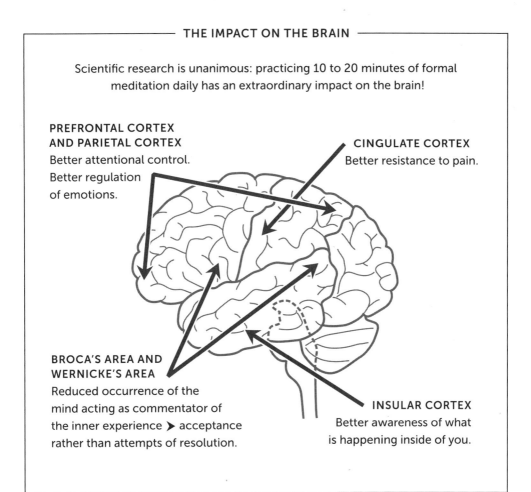

THE IMPACT ON THE BRAIN

Scientific research is unanimous: practicing 10 to 20 minutes of formal meditation daily has an extraordinary impact on the brain!

PREFRONTAL CORTEX AND PARIETAL CORTEX
Better attentional control. Better regulation of emotions.

CINGULATE CORTEX
Better resistance to pain.

BROCA'S AREA AND WERNICKE'S AREA
Reduced occurrence of the mind acting as commentator of the inner experience ➤ acceptance rather than attempts of resolution.

INSULAR CORTEX
Better awareness of what is happening inside of you.

These times of formal practice aside, applying *mindfulness* skills in everyday life allows us to live our lives fully.

This informal practice of *mindfulness* can be done during any daily activity. We see a lot of routine activities as a means to an end, a step before moving on to the next activity.

Doing routine activities mindfully gives each of them our total attention so that they become ends in themselves. For example, when you wash your hands, wash your hands. Don't do it to have clean hands before moving on to another activity, but for the action itself. Be aware of the sensation of water on your skin, the movements of your hands, the smell of the soap, the sound of running water, and so on.

Often, in the course of the various actions that we do, we're under the influence of the involuntary inner dialogue produced by the mind. The mind is constantly trying to hide the present moment behind the past or the future. The problem isn't that the mind works this way; it's unavoidable for every human being on Earth. The problem lies in the fact that we are mostly unaware of it and that we identify ourselves with the mind. This encourages us to live almost exclusively according to memory and anticipation, and it distances us from the present moment.

> " Nothing has happened in the past; it happened in the Now. Nothing will ever happen in the future; it will happen in the Now. "
>
> —ECKHART TOLLE

The present moment is:

- the only moment that exists! There has never been and there will never be a time when your life will not take place *now*, in *this* moment.

Let's do a little experiment. Try, now, to:

- drink a glass of water yesterday . . .
- brush your teeth tomorrow . . .

Unfortunately, it's not uncommon for people to spend their lives waiting to start living: "When I have a new job," "When I meet the right person," "When I finish this project." Your mind will always suggest better future conditions for "*really* starting to live": be aware that this is actually endless. If you wait to live, you may find yourself on death's doorstep realizing that you haven't lived at all.

- the only moment that allows you to perceive mental events as they are, *temporary*, independent of you.

You are like the sky, and mental events are like the clouds. Only in the present moment can you observe that the clouds don't make up the sky. The sky welcomes the passing clouds, without being affected.

- the key to your freedom. Some people believe that by exploring and delving into the past, they'll understand "the reason why they currently operate the way they do," and thus be freed from the burdens of the past. This is the biggest illusion of all! This path leads to a bottomless pit that will bring you nothing. Only the present moment can lead to freedom. Certainly your hooks were created by past, and often repeated, experiences, but the act of observing these mental events, as they appear to you in the present moment, makes it possible to reduce their impact—and, gradually, their frequency.

How can you practice returning to the present moment in everyday life?

- *Connect regularly to what's going on inside you*: What's going on inside me in this moment?

- *Observe your mind's tendency to flee from the present moment.* Have you experienced moments that were important to you but that you didn't enjoy because you were occupied with your thoughts, such as "he/she is going to leave soon," "it's almost the end of the weekend," or "if only I had . . ."?

The mind repeatedly shows you memories of the past (pleasant or unpleasant) or shows you premonitions of the future (by showing you a better or worse future than the present moment). All of this is only illusion!

- *Come back, as best as you can, and as many times as necessary, to the present moment.* As soon as you observe that you're no longer present and that your mind has brought you to the past or the future, you are present once again! By observing your mind, you free yourself from its control. This will further enhance your conscious use of the mind as a tool of rational awareness.

It's the difference between choosing to use a computer as a means of creation that's effective in a defined moment, and having ceaseless images coming from the computer at all times (and drifting from image to image thinking they're the true reality). The mind is like this computer.

> *The key is being present, moment by moment.*

Finally, the mind weighs down our existence with stories from the past and concerns about the future. Refocus on the present moment, and ask yourself, "What problem do I have right now?" Not the problem your mind tells you that you may have next year, in two days, or in ten minutes, but *right now*. It's a powerful question that requires a response that doesn't come from the mind.

❝Worry never robs tomorrow of its sorrow, it only saps today of its joy!❞
—LEO BUSCAGLIA

The Feeling of Expertise

This is feeling competent at something in particular. It could be cooking, playing a musical instrument, having a talent for film-making, being skilled at your profession, caring for and decorating your home, or anything else.

Developing our skills enhances our self-confidence. It also helps counterbalance devaluing thoughts ("I'm bad at this, I'm no good, I don't know how to do anything") present in moments of high vulnerability. Developing our natural skills is a way to find the loveliest part of ourselves, our most joyful, peaceful nature, for the good of others. For example, your job might be challenging, but outside of work, you've been practicing the guitar and have become quite good at it. Therefore, in a state of mindfulness, you know that there is also something positive in your life and that it's not only difficulties. Playing music is a way to bring to light your deepest nature, who you really are, for the sake of others.

Identify and list your current areas of expertise.

➤ ME _____

_____

Identify and list areas of expertise that you could start or continue to develop.

➤ ME _____

_____

Your Personal Strengths

These are the positive traits that characterize you and that you naturally possess. What are your strengths? List three strengths that come to mind.

➤ ME _____

_____

List three accomplishments. These are three small or big accomplishments that you're proud of. For each accomplishment, ask yourself: what two strengths enable you to be successful? What strengths made these accomplishments possible?

➤ ME _____

_____

Every time you succeed at something, it's because you used your gifts. You put your gifts at your service. Ask three people who are close to you what your strengths are.

Their responses: _____

_____

_____

Go to the VIA Institute on Character's website (https://www.viacharacter.org) and take the survey to determine your main strengths.

The result of the survey appears as a list of strengths, ranked in order of importance for you. Focus on the first five on the list: these are your main strengths.

> *An intense relationship should never be the only relationship in which a person is invested.*

Your Support Network

Developing a *strong support network* helps to *reduce your emotional vulnerability*.

What is a strong support network? It's a group of caring people (friends or family or both) who I know I can count on and with whom I spend the moments that embody what is important to me. A group with whom I feel a relational stability, and toward whom I don't have unrealistic expectations. I can simply enjoy shared moments in the present moment, knowing that this group is a support for me in life. It's an environment in which I feel revitalized and safe.

Many individuals with borderline personality disorder tend to seek out strong, extremely close relationships. This can lead to relational exclusivity and unrealistic expectations about the relationship. The risk is that this person's happiness is determined by the intense emotional experiences coming from this relationship. This type of relationship inevitably leads to feelings of insecurity, relational instability, and increased emotional vulnerability.

This doesn't mean that an intense relationship shouldn't exist in a person's life. But this relationship should be part of a larger support network. An intense relationship should never be the only relationship in which a person is invested. In chapter 21, you'll discover the keys for creating a strong support network.

Gratitude

Scientific studies are unanimous on this point: gratitude is a *main ingredient of happiness*.[12]

What is gratitude? It's an orientation of the mind toward gratefulness; it's an ability to be thankful (to life, God, the holy beings, the Universe . . . depending on our beliefs) for the little things that embellish our daily lives. It may be the sight of a clear blue sky, birdsong, a nice hot cup of coffee, the smile of a stranger in the street, a phone call from a friend, a hug from someone we're close to, or the presence of a person in our life whom we love.

As you know, it's not the big things. Quite the opposite, gratitude is about shining a light on all the little things that surround us and to which we don't (or no longer) pay attention. It's a way to be aware of all the things we're constantly receiving from others, in a sort of huge contribution network. It's a way of focusing on all the gifts from life and others.

Imagine . . . You've been blind for a decade, and suddenly you can see again! How would you look at what's around you? In what way? With what kind of attention?

You've just been reunited with your loved ones after being away for a long time. How would you enjoy each moment spent by their sides?

Be in touch with your surroundings as if you found yourself there again after being gone for a long time.

Another perspective What is part of your daily life that you wouldn't give up for a million dollars? Your legs perhaps? Your arms? Someone in your life who's very important to you? What else?

➤ ME _____

These aspects of your life are priceless, aren't they? What you already have is worth more than all the money in the world. You can be grateful for that. Change your perspective on the aspects making up your daily life: consider them a gift and not something you're owed. To help you, for each of these aspects, ask yourself, "What would my life be like if I didn't have that?"

“Walking on both legs or taking a hot shower doesn't make us feel happier, until we break a leg or our water heater breaks: deprivation then reveals the invisible sources of happiness.” —CHRISTOPHE ANDRÉ

To develop this skill of gratitude, we recommend that you keep a *gratitude journal*. Every day, write down *three things* you can be grateful for that day, three things for which you can say "thank you." For each thing, explain in detail what you feel gratitude for and what makes you grateful for it.

Resilience

Like every human being, you sometimes encounter difficulties, problems, and setbacks—situations in which you might think, "I hate my life."

Start by replacing the word "problem" with "challenge" or "opportunity." We'll train ourselves to open the field of our awareness to see the bigger picture, to open the field of possibilities.

We can't see the big picture of our life; it appears only in fragments. However, we can be certain that the picture as a whole is harmonious and that there is a reason for every element that is revealed to us. According to the proverb, "God never closes one door without opening another" (you can replace "God" with "life" or "the Universe" or whatever speaks to you most).

A challenge consistently produces a *blessing* in disguise. It's a blessing that isn't immediately visible and that we'll have to go find.

To get new answers, we need to change the questions that we ask ourselves. When we're faced with a challenge, we might be tempted to ask ourselves: "But why me? What did I do to deserve this?" Instead, we should ask:

- What is the blessing in this situation?
- What advantages does this situation offer me?
- What does this situation teach me?
- What does this situation allow me to work on or improve in myself?
- What will this allow me to do differently next time?
- What new opportunity will this situation open up for me?

An opportunity can be a new offer, a new encounter, returning to yourself and to what is really important, or strengthening relationships with family members or friends. This opportunity is always a chance for inner growth, by exercising your skills for managing painful internal events.

Think of a painful situation that you've experienced in the past such as a breakup, a job loss, or a rejection. What did this event allow to appear in your life that you wouldn't have experienced otherwise?

The event was: _____

The blessing in disguise that emerged: _____

> CANDACE *I always thought that I'd be an engineer (because that's what my father always wanted me to be). To that end, I had to take a scientific prep course after high school. I didn't register in time . . . It was too late for that year! I'll let you imagine the brutal argument that followed with my father . . . It was like the world was ending! It made me wonder what I really wanted to do, and I passed the nursing school entrance exam! I feel fulfilled by being a nurse. This job is a good fit for me. In retrospect, forgetting to register for the prep course is the best thing that could've happened to me (even if, at the time, it was a horrible situation!).*

The Story of the Chinese Farmer and the White Horse

A Chinese farmer aroused the envy of the wealthiest people in the land because he owned a magnificent white horse. Whenever someone offered to pay him a fortune for the animal, the old man would reply, "This horse is much more than an animal to me; it's a friend. I cannot sell it."

One day, the horse disappeared. The neighbors gathered in front of the empty stable to give their opinion: "It's no surprise that someone would steal your horse. Why didn't you sell it?" The farmer was doubtful. "Let's not exaggerate," he said. "We can say that the horse is no longer in the barn. That's a fact. The rest is only speculation on your part. How do we know if it's good or bad fortune?" People made fun of the old man. They had long regarded him as a simple-minded person.

Fifteen days later, the white horse returned. He hadn't been stolen—he had simply run away and now came back with a dozen wild horses. The villagers gathered again.

"You were right, it wasn't bad fortune but a blessing."

"I wouldn't go that far," said the farmer. "All we can say is that the white horse has returned. How do we know if it's good or bad luck?"

The villagers dispersed, convinced that the old man was talking nonsense. Receiving twelve beautiful horses was unquestionably a gift from heaven. Who could deny that?

The farmer's son began training the wild horses. One of them threw him to the ground and trampled him. The villagers came once again to give their opinion: "Poor friend! You were right, these wild horses did not bring you good luck. Now your only son is crippled. Who will help you in your old age? We pity you."

"Come on," retorted the farmer, "not so fast. My son has lost the use of his legs, that's all. Who can say what that will bring us? Life happens in small pieces. No one can predict the future."

Some time later, war broke out and all the young men in the country were drafted into the army, except the invalid.

"Old man," the villagers lamented, "you were right. Your son can't walk anymore, but he is still with you while our sons are going to get killed."

"I beg you," replied the farmer, "don't judge hastily. Your young people are serving in the army and mine stays at home, that's all we can say. God alone knows whether that's good or bad."

Invigorating Routines: Morning and Evening

The first hours of our day determine the tempo of the rest of the day. In the same way, the last things we do in the evening have an impact on the quality of our sleep and the state in which we wake up the next morning. We suggest bookending your day with *two invigorating routines*: a routine in the morning and one in the evening.

The Morning Routine

- *Silent formal meditation*: Set a timer for ten minutes. During this meditation, focus on your inner experience, moment by moment.

- *Gratitude*: Write at least three things in your gratitude journal that you are grateful for. Get in touch with the feeling that this creates.

- *Get in touch with what is important to you*:
  - by rereading the right-hand part of your matrix, p. 40;
  - by creating a vision board. The brain is made up of images. You could assign a photo to represent each item on the right-hand side of your matrix. You could even create a video that scrolls through your photos one by one and synchronize it with inspiring music to increase the emotional impact.

The Evening Routine

- *Silent formal meditation*: Set a timer for ten minutes. During this meditation, focus on your inner experience, moment by moment.

- *Gratitude*: Write at least three things in your gratitude journal that you are grateful for today.

What small or big things did you experience today for which you can say "thank you"? Get in touch with the feeling that this creates.

PRACTICAL APPLICATION

Exercise for the Coming Week

Identify behaviors that allow you to reduce your emotional vulnerability. The daily experience of borderline personality disorder resembles a succession of relational stressors, experienced as major storms. Putting strategies in place to reduce emotional vulnerability will allow you to navigate more tranquil waters on a daily basis.

Day	New daily habits to reduce your vulnerability factors	Areas of expertise you've invested	Personal strengths used
1			
2			
3			
4			

5		
6		
7		

DISTRESS: WHAT IS IT?
HOW DO WE COPE WITH IT?

WHAT IS DISTRESS?

Distress is a state of psychological crisis in which the *emotional stress* seems too high to be regulated. This state of crisis is generally associated with impulsive behavior seeking short-term relief ("I need it to stop at any price, whatever the consequences may be").

How It Happens

It can overwhelm me from one moment to another ("all of a sudden I felt really bad, terrible even"). However, it's *most often* a state of *latent stress* that was present, unregulated, and unacknowledged that a minor triggering event will amplify. It's the straw that broke the camel's back. In other words, even when we have the impression that "it came up out of the blue," it's possible to see that in reality, a succession of preexisting emotions were not taken into account earlier on.

Therefore, it's *most often* possible to avoid these times of distress. This is done by being *aware*, moment by moment, of what is happening inside of us. The skills you need have all been described in previous chapters.

PRACTICAL APPLICATION: DISTRESS FOR ME _____

What does distress evoke for you? How would you define it for yourself?

➤ ME _____

_____

_____

_____

At what level of emotional stress do you feel distressed? *(Circle the number on the scale below, with 0 corresponding to the absence of emotional stress [a totally relaxed state] and 10 to the greatest emotional stress imaginable [an extremely stressed state].)*

0	1	2	3	4	5	6	7	8	9	10

At what level of emotional stress are you currently, at this very moment? *(Circle the number on the scale below.)*

0	1	2	3	4	5	6	7	8	9	10

Generally, people with borderline personality disorder feel that distress occurs at a stress level of around 7/10. Of course, this value is purely subjective; what is important is that you can define yours.

HOW TO MANAGE A TIME OF DISTRESS EFFECTIVELY

When your emotional stress indicates that you're in distress, the goal is to experience the state of crisis without aggravating the situation. It's only once the emotional stress becomes less intense that you'll be able to resolve the problem.

To do this, we're going to show you some skills that will help you tolerate times of distress. This set of skills will make up your first aid kit, or tolerance kit. If you use the emotion regulation skills from the previous chapters on a daily basis, then you'll only need the distress tolerance skills on occasion. The more *effectively you regulate your emotions on a daily basis*, the less you'll need the *"distress tolerance"* first aid kit.

What to Know before Using the Tolerance Kit

- Distress is *transient*. It will pass by definition. All human beings experience it in their lives.
- Getting through distress amounts to *waiting for the emotional stress to become less intense*, without hurting you or making you struggle in an area of life that's important to you (relationships, work, and so forth).
- Distress tolerance strategies should be applied *while being fully present in what you're doing*. If your mind brings you back to the present difficulty that is the source of your current state of

distress, choose, with kindness, to return to what you've chosen to implement for getting through the moment.

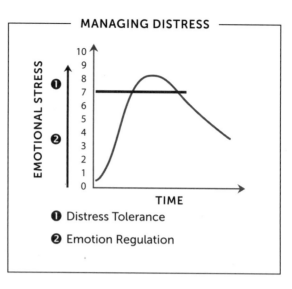

- In a state of crisis, your mind will suggest (or sometimes order) that you do what you've done for years in this situation—things that sometimes work effectively to quickly reduce stress. However, you've made the decision to train yourself to do things differently in order to improve your life in a sustainable way.

- Some strategies won't work as well or as fast as you would've hoped. *Try again!* Try a sequence of several strategies. We guarantee that, afterward, you'll be proud of getting through the crisis in this way.

- It's possible that you'll sometimes go back to your old behaviors to get through a crisis. That's normal. Even if you temporarily go back to an old way, the important thing is to *refocus yourself* as quickly as possible in the right direction. And that alone is a huge victory.

PRACTICAL APPLICATION

1. What are the behaviors (the upper left part of the matrix) that you tend to implement, without thinking, when you're in distress?

These could be:

- your current behaviors in a state of crisis

- your occasional behaviors

- your desired behaviors

It's these behaviors (the upper left part of the matrix), whose sole purpose is to reduce the emotional stress as quickly as possible, that are:

- moving you away from your values, from what is important to you

– not allowing you to act consistently with who you'd really like to be

– preventing you from taking care of yourself

CANDACE	ME
– Bulimic episode – Punching walls – Harassing others – Cutting myself – Alcohol – Smoking or vaping pot	

2. Can you identify how these problematic behaviors do not take care of you or your values? What do they affect? Which areas of life are negatively impacted by these behaviors?

CANDACE	ME
– Having self-respect – Taking care of my body – Taking care of my relationships – Making progress toward effectively managing emotions	

3. Can you identify or check off on the list of strategies below the behaviors you would be willing to try out the next time you feel distressed?

First Group of Strategies: Calming Down Using the Five Senses
This first group of distress tolerance skills is based on the principle of calming yourself down by using the five senses. Therefore, you'll bring all of your attention, in a state of mindfulness, to the physical sensations that you'll perceive through your sensory organs.

Hearing

☐ Singing

☐ Listening to a soothing playlist or one that provokes pleasant emotions

☐ Listening to nature sounds

☐ Playing a musical instrument

☐ Watching a recording of a concert

☐ Other: _____

Touch

- [ ] Having physical contact with someone
- [ ] Petting an animal
- [ ] Feeling a plush toy or a piece of fabric

- [ ] Taking a bath
- [ ] Massaging my body
- [ ] Squeezing a rubber ball
- [ ] Other: _____

Taste

- [ ] Drinking something chosen specifically for its taste or physical qualities (hot, cold, sweet, acidic, fizzy, and so on)
- [ ] Eating something chosen for its taste or physical qualities (hot, cold, soft, crunchy, sweet, sour, spicy, and so on)

- [ ] Other: _____

Smell

- [ ] Smelling a spice, food, flower, beauty product (soap, body cream, and so on)
- [ ] Smelling natural scents
- [ ] Spraying perfume
- [ ] Lighting a stick of incense

- [ ] Smelling someone's scent or the scent of something comforting (my mother's scarf, pine scent from my childhood home, and so on)
- [ ] Other: _____

Sight

- [ ] Watching a slideshow (inspiring images, photos of nature, baby animals, and so on)
- [ ] Looking at old photos
- [ ] Watching a movie or TV series

- [ ] Looking at a natural landscape
- [ ] Looking at my vision board (refer to chapter 11, p. 127)
- [ ] Other: _____

Second Group of Strategies: Distracting the Mind

This second group of distress tolerance skills is based on the principle of distracting the mind by distancing it from whatever is causing the distress, while also trying to change the emotional response. Distraction allows you to fill the short-term memory with thoughts, images, and sensations, thwarting those that activate and reactivate emotional stress. So you will bring all of your attention to the activity you have chosen, in a state of mindfulness.

Pleasurable Activities

- [ ] Being with my pet
- [ ] Watching funny videos
- [ ] Going out for some fresh air
- [ ] Putting on makeup, painting my nails
- [ ] Playing sports
- [ ] Taking a bath
- [ ] Going to the hairdresser
- [ ] Organizing things
- [ ] Cleaning the house
- [ ] Cooking
- [ ] Watching a TV series
- [ ] Drinking a cold drink
- [ ] Reading a book
- [ ] Taking photos
- [ ] Other: _____

Other Pleasurable Activities

Identify what activities you could implement in times of distress. These are activities that you like and that can be implemented rather easily.

- [ ] _____

Giving to Others

This is about turning to another person, a loved one or someone else, to give them your help or your presence. It's about being able to disconnect yourself from your problems by putting your mind at the service of someone else.

- [ ] Giving to: _____

Escaping

Physically: Going for a walk or leaving the place related to the crisis in order to reduce contact with emotional stimuli.

- [ ] Physically escaping

Perspective

Ask yourself: Will this situation still matter in five years?

- [ ] Perspective

Unwinding

- [ ] Going for a run
- [ ] Doing a set of pushups or sit-ups
- [ ] Dancing
- [ ] Singing (karaoke on YouTube)
- [ ] Other: _____

Third Group of Strategies: Improving the Present Moment

Mental Imagery

This is about projecting ourselves into a reality other than the one we experience, while knowing that it's only a mental projection and not reality. This will keep our mind busy transporting us to pleasant places.

The act of projecting ourselves somewhere else also tells us that reality is changeable and that the current painful situation is not permanent.

☐ Projecting yourself into another setting, a pleasant place full of memories *(for example, imagining myself in a pleasant moment that's planned for a few days from now, like a trip with friends to the mountains, or to a place that reminds me of happy times and where I'll be able to return again)*

☐ Creating a safe place in your mind

> To do this, close your eyes and create a place for yourself that's the most comfortable and safe you can imagine. Envision yourself walking on a path that draws you toward a place that exudes calm and serenity. At one point, you find yourself in front of a blank canvas on which you can paint the place that's in your mind. You imagine the place: its decor, smells, sounds, and so on.

> Whenever you'd like, imagine that you leave this peaceful place through a door that only you alone can reopen. You can come back to this place whenever and as often as you want and feel at peace immediately.

☐ Making "films" for yourself *(imagining myself in another life—a total fantasy life—in which I could be a completely different person from who I am in real life. I could be famous, an expert in a cutting-edge field that would be a dream come true for me, a lottery winner, or anything else I can imagine)*

Relaxation

Changing the body's response in a state of crisis by using relaxation techniques, such as: breathing slower, contracting/relaxing muscles, and so forth.

☐ Relaxing

PREPARING YOUR DISTRESS TOLERANCE KIT _____

Gather all the things you'll need for the strategies you selected to apply in a time of crisis (vaporizer, camera, music playlist, herbal tea, and so on.). In fact, to maximize your chances of success in implementing new behaviors, you have to have *prepared everything in advance.*

Exercise for the Coming Week

If you experience a time of distress in the next few days, complete the table below.

Remember, your first priority should be to try to apply the emotion regulation skills.

If you can't apply these skills because the stress is too pervasive, then experiment with the new strategies you checked off on the list.

In a state of mindfulness, apply the strategy you chose to calm you down, bringing all of your attention to sensory perceptions.

As soon as the stress has died down, use the emotion regulation skills. Otherwise the emotional stress will certainly come back again and probably even more intensely, because the emotion was not recognized, validated, and accepted.

DAY 1. SITUATION:											
Emotional Stress	0	1	2	3	4	5	6	7	8	9	10
Did you use the self-guided acceptance exercise?	Yes: what was the outcome?										
	No: what was the obstacle?										
Did you use a new distress tolerance strategy?	Yes: which one(s) and what was the outcome?										
	No: what was the obstacle?										

DAY 2. SITUATION:

Emotional Stress	0	1	2	3	4	5	6	7	8	9	10

Did you use the self-guided acceptance exercise?

Yes: what was the outcome?

No: what was the obstacle?

Did you use a new distress tolerance strategy?

Yes: which one(s) and what was the outcome?

No: what was the obstacle?

DAY 3. SITUATION:

Emotional Stress	0	1	2	3	4	5	6	7	8	9	10

Did you use the self-guided acceptance exercise?

Yes: what was the outcome?

No: what was the obstacle?

Did you use a new distress tolerance strategy?

Yes: which one(s) and what was the outcome?

No: what was the obstacle?

DAY 4. SITUATION:

Emotional Stress	0	1	2	3	4	5	6	7	8	9	10

Did you use the self-guided acceptance exercise?

Yes: what was the outcome?

No: what was the obstacle?

Did you use a new distress tolerance strategy?

Yes: which one(s) and what was the outcome?

No: what was the obstacle?

DAY 5. SITUATION:

Emotional Stress	0	1	2	3	4	5	6	7	8	9	10

Did you use the self-guided acceptance exercise?

Yes: what was the outcome?

No: what was the obstacle?

Did you use a new distress tolerance strategy?

Yes: which one(s) and what was the outcome?

No: what was the obstacle?

DAY 6. SITUATION:

Emotional Stress	0	1	2	3	4	5	6	7	8	9	10

Did you use the self-guided acceptance exercise?

Yes: what was the outcome?

No: what was the obstacle?

Did you use a new distress tolerance strategy?

Yes: which one(s) and what was the outcome?

No: what was the obstacle?

DAY 7. SITUATION:

Emotional Stress	0	1	2	3	4	5	6	7	8	9	10

Did you use the self-guided acceptance exercise?

Yes: what was the outcome?

No: what was the obstacle?

Did you use a new distress tolerance strategy?

Yes: which one(s) and what was the outcome?

No: what was the obstacle?

CHAPTER 13

DISTRESS TOLERANCE SKILLS: ARE THEY REALLY BENEFICIAL?

You may sometimes wonder if these new coping strategies for crises are really beneficial. For that matter, your mind will strongly be making you doubt it and will be pushing you to go back to the old strategies during difficult times.

That's perfectly normal. All human minds work this way.

To prevent your mind from tricking you during more difficult times, let's explore the advantages and disadvantages of your usual strategies compared to the new distress tolerance strategies.

▷ CANDACE She filled in the table below. Circle what you agree with, and complete it if necessary.

Applying the new distress tolerance strategies

ADVANTAGES	DISADVANTAGES
In the short term: – reduces distress – reassures our loved ones – reduces guilt, shame	In the short term: – _____ – _____
In the long run: – increases self-esteem (choice made mindfully) – increases skills	In the long run: – _____ – _____

Applying the old behaviors (self-damaging)

ADVANTAGES	DISADVANTAGES
In the short term: – relief – effective – known strategies – reduces physical injuries and harm	**In the short term:** – physical injuries and harm – increases guilt – reduces self-esteem – _____
In the long run: – _____ – _____ – _____	**In the long run:** – scars – exhausts the people in our life – depression – social withdrawal – _____

PRACTICAL APPLICATION: YOUR DISTRESS TOLERANCE MATRIX _____

Each quadrant of the matrix on the next page is assigned a number corresponding to one of the four questions below. Fill in the matrix with your responses.

1. Write down the emotional stress number above which you feel distressed (see chapter 12, p. 131).

2. Write down the problematic behaviors that you tend to implement during times of distress (you identified these in the previous chapter, p. 133).

3. Write down your first intention: self-guided acceptance exercise (found in chapter 9, pp. 101–3). Write down the new distress tolerance strategies you have tried in recent weeks that have been effective in helping you get through a time of distress.

4. Using the completed "Advantages/Disadvantages" table at the beginning of this chapter, identify:

- in what ways it makes sense for you to apply new distress tolerance strategies

- in what ways that takes care of you or those close to you

- in what ways that allows you to be consistent with the person you really want to be

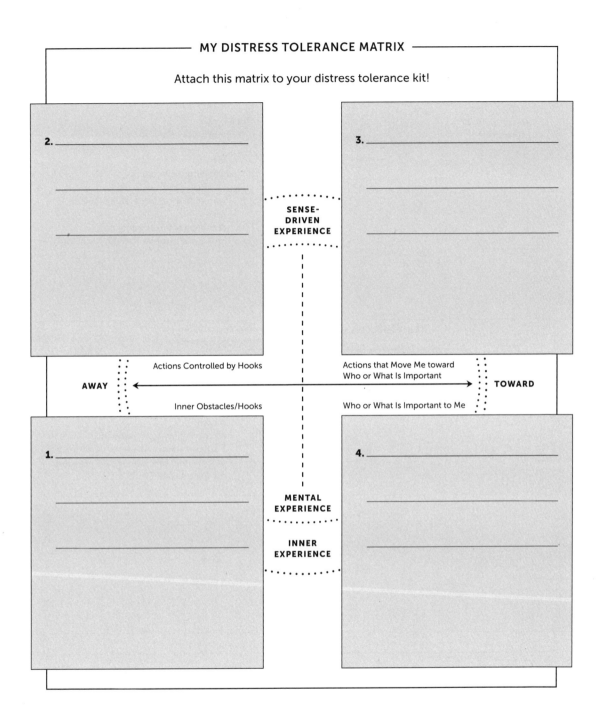

MY DISTRESS TOLERANCE MATRIX

Attach this matrix to your distress tolerance kit!

2. _____

3. _____

SENSE-DRIVEN EXPERIENCE

Actions Controlled by Hooks

AWAY ← — — — — — → **TOWARD**

Actions that Move Me toward
Who or What Is Important

Inner Obstacles/Hooks

Who or What Is Important to Me

1. _____

4. _____

MENTAL EXPERIENCE

INNER EXPERIENCE

CANDACE'S DISTRESS TOLERANCE MATRIX

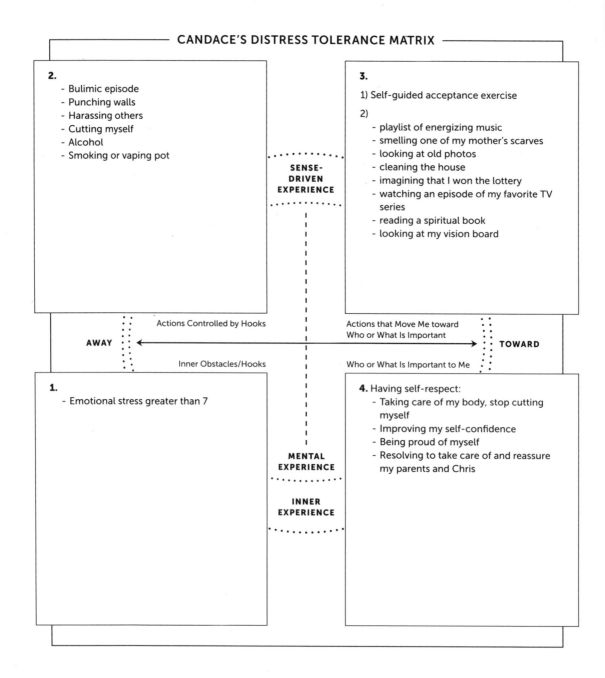

2.
- Bulimic episode
- Punching walls
- Harassing others
- Cutting myself
- Alcohol
- Smoking or vaping pot

3.

1) Self-guided acceptance exercise

2)
- playlist of energizing music
- smelling one of my mother's scarves
- looking at old photos
- cleaning the house
- imagining that I won the lottery
- watching an episode of my favorite TV series
- reading a spiritual book
- looking at my vision board

SENSE-DRIVEN EXPERIENCE

Actions Controlled by Hooks

Actions that Move Me toward Who or What Is Important

AWAY ←——————————————→ **TOWARD**

Inner Obstacles/Hooks

Who or What Is Important to Me

1.
- Emotional stress greater than 7

4. Having self-respect:
- Taking care of my body, stop cutting myself
- Improving my self-confidence
- Being proud of myself
- Resolving to take care of and reassure my parents and Chris

MENTAL EXPERIENCE

INNER EXPERIENCE

WHAT IS DISSOCIATION?

DISSOCIATIVE SYMPTOMS

During emotionally charged times, more than two individuals out of three with borderline personality disorder experience *dissociative symptoms*.

Dissociation is a distortion of one's perception of reality, the manifestations of which can vary depending on the person and the context in which it appears. This is one of the criteria for a borderline personality disorder diagnosis. However, just like for the other criteria, *it's not systematically found in all individuals with borderline personality disorder*, since a diagnosis is made based on five out of the list of nine criteria being met (refer to chapter 2, p. 42).

Dissociation is a complex phenomenon whose symptoms can vary greatly. The most common forms of dissociation found in borderline personality disorder are:

- *Time distortion.* In this state, time seems to move either very quickly or very slowly.

- *Depersonalization.* In this state, you feel like a stranger to yourself. You can observe yourself going through the motions of living as if you had no control over your actions and while feeling as if things aren't real.

- *Amnesia.* This is memory loss concerning certain periods of life or certain aspects of an event but not all. It can concern the past but also the present.

- *Derealization.* In this state, the environment and the people in it seem unreal, like they've become foreign, unknown, or distant.

- *Changes in self-perception.* In this state, some components of your personality are experienced as "not oneself"; in other cases, you may feel that you have multiple identities, as if you were several people.

Dissociation can be seen as a survival mechanism in the face of a situation experienced as too emotionally painful (or the reminder of such a situation).

Therefore, the brain protects itself by not integrating part of the traumatic experience.

For example, someone may remember a painful childhood event as not really being their own memory, thus preventing them from incorporating it into their conscious personal history. The dissociative reaction therefore initially has a protective function in the face of life events perceived as traumatic.

However, later, these dissociative symptoms may tend to repeatedly trigger that person, whenever "triggers" recalling the initial trauma occur. In fact, this defense strategy will be initiated when an anticipated risk of reliving, in the present, the painful and traumatic emotions of the past occurs.

What Risk Does Dissociation Pose?

When a person is dissociating, they are no longer reacting to the reality of the present moment but are reacting automatically when confronted with warning signs that they associate with past trauma. It can therefore result in behavior that is not adapted to the reality of the situation through *loss of control and lucidity*. It's in this context that impulsive, aggressive, isolating behaviors—toward oneself or toward others—can develop rather than behaviors based on conscious choices.

WHAT IS THIS DISSOCIATIVE STATE LIKE FOR ME?

Let's start by exploring how you experience dissociation. To do this, carefully read the words below and check the box next to the ones that correspond to your experience.[1]

☐ Do you sometimes feel like you're standing next to yourself, or seeing yourself doing something, as if you were looking at another person?

- [ ] Do you sometimes notice that you don't have any memories of certain important events in your life?
- [ ] Do you sometimes feel unreal relative to your environment or the people around you?
- [ ] Do you sometimes feel like your body doesn't belong to you?
- [ ] Do you ever remember a past event and feel it as strongly as if you were living it right now?
- [ ] Do some memories sometimes seem unreal to the point that you don't know anymore whether you dreamed them or whether they really happened?
- [ ] Have you ever found that familiar places look foreign to you?
- [ ] Do you ever feel so immersed in your imagination that it feels as if it were really happening?
- [ ] Do you ever react so differently from one moment to another that sometimes it feels like you're several different people?
- [ ] Do you sometimes not know if you really did something or if you only thought about doing it?
- [ ] Do you sometimes hear voices in your head commenting on what you're doing or even telling you to do things?

If you can, give an example of a dissociative symptom that you've experienced recently:

➤ ME _____

▷ CANDACE *In times of intense stress, I suddenly feel like I'm here without being here. I know I should be affected by the situation, but nothing else seems to reach me. I don't even know if what I'm hearing is real or imaginary, if people are really there or if I'm imagining all of it.*

Can this state affect your behavior? If so, how?

➤ ME _____

▷ CANDACE *Yes, it's pretty scary, because I realize it's strange, but I can't do anything about it. I put up with the situation without controlling anything until this state passes. I feel like I can't make decisions. Even my friends notice that I'm not really there anymore.*

What Can We Do about This Dissociative State?

In dissociation, it's as if you're not integrating some of the present experience.[2] As a result, one way to overcome many of your dissociative symptoms will be to develop your ability to consciously live in the present moment, to be aware here and now.

Therefore, in the therapeutic strategies we offer you, we won't try to explore what's at the origin of your dissociative state; rather we'll try to free you from the control this dissociative state has over you. Let's stop automatic and uncontrollable reactions.

The solution is *mindfulness*. It's learning to be fully present *here and now* in order to increase awareness of the current situation, be able to make choices consistent with your values whatever the situation may be, and not live hooked by the past.

PRACTICAL APPLICATION

Exercise One: Learning to Be Present
Step One
Choose *three objects* in your environment, and for each of these objects, identify three of their characteristics.

▷ CANDACE
Object: *a chair*
Its characteristics: *brown, smooth, cold*

➤ ME
Object 1: _____

Its characteristics: _____

Object 2: _____

Its characteristics: _____

Object 3: _____

Its characteristics: _____

Now become aware that you are here, *right now*, in the presence of these objects. Look at and name these three objects. They are around you, right now, here, and you are safe in this moment.

Step Two

Focus on *three sounds* in your environment, and name three of their characteristics.

▷ **CANDACE**

Sound: *bird chirping outside my window*

Its characteristics: *irregular, piercing, distant*

▶ **ME**

Sound 1: _____

Its characteristics: _____

Sound 2: _____

Its characteristics: _____

Sound 3: _____

Its characteristics: _____

Now become aware that you are here, *right now*, listening to these three sounds. Listen to and name these three sounds. They are around you, right now, here, and you are safe in this moment.

Step Three

Touch *three things* in your environment, and name three of their characteristics.

▷ **CANDACE**

Thing: *a pen*

Its characteristics: *smooth, light, hard*

▶ **ME**

Thing 1: _____

Its characteristics: _____

Thing 2: _____

Its characteristics: _____

Thing 3: _____

Its characteristics: _____

Now become aware that you are here, *right now*, touching or holding these objects. Touch and name these three objects. They are around you, right now, here, and you are safe in this moment.

Do this exercise at least twice a day. Feel free to change the objects, sounds, and things so you don't get bored and so you'll be fully aware of what you're doing.

▷ **CANDACE** She chose to do her exercise in the morning shortly after waking up and in the middle of the afternoon.

How about you? What times have you chosen?

➤ **ME**
1st time: _____

2nd time: _____

Exercise Two: Identifying Your Anchors to the Present Moment
Anchors are the objects, smells, tastes, and sounds that allow you to experience these sensations by being fully aware of the fact that you are in the present moment.

Step One
Walk around your home and find three things that you can see and that are always there.

➤ **ME** My three things: _____

Find three sounds that you can hear and that are always there.

➤ **ME** My three sounds: _____

Find three scents or flavors that you can smell or taste and that are always there.

➤ **ME** My three scents/flavors: _____

List your current anchors, because in moments of stress they will help you realize that you are in the present moment, that these anchors are there, here and now, with you, in your house and that you are safe.

CANDACE	ME
– Rocking chair	
– Fish tank	
– Photo of Mia	
– Perfume	
– Soap	
– Old book	
– Plaid polar fleece	
– Computer keyboard	

Step Two

You can go buy an anchoring object or a few of them, so you can always have these objects with you. Then, in moments of stress, in moments when you're particularly likely to lose control, you'll be able to look at them or touch them, while bringing all of your attention to these objects and to the fact that you're in contact with them here and in this moment. They can help you become fully anchored to the present, to reality. Feel free to choose objects that are associated with different parts of your personality.

CANDACE'S ANCHORS	MY ANCHORS
– A giraffe keychain that reminds me of the times when I was a kid and loved going to the zoo to feed them with my sister. – A small amethyst that I brought back from one of my trips and that I slip into my pocket.	

Exercise for the Coming Week

Do the "Learning to Be Present" exercise twice a day at the times of your choice. Create your list of anchors and choose at least two anchoring objects that you'll keep with you all the time. Pay attention to the occurrence of dissociative symptoms. If you become aware of this happening, identify the form they're taking, then choose to anchor yourself to the present with your anchoring objects.

CHAPTER 15

BORDERLINE PERSONALITY DISORDER AND INTERPERSONAL RELATIONSHIPS

INTERPERSONAL RELATIONSHIPS: WHAT DIFFICULTIES DO PEOPLE WITH BORDERLINE PERSONALITY DISORDER HAVE?

People with borderline personality disorder tend to be absolutist and function in a binary way that is "all or nothing" or "black or white" (**idealization/devaluation**).

They will tend to **hyperinvest very quickly and intensely in relationships.** They give a lot of themselves with expectations of reciprocity to match their own level of investment. They often look for **strong, extremely close relationships.** And since the other person generally doesn't measure up to their expectations, they are often disappointed. Therefore, relationships will often be intense but unstable over time. In fact, *the disappointment* in the relationship will often lead either to an abrupt and decisive end to the relationship, or to distinct, temporary shifts between phases of distance and phases of intense relational investment, according to how the daily events experienced in the relationship are interpreted.

Even when there's no external event altering the relationship, thoughts like, **"I'm not interesting enough to be loved"** or **"He/she will leave me one day,"** can create so much pain that individuals with borderline personality disorder will **test the boundaries of the relationship** to see the extent to which the other person will remain reliable in this relationship. This can result in **extreme relational behaviors** such as emotional blackmail, threats, and so on.

Relationships are truly *central* to individuals with borderline personality disorder, either to compensate for a **chronic feeling of emptiness** or to experience strong emotions caused by closeness in relationships. In this context, they will often be on the lookout for the slightest signs of rejection or **abandonment.**

Analyzing each behavior of the other person through this filter will inevitably increase the likelihood that they'll find what they're looking for. In addition, their internal attributional style shows a tendency to interpret external events as having a direct link to themselves (example: "Sophie seems upset today; she's going to criticize me for something.").

It thus appears that the importance of relationships, in conjunction with this permanent relational insecurity, leads to *mental pain* that is sometimes very significant. These unpleasant and pervasive emotions and feelings sometimes lead to behaviors aimed at alleviating emotional stress in the (very) short term, but they are detrimental to relationships and self-respect in the long term: **excessive obsessive thoughts about the relationship, explosive behavior, excessive demands for reassurance (multiple calls, repeatedly sending text messages), begging or threatening the other person, or exaggerated tolerance for other people's behaviors that may be harmful and undermine one's own integrity.**

In the long term, these types of behaviors can lead to the much-feared result of rejection or abandonment by causing the other person to distance themselves or to end the relationship. This leads to an even greater fear of being abandoned in future relationships. In addition, excessive reassurance-seeking behaviors frequently lead to **shame** (of oneself as a person).

This will then further increase the familiar feeling of fear of not being loveable enough as a person. Finally, the all-or-nothing mindset serves as an attempt to impose a stable and predictable framework on reality, when in fact reality is actually uncertain and complex.

At the opposite extreme, in order to protect themselves from *abandonment* perceived as inevitable (**"mistrust," "I'm not interesting enough to be loved"**), some individuals with borderline personality disorder avoid all intimate relationships, whether platonic or romantic, most of the time, which leads to relational isolation. In fact, the constraints of isolation are perceived as less painful than a breakup would be after a sincere emotional investment.

Individuals with borderline personality disorder are thus stuck in their own loop.

Do you recognize that you're stuck in this loop?

— What hooks frequently tend to appear for you in relationships?
   (Circle the hooks, in the lower left part of the matrix on the next page, that correspond to what appears for you. You can add any that aren't already listed.)

— What can we see you do when these hooks appear and you take the bait? (*Circle the behaviors, in the upper left part of the matrix below, that correspond to what you tend to do. You can add any that aren't already listed.*)

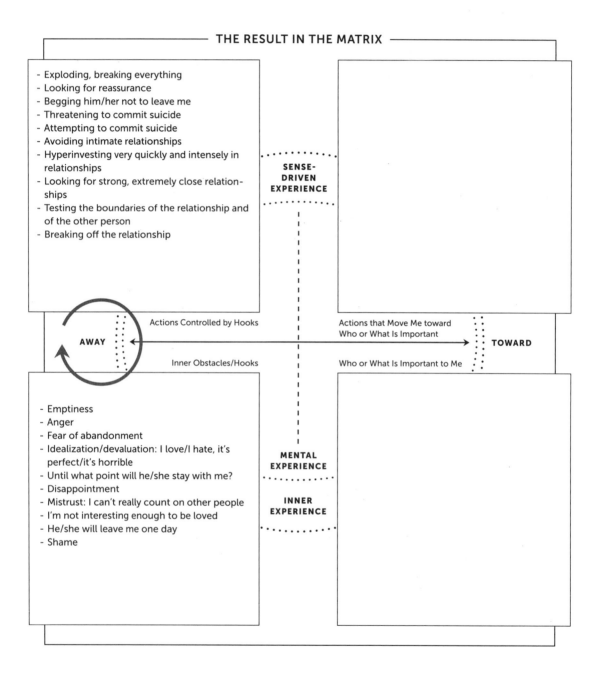

THE RESULT IN THE MATRIX

- Exploding, breaking everything
- Looking for reassurance
- Begging him/her not to leave me
- Threatening to commit suicide
- Attempting to commit suicide
- Avoiding intimate relationships
- Hyperinvesting very quickly and intensely in relationships
- Looking for strong, extremely close relationships
- Testing the boundaries of the relationship and of the other person
- Breaking off the relationship

SENSE-DRIVEN EXPERIENCE

AWAY

Actions Controlled by Hooks

Actions that Move Me toward Who or What Is Important

TOWARD

Inner Obstacles/Hooks

Who or What Is Important to Me

- Emptiness
- Anger
- Fear of abandonment
- Idealization/devaluation: I love/I hate, it's perfect/it's horrible
- Until what point will he/she stay with me?
- Disappointment
- Mistrust: I can't really count on other people
- I'm not interesting enough to be loved
- He/she will leave me one day
- Shame

MENTAL EXPERIENCE

INNER EXPERIENCE

INVENTORY OF YOUR RELATIONSHIPS

Intense emotional reactivity varies according to the different characteristics of the relationship:

- your *investment* in this relationship
- your *level of satisfaction* in this relationship
- the balance in this relationship
- the feeling of *security* in this relationship

Now we're going to help you clarify your relational landscape (you'll find the table to fill in at the end of the instructions, on p. 158; it consists of five columns.

First Column ("Name")

List the people close to you who are important to you or who are taking up space in your life (by spending time with that person, talking about that person, or even thinking excessively about that relationship). These people can belong to different circles: partner, family member, friend, co-worker, neighbor, and so on.

Second Column ("Level of Personal Investment")

Evaluate your investment in the relationship, giving it a score between 12 and 84 by using the following questionnaire (the Unidimensional Relationship Closeness Scale). For each item in this questionnaire, rate how much you agree with the statement by selecting a score from 1 to 7 (1 meaning you strongly disagree and 7 meaning you strongly agree). Then add up the scores.

1. My relationship with him/her is close.

| 0 | 1 | 2 | 3 | 4 | 5 | 6 | 7 |

2. When we are apart, I miss him/her a great deal.

| 0 | 1 | 2 | 3 | 4 | 5 | 6 | 7 |

3. He/she and I disclose important personal things to each other.

| 0 | 1 | 2 | 3 | 4 | 5 | 6 | 7 |

4. He/she and I have a strong connection.

| 0 | 1 | 2 | 3 | 4 | 5 | 6 | 7 |

5. He/she and I want to spend time together.

0	1	2	3	4	5	6	7

6. I'm sure of my relationship with him/her.

0	1	2	3	4	5	6	7

7. He/she is a priority in my life.

0	1	2	3	4	5	6	7

8. He/she and I do a lot of things together.

0	1	2	3	4	5	6	7

9. When I have free time I choose to spend it alone with him/her.

0	1	2	3	4	5	6	7

10. I think about him/her a lot.

0	1	2	3	4	5	6	7

11. My relationship with him/her is important in my life.

0	1	2	3	4	5	6	7

12. I consider him/her when making important decisions.

0	1	2	3	4	5	6	7

Third Column ("Satisfaction in the Relationship")

For each of the individuals listed in the left-hand column of the table, rate your satisfaction with this relationship, giving it a score between 1 and 7, 1 meaning that this relationship is not satisfying at all and 7 meaning that it's very satisfying.

Fourth Column ("Balance: My Needs/Their Needs")

For each person listed in the left-hand column of the table, toward which side does the scale tilt most of the time?

- *"My Needs"*: these are things that are important to me, the things I want to do or that I expect to happen. It's what the priority is for me (and even, what I *feel* I'm receiving in this relationship, even if I don't necessarily ask for it at this level).

- *"Their Needs"*: these are what the other person wants me to do for them, what they want to see happen. This is what they ask of me (or even, what I *feel* I'm giving in this relationship, even if it isn't necessarily asked of me at this level).

- *When "their needs" take up more space and tip the scales:* When satisfying the other person's needs in a relationship is the priority or happens more frequently, you tend to go beyond your personal boundaries to satisfy that person and thus obtain their approval. In any event, be aware that you will eventually damage the quality of the relationship. Indeed, if a person is overwhelmed, they will explode or try to end this situation at one time or another. This often results in giving up, the relationship ending, or impulsively distancing yourself from the other person.

- *When "my needs" take up more space and tip the scales:* If having your needs met in a relationship is the priority or happens more frequently, the other person will be overwhelmed and may not feel heard, understood, or sufficiently taken into account, which may also end up ending the relationship. The tolerable level of meeting someone's needs varies over time and from person to person. In a way, this level depends on the person's usual (or current) energy level, the amount of help and support provided by their environment, and their emotional state.

- *"Balance":* This means you consider that there is a balance between your needs and their needs.

Fifth Column ("Security of the Relationship")

For each person listed in the left-hand column of the table, evaluate your level of security in this relationship by giving it a score between 1 and 7, with each end of the range meaning:

1. Relationship experienced as *completely "insecure"*: obsessive thinking regarding the possibility that the relationship will end or is not actually living up to expectations or of the quality expected. The duration and frequency of these thoughts can help you choose a rating, but also consider: your perceived impatience while waiting for a response from that person or while waiting for the result of a reassurance-seeking behavior; the level of perceived emotional stress after or during an interaction with that person that is associated with the fear of doing the wrong thing, not measuring up, disappointing them, as if you feel that the relationship depends more on the quantity or quality of things you do for that person than on who you are.

7. Relationship experienced as *completely "secure"*: absolute confidence in the quality of the relationship, its likely duration over time, and its ability to measure up to expectations. You feel accepted and loved for who you are.

PRACTICAL APPLICATION

Your Relational Landscape Table

Name	Level of Personal Investment	Satisfaction in the Relationship	Balance: My Needs/ Their Needs	Security of the Relation- ship

Analyze your table

Which relationships do you experience as safe and balanced?

Which relationships do you experience as off-balance? In what sense? Are these off-balance relationships "secure" or "insecure"?

Perhaps, by looking at your table, you'll be able to draw a connection between one (or more) relationship(s) that are experienced as "insecure" and associated with an imbalance in terms of the other person's needs. That means being ready to go beyond your personal boundaries in order to strengthen the relationship, without necessarily meaning that this will be enough.

Interpersonal effectiveness is more likely to be distorted in these relationships, where the priority, even sometimes unconsciously, is to maintain the relationship— often to the detriment of respect for one's own boundaries, feelings, or desires. These relationships have the highest likelihood of inducing a lack of interpersonal effectiveness, not necessarily because of a lack of competence in this area, but rather because of behavior under the control of hooks.

LET'S WORK TOGETHER ON A SECURE RELATIONSHIP _____

Now we invite you to fill out a matrix about someone important to you, with whom your relationship feels "secure"/"harmonious." If possible, choose a relationship in which the balance between "their needs" and "my needs" is in equilibrium, or in which the balance tilts in favor of "my needs." To do this, refer to the relational landscape table that you just completed.

Fill in the matrix that follows by following the instructions below.

1. Write down the name of someone important to you, with whom your relationship feels "secure" *(refer to the previous table).*

➤ ME _____

2. Write down the important ways in which you could take a little more care of this relationship, to invest yourself in it a little more, and so on. What do you share with this person? Why is this relationship really important to you?

➤ ME _____

Review the score associated with your satisfaction in this relationship (third column of the table). Imagine . . . you get into a time machine and you're sent into the future three months from now. You meet the "you" of the future, who rates the satisfaction in this relationship two points higher! You're pleased to see this improvement in the relationship and ask the "you" of the future:

What has changed in this relationship? What is different compared to three months ago?

➤ ME _____

3. What are the inner obstacles that tend to arise for you that make you suffer and prevent you from moving toward that person the way you would like to—or as much as you would like to? What are your thoughts? What are your emotions?

➤ ME _____

4. When you're in touch with these thoughts and emotions, it's unpleasant. Where do you feel this in your body? How would you describe this sensation? *(It's important to describe it precisely so that when we experience this unpleasant sensation, we can recognize that we're reacting physically to these particular thoughts and emotions.)* Get in touch with these feelings for a few moments.

➤ ME _____

5. When you're in touch with these feelings, what does it make you want to do? If you completely latch onto what is written down in the lower left part of the matrix, what does it push you to do in the moment? *(These may be things you do or don't do—but that you strongly feel like doing in the moment.)*

These are the things you tend to do more to move away from what you don't want to think or feel, or under the control of what you don't want to think or feel, rather than to move toward that relationship in the way that is important to you.

➤ ME _____

6. Write down what you are doing or what you could do to move toward that person in the way you would like to. What would the person you'd really like to be do? *(This behavior should be a little different from what you usually do and should still take care of you.)*

➤ ME _____

Reread what your "me of the future" wrote down as being different in the improved relationship three months from now. What could you do in the days to come to move in this direction to improve your satisfaction in the relationship?

➤ ME _____

7. If the step is too big or too difficult to do as it is, what can you do to make it easier? What can you do that takes care of you and that in the bigger picture enables you to take the step that's important to you later on?

➤ ME _____

8. In the hours and days to come, what might we see you do specifically to move in this direction?

➤ ME _____

Reread the right-hand side of your matrix.

9. What does it make you feel in your body? Where? How would you describe it?

➤ ME _____

Does this make more sense than what is written on the left-hand side of the matrix?

If YES, would you agree to leaving a little room for inner obstacles (written in the lower left part of the matrix) should they arise for you, quit fighting them, and take the small step that you've identified in the upper right of your matrix, because it allows you to move forward toward a life that has meaning for you?

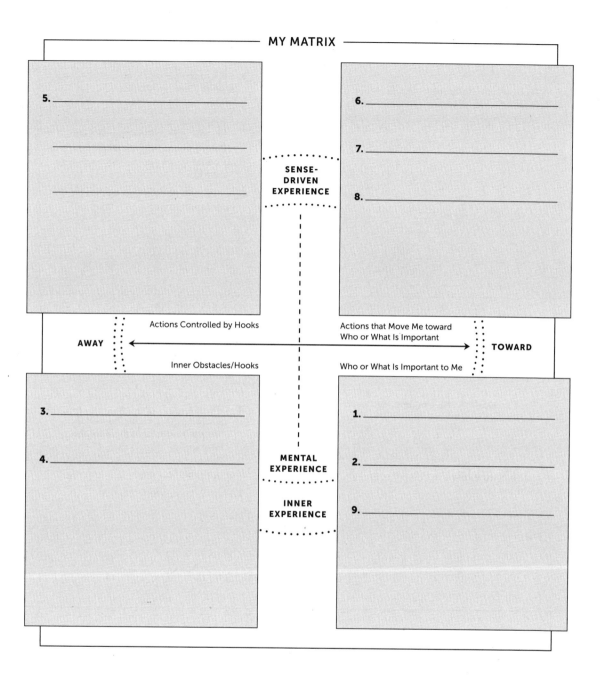

So, for the hours and days ahead, watch what happens. If you aren't able to take the small step, don't worry. The simple act of having written it down in the matrix is already a way you're moving forward in that direction. And if you did take the small step, great! In that case, observe the difference in your feelings. Could it be related to pushing yourself beyond your limits, pride, and consistency with your values?

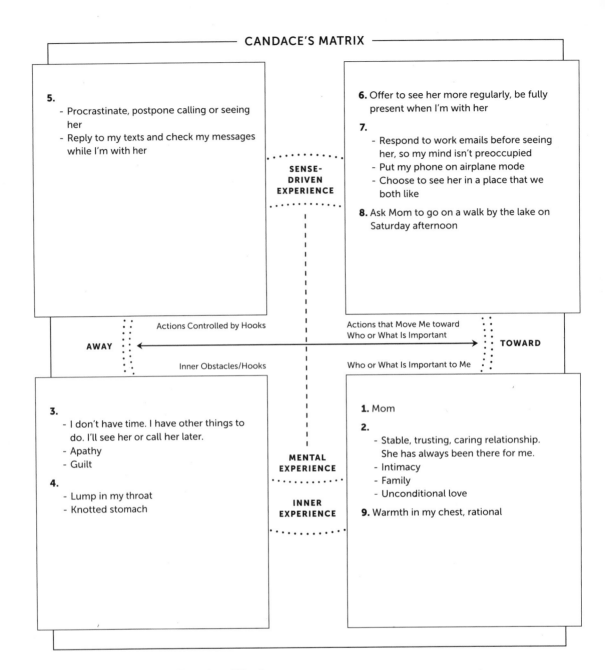

5.
- Procrastinate, postpone calling or seeing her
- Reply to my texts and check my messages while I'm with her

6. Offer to see her more regularly, be fully present when I'm with her

7.
- Respond to work emails before seeing her, so my mind isn't preoccupied
- Put my phone on airplane mode
- Choose to see her in a place that we both like

8. Ask Mom to go on a walk by the lake on Saturday afternoon

SENSE-DRIVEN EXPERIENCE

Actions Controlled by Hooks

Actions that Move Me toward Who or What Is Important

AWAY

TOWARD

Inner Obstacles/Hooks

Who or What Is Important to Me

3.
- I don't have time. I have other things to do. I'll see her or call her later.
- Apathy
- Guilt

4.
- Lump in my throat
- Knotted stomach

MENTAL EXPERIENCE

INNER EXPERIENCE

1. Mom

2.
- Stable, trusting, caring relationship. She has always been there for me.
- Intimacy
- Family
- Unconditional love

9. Warmth in my chest, rational

Exercise for the Coming Week

Every night identify:

– one or more steps you've taken during the day toward someone with whom you have a harmonious relationship that is important to you. Write down the feeling associated with doing this small step.

– one or more steps that you could take the next day toward someone (it could be a different person each day) with whom you have a harmonious relationship that is important to you.

Remember! Small steps indicate *directions*, not goals. If you didn't take the small step that you wrote down the night before, don't worry about it. The fact of having written it down and anticipating it is already a step in the right direction. This small step may happen at another time or in another way.

Now identify what obstacles arose:

- What thoughts, feelings, or emotions prevented you from taking the small step?
- If fears arose, which ones?
- If obsessive thoughts arose, which ones?

Can you see that the fact that you bit the hook has changed your trajectory away from the small step that was originally planned?

DAY 1

Today's small step	Small step: Feeling:
If yesterday's small step didn't happen	Planned small step: Obstacle(s): What I did next:
Tomorrow's small step	

DAY 2

Today's small step	Small step: Feeling:
If yesterday's small step didn't happen	Planned small step: Obstacle(s): What I did next:
Tomorrow's small step	

DAY 3

Today's small step	Small step: Feeling:
If yesterday's small step didn't happen	Planned small step: Obstacle(s): What I did next:
Tomorrow's small step	

DAY 4

Today's small step	Small step: Feeling:
If yesterday's small step didn't happen	Planned small step: Obstacle(s): What I did next:
Tomorrow's small step	

DAY 5

Today's small step	Small step: Feeling:
If yesterday's small step didn't happen	Planned small step: Obstacle(s): What I did next:
Tomorrow's small step	

DAY 6

Today's small step	Small step: Feeling:
If yesterday's small step didn't happen	Planned small step: Obstacle(s): What I did next:
Tomorrow's small step	

DAY 7

Today's small step	Small step: Feeling:
If yesterday's small step didn't happen	Planned small step: Obstacle(s): What I did next:
Tomorrow's small step	

MY SECURE RELATIONAL LANDSCAPE

UNDERSTANDING INTERPERSONAL RELATIONSHIPS THROUGH A GAME

We're going to learn to characterize the relationships with the people around you, whether these are secure or insecure attachments. To do this, we're going to play a card game! This relational card game will be as realistic as possible and will include all the relationships identified in the table in the previous chapter.

It's the game of your current relationships. And as always, reality is constantly changing! This card game will therefore evolve over time, in the same way that you'll evolve over time.

There are two categories of cards:

1. *"Security" cards:* We experience these relationships as stable, reassuring, and harmonious (we feel respected and loved in a way that measures up to our expectations).

2. *"Insecurity" cards:* We experience these relationships as unstable, distressing, and insecure; they can be satisfying or not, relative to what we expect from a relationship.

SECURITY CARDS: BASIC PRINCIPLES OF THE GAME

Let's focus this week on the security cards.

Card Profile
Front: The relationship's strengths
Start by writing the person's name in the place indicated on the card shown in the box on the next page, and next to it write this relation-

ship's scores from the "relational landscape" table in chapter 15, p. 158. Next write down the relationship's strengths according to the following instructions.

- *Its length:* How long have you been in this relationship?
- *Significant life areas you share:* What life areas do you share? This is time spent together or interacting (a source of fulfillment and satisfaction) in an area of life that has meaning for you. These are life areas or values that you really enjoy sharing with this person. Sharing these important things with them makes investing in these areas even more meaningful for you.

For example, two brothers work in the same family business, only because they inherited it and not because of any shared passion for it, and they work in a toxic environment in which they avoid crossing each other's path. This area of life should not be written on the card. The opposite is true of two friends who are passionate about sewing and who create a company together, which allows them to enjoy their shared passion, share common values, and spend even more time together. Here, clearly, the life area adds to the strength of the relationship. And there are all sorts of situations that exist in between these two examples.

- *Common and shared values, what is important:* these are shared values that play a role in the relationship, allowing each person to move toward what is important and meaningful, and allowing each person to embody the kind of person they really want to be.
- *This person's character strengths that serve the relationship:* these are the character strengths that the person brings to your relationship or to you that enable you to move toward something that's important to you.
- *The great things this person has done for me:* these are times this person has gone above and beyond to improve the quality of the relation-

┌──────── SECURITY CARD: FRONT ────────┐

NAME ❶ / ❷ / MN❸TN / ❹

The Relationship's Strengths
- Its length
- The significant shared life areas
- Common and shared values, what is important
- This person's character strengths that serve the relationship
- The great things they've done for me
- The great things I've done for them

❶ Level of personal investment

❷ Satisfaction in the relationship

❸ Balance: my needs/their needs

❹ Security of the relationship

ship. Think of the positive significant events during the times you've shared that are the most indicative of this person's investment in the relationship. Write down only the observable positive events that took place. You can add an objective detail to make them less abstract (date, name, outcome, and so on).

- *The great things I've done for this person:* these are times you've gone above and beyond to improve the quality of the relationship. Think of the positive significant events during the times you've shared that are the most indicative of your investment in the relationship. This is everything you've already done to improve the quality of the relationship. Write down only the observable positive events that took place. You can add an objective detail to make them less abstract (date, name, outcome, and so on).

Back: The relationship's limitations

Imagine . . . You interview someone outside of the relationship, someone who cares deeply for you and this relationship. Suddenly, she says to you, "This relationship is really inspiring. This relationship is so important to you that you accept this about them." What is she talking about? What could "this" be?

Write it on the back of this person's card.

All human beings have limitations or weak points. These limitations coexist with strengths. In practicing mindfulness, do you agree to *accept this person's limitation* in order to nurture this important and secure relationship?

PRACTICAL APPLICATION

Matrix: Let's work once again on a secure relationship with the security card game

Now we invite you to fill out a matrix about someone important to you (someone other than whom you chose in the previous chapter), with whom your relationship feels "secure"/"harmonious." If possible, choose a relationship in which the balance between "their needs" and "my needs" is in equilibrium or in which the balance tilts in favor of "my needs." To do this, refer to the relational landscape table (chapter 15, p. 158).

CANDACE'S SECURITY CARD

FRONT	BACK

MELANIE   61 / 6 / MN   TN ⊥★ / 6

The Relationship's Strengths
- *Its length:* 5 years
- *The significant shared life areas:* painting, art
- *Common and shared values, what is important:* creativity, sharing, closeness
- *Her character strengths that serve the relationship:* attentive, considerate
- *The great things she's done for me:* In Last year, she helped me file paperwork when I was having a hard time. Two months ago she told Mrs. Pigort that she would only exhibit her paintings in the gallery if I did it with her.
- *The great things I've done for her:* In May, I organized a surprise birthday party for her. Last summer, I was there for her, day or night, when she broke up with Patrick.

The Relationship's Limitations
- The fact that she's sensitive, she gets offended easily
- The fact that she's often late
- She talks a lot!

1. Write down the name of someone important to you, with whom your relationship feels secure.

⮞ ME _____

2. Write down the important ways in which you could take a little more care of this relationship, to invest yourself in it a little more, and so on. What do you share with this person? Why is this relationship really important to you?

⮞ ME _____

Review the score associated with your satisfaction in this relationship (third column of the table). Imagine . . . you get into a time machine and you're sent into the future three months from now. You meet the "you" of the future, who rates the satisfaction in this relationship two points higher! You're pleased to see this improvement in the relationship and ask the "you" of the future: What has changed in this relationship? What is different compared to three months ago?

⮞ FUTURE ME _____

Fill in the matrix below with the answer that corresponds to each question number.

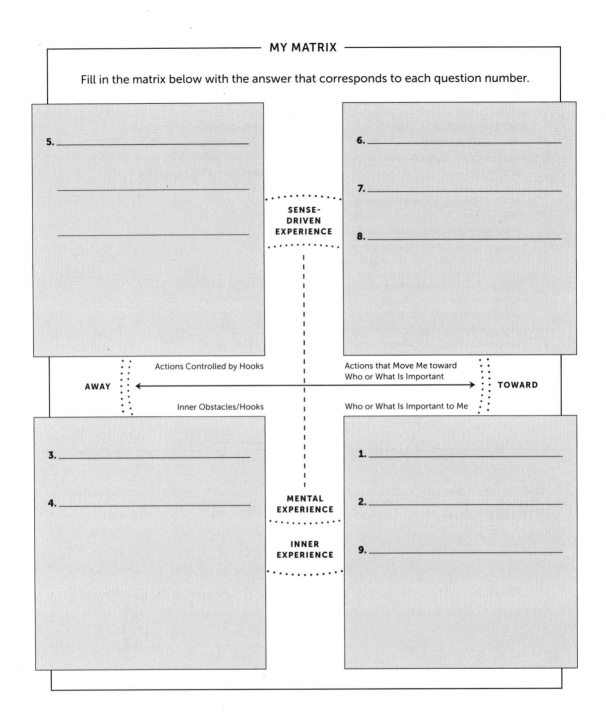

5. _____

_____

_____

6. _____

7. _____

SENSE-DRIVEN EXPERIENCE

8. _____

Actions Controlled by Hooks

Actions that Move Me toward
Who or What Is Important

AWAY ◄—————————————————————► **TOWARD**

Inner Obstacles/Hooks

Who or What Is Important to Me

3. _____

1. _____

4. _____

2. _____

MENTAL EXPERIENCE

INNER EXPERIENCE

9. _____

3. What are the inner obstacles that tend to arise for you that make you suffer and prevent you from moving toward that person the way you would like to—or as much as you would like to? What are your thoughts? What are your emotions?

▶ ME _____

4. When you're in touch with these thoughts and emotions, it's unpleasant. Where do you feel this in your body? How would you describe this sensation? *(It's important to describe it precisely so that when we experience this unpleasant sensation, we can recognize that we're reacting physically to these particular thoughts and emotions.)*

Get in touch with these feelings for a few moments.

➤ ME _____

5. When you're in touch with these feelings, what does it make you want to do? If you completely latch onto what is written down in the lower left part of the matrix, what does it push you to do in the moment? These may be things you do or don't do (but that you strongly feel like doing in the moment). *(These are the things you tend to do more to move away from what you don't want to think or feel, or under the control of what you don't want to think or feel, rather than to move toward that relationship in the way that is important to you.)*

➤ ME _____

6. Write down what you are doing or what you could do to move toward that person in the way you would like to. What would the person you'd really like to be do? *(This behavior should be a little different from what you usually do and should still take care of you.)*

➤ ME _____

Reread what your "me of the future" wrote down as being different in the improved relationship three months from now (item 2 above). What could you do in the days to come to move in this direction to improve your satisfaction in the relationship?

➤ ME _____

7. If the step is too big or too difficult to do as it is, what can you do to make it easier? What can you do that takes care of you and that in the bigger picture enables you to take the step that's important to you later on?

➤ ME _____

8. In the hours and days to come, what might we see you do specifically to move in this direction?

➤ ME _____

Reread the right-hand side of your matrix.

9. What does it make you feel in your body? Where? How would you describe it?

➤ ME _____

Does this make more sense than what is written on the left-hand side of the matrix?

If YES, would you agree to leaving a little room for inner obstacles (written in the lower left part of the matrix) should they arise for you, quit fighting them, and take the small step that you've identified in the upper right of your matrix, because it allows you to move forward toward a life that has meaning for you?

So, for the hours and days ahead, watch what happens. If you aren't able to take the small step, don't worry. The simple act of having written it down in the matrix is already a way you're moving forward in that direction.

And if you did take the small step, great! In that case, observe the difference in your feelings. Could it be related to pushing yourself beyond your limits, pride, and consistency with your values?

Exercise for the Coming Week
Every night identify:

- one or more steps you've taken during the day toward someone with whom you have a harmonious relationship that is important to you. Write down the feeling associated with doing this small step.

- one or more steps that you could take the next day toward someone (it could be a different person each day) with whom you have a harmonious relationship that is important to you.

Remember! Small steps indicate *directions*, not goals. If you didn't take the small step that you wrote down the night before, don't worry about it. The fact of having written it down and anticipating it is already a step in the right direction. This small step may happen at another time or in another way. Now identify what obstacles arose:

- *What thoughts, feelings, or emotions prevented you from taking the small step?*
- *If fears arose, which ones?*
- *If obsessive thoughts arose, which ones?*

Can you see that the fact that you bit the hook has changed your trajectory away from the small step that was originally planned?

DAY 1

Today's small step	Small step: Feeling:
If yesterday's small step didn't happen	Planned small step: Obstacle(s): What I did next:
Tomorrow's small step	

DAY 2

Today's small step	Small step: Feeling:
If yesterday's small step didn't happen	Planned small step: Obstacle(s): What I did next:
Tomorrow's small step	

DAY 3

Today's small step	Small step: Feeling:
If yesterday's small step didn't happen	Planned small step: Obstacle(s): What I did next:
Tomorrow's small step	

DAY 4

Today's small step	Small step: Feeling:
If yesterday's small step didn't happen	Planned small step: Obstacle(s): What I did next:
Tomorrow's small step	

DAY 5

Today's small step	Small step: Feeling:
If yesterday's small step didn't happen	Planned small step: Obstacle(s): What I did next:
Tomorrow's small step	

DAY 6

Today's small step	Small step: Feeling:
If yesterday's small step didn't happen	Planned small step: Obstacle(s): What I did next:
Tomorrow's small step	

DAY 7

Today's small step	Small step: Feeling:
If yesterday's small step didn't happen	Planned small step: Obstacle(s): What I did next:
Tomorrow's small step	

CHAPTER 17

MY INSECURE RELATIONAL LANDSCAPE

MANAGING DIFFICULT RELATIONSHIPS

Using the matrix for interpersonal relationships will allow you to progressively and truly embody the person you want to be in your relationships, according to who you really are deep down.

Moving toward stable and tranquil relationships is sometimes very difficult when you have borderline personality disorder. When it comes to interpersonal relationships, the discomfort caused by leaving the comfort zone is even greater in this life area than in other areas. In fact, relationships are often very important to individuals with borderline personality disorder, and as a result, hooks may be so attractive and they take the bait so often that it becomes difficult to practice mindfulness.

In this life area, emotion mind easily remains dominant, and experiential avoidance behaviors (that is, the upper left part of the matrix) are more intense. Therefore in order to move forward, it'll be necessary to avoid "going around in circles" or avoid "taking a step backward each time we take a step forward," and to choose to take even smaller small steps than in other life areas.

We must take into account that in interpersonal relationships emotions are increased tenfold. The main thing is to stay oriented in the same direction and to double your kindness toward yourself when the small step isn't made. It's already a step forward to work on it and express the intention to change something.

Finally, when an imbalanced interpersonal situation begins to hinder our quality of life, the more we act in keeping with the reality of the situation—and not according to what we'd like the situation to be—the more the pain becomes tolerable. For example, if a relationship disappoints me—I invest a lot without it being reciprocated (or what's returned is dissatisfying for me)—it's useless to persist in wanting to change it for months and years.

The most effective thing to do is to accept that this relationship is what it is, and that with all the effort and energy already invested in it, if something were going to change, it would have happened already. So, either I have the possibility to extract myself from this situation (end the relationship, distance myself, and so on), or I do the most effective thing, which is to accept this relationship as it is and for what it is, embodying as best as I can the person I would be proud to be in this situation.

The more we act in keeping with the reality of the situation, the more the pain becomes tolerable.

In fact, the situation is painful in itself because there is a gap between expectations and reality, but this situation will advance from pain to suffering if it's kept going, if we make decisions that go against reality, or if we persist in trying to change the situation so that it becomes what we expect. All this only makes the problem last. It keeps the problem going and amplifies it. We lie to ourselves so we don't have to confront something difficult. This is how "pain" + "nonacceptance of this pain" becomes "suffering."

Therefore, the most effective thing to do is to play the card that we actually have in our hand and not act as if we had another one that we like more, but that in reality we don't have.

For example, if the relationship with my sister is difficult, and it doesn't meet my expectations, then I can try to change things. For a while, usually several years, I probably acted with the hope of being able to make it better fit what I expect from a relationship between sisters. I probably told her many times what disappoints me; sometimes I acted as if she were the sister I dreamed of, and then I was disappointed again and again. I was annoyed with her, I was probably mad at her, or I lost my temper every time she didn't meet my expectations. But, in the end, if I invested a lot of energy for years without being able to change anything, it's because in reality I can't change my sister. In the same way I can't really "walk away" from my life either; she's family, even if it's disappointing.

Then the most effective thing to do is to tell myself: that's the way she is, even if I don't like that she's like that. From now on, I'm going to stop living in the illusion that she can be different, and I'll behave like the sister that I would be proud to be in *this* situation.

This could mean that I don't sulk or lose my temper anymore (the upper left part of the matrix) because that doesn't uphold the image I have of myself or lead to a sense of personal pride.

Instead, I'll choose to act as best as I can—like the person I would like to be—consistent with who I am and while respecting myself, according to what can be done in this relationship (as it is and not as what I tell myself it should be).

INSECURITY CARDS: BASIC PRINCIPLES OF THE GAME

Now let's create our insecurity cards

They designate the relationships in which:

- I honor the needs of the other person to the extreme, without taking into account my boundaries, my expectations, or my interests.

- I too often act under the control of my hooks in this relationship, and it even influences other areas of my life.

- I experience this relationship as unstable, distressing, and insecure. I may spend a lot of time obsessively thinking about this relationship.

- I do not feel respected or loved in a way that measures up to my expectations in this relationship.

Card Profile

Front: The relationship's strengths

This side of the card is identical for the security card and the insecurity card. Read pp. 166–68 for instructions on how to fill it out.

Back: The relationship's limitations

The back is different for the two types of cards. For this side of the insecurity card, don't worry if you can't fill in each item. Write something down only if you observe behaviors in this person that bring about thoughts, feelings,

---

INSECURITY CARD: BACK

NAME ❶ / ❷ / MN❸TN / ❹

The Relationship's Limitations
- Their behaviors that harm the relationship
- What hooks do these behaviors bring about for me?
- How does this move me away from my values, from what is important to me?
- Negative significant events
- What are the significant differences between my expectations and reality?

❶ Level of personal investment
❷ Satisfaction in the relationship
❸ Balance: my needs/their needs
❹ Security of the relationship

FRONT

BACK

OLIVIA   45 / 2 /  TN / 2

The Relationship's Strengths

- *Its length:* 4 years
- *The significant shared life areas:* work
- *Common and shared values, what is important:* exchange of professional experiences, focus on the relationship with patients
- *Her character strengths that serve the relationship:* open-mindedness
- *The great things she's done for me:* she organized a surprise party with my department colleagues to celebrate my 30th birthday, and they all contributed to give me an iPad. She regularly offers to take my night shifts for me.
- *The great things I've done for her:* I have, on several occasions, done complex patient care in her place because she often doesn't feel confident doing it. I mediated a situation for her, in which a family was raised questions about the death of a relative, which helped avoid unwarranted litigation.

The Relationship's Limitations

- *Her behaviors that harm the relationship:* We have a special relationship at work, but she never calls me (except when she wants to swap shifts) or ask me to spend time with her outside of work.
- *What hooks do these behaviors bring about for me?* She doesn't care about me, she uses me, I'm uninteresting, shame, anger
- *How does this move me away from my values, from what is important to me?* Self-respect, my conversations with my close friends often revolve around her
- *Negative significant events:* 1. She didn't invite me to a party at her house with other colleagues. 2. When my grandfather passed away, I was looking for someone to take my shift on a Sunday so I could stay with my family. She told me she couldn't, but it was just so she could spend a few hours with her boyfriend. 3. We regularly share ideas for improving the department, but in meetings, she always sides with the most influential colleagues or managers, even if it's not what we discussed together.
- *What are the significant differences between my expectations and reality?* I'm looking for a close and trustworthy relationship on a professional and friendly level. But I have the feeling that she isn't looking for a friendly relationship with me, and I feel I can't trust her completely.

or emotions that will often control or influence your behavior. In turn, these behaviors serve to move you away from these painful hooks rather than to allow you to dedicate yourself to the areas that are important to you in the way you would like.

- *Their behaviors that harm the relationship:* what they do that hurts me, that I cannot understand from my perspective or in terms of my expectations of a quality relationship. These behaviors are done voluntarily, or involuntarily, to hurt the relationship.

- *What hooks do these behaviors bring about for me?* These are my thoughts, feelings, and emotions related to the behaviors of this person that harm the relationship.

- *How does this move me away from my values, from what is important to me?* What are the values that I cannot embody in this relationship because the hooks are so painful? How can I be the person I would really like to be right now? How will these hooks prevent me from dedicating myself to other important life areas in the way I would like to or as I could if these hooks weren't there?

- *Negative significant events*: what this person did that really hurt me, who made terribly painful hooks emerge for me. Don't hesitate to write down concrete details, such as dates, names, and places.

- *What are the significant differences between my expectations and reality?* In a few words, write down what is disappointing in this relationship that is nevertheless important to you or takes up space in your life.

> *These behaviors serve to move you away from these painful hooks rather than to allow you to dedicate yourself to the areas that are important to you.*

MATRIX: LET'S WORK ON YOUR INSECURE RELATIONSHIPS WITH THE INSECURITY CARD GAME

Before continuing on in this chapter, we're going to ask you to differentiate between two scenarios in your insecure relationships.

1. The relationship feels insecure even though it's satisfying

What you experience in the relationship is in line with your relational expectations. You embody your values and can invest in the areas of life that are important to you. However, at times, internal obstacles (such as: "I'm afraid this won't last, I'm not interesting enough to invest in this relationship, I don't matter to them as much as they matter to me") arise for you. It's very likely that these fears are related to your personal story. Therefore, identify these inner obstacles as mental phenomena and not as the reality of the situation. They are the drawback of the importance this relationship has for you. This relationship means so much that it scares you to conceive of a life without it.

In this scenario, fill in your matrix as if it were a secure relationship, because investing in such a relationship has meaning and takes care of you. Therefore, look back to chapter 16, pp. 169–72, and take a closer look at number 3. Take the time to identify your inner obstacles that are related to this relational insecurity.

2. The relationship feels insecure and dissatisfying

There are significant differences between your relational expectations and the reality of the situation. You've probably put a lot of energy into wanting to change this relationship, to doing actions on the right-hand side of your matrix, but the problem is still there. Not only does this relationship not meet your expectations, but on top of that, it probably doesn't take care of you. Since we're working on significant relationships or relationships that take up space, it's highly likely that it also hooks you so often that you aren't able to invest your values any longer in the way you would like to in this relationship, and that this even interferes with other areas of your life.

PRACTICAL APPLICATION _____

Choose a person from the insecurity card game with whom your relationship is dissatisfying.

1. Write down your name. Taking care of yourself within this relationship is the priority that's important today (you can write down the name of the person in parentheses with whom the relationship is difficult).

➤ ME _____

2. What are the inner obstacles that tend to arise for you related to this relationship?

- What difference do you see between your expectations and what the relationship brings you in reality?
- What are your thoughts, feelings, and emotions about this?
- What thoughts and feelings underlie the insecurity in this relationship (fear of abandonment, disproportionate attachment, fear of the power

this person has over you, terror as soon as the relationship seems more uncertain, feeling of not being respected, of not being loved for who you are but only for what you do)?

- What are the thoughts or beliefs that will lead to an impulse to hyperinvest—trying to get in touch with that person too often—but that prevent you from embodying the person you would like to be and of whom you would be proud?

- What are the thoughts or beliefs that will lead to an impulse to abruptly reject the person (avoid them, sulk), but that prevent you from embodying the person you would like to be and of whom you would be proud?

➤ ME _____

3. Get in touch with how it feels in your body when you're in contact with these obstacles. Where do you feel it in your body? How would you describe it in a few words?

➤ ME _____

4. Write down what you do or tend to do when these obstacles arise for you. These are things that you do more to move away from these obstacles, or under the control of these obstacles, rather than to take care of yourself, respect yourself, or move toward what is important to you. It may be things you do that you're ashamed of afterward (or later on), that do not respect you as a person, or that move you away from a sense of pride.

➤ ME _____

5. What might we see you do to take care of yourself in this relationship? What would the person you'd like to be do? What would you do if you respected yourself as a person? If you acted in a way in this relationship that showed pride in yourself, what would we see you do?

➤ ME _____

You'll need to list your objective personal limitations and number them. *Choose doable small steps* that don't go beyond what is currently tolerable for you, that only widen the comfort zone. In this case, you can choose small steps that are articulated in the negative: for example, no longer doing a particular excessive or constantly asked-for favor; turning off my phone at times to guarantee myself some time without contact with someone; no longer implementing excessive reassurance-seeking behaviors such as sending off-topic emails or text messages to ensure the quality or longevity of the relationship; not putting my priorities after those of the other person; allowing myself to think differently and to express it; knowing how to ask for help when I need it; and so on.

We must take into account that in interpersonal relationships emotions are increased tenfold. The small steps have to be tiny steps, but there can be a lot of them. A difficult relationship that's lasted many years can't improve in just a few days. The essential thing is to not move backward as soon as we've moved forward. We need to continue in the same direction so that we don't take a step backward; we also need to show ourselves a lot of kindness when the tiny step doesn't happen. *Not moving backward is a victory in itself!*

6. Take another look at each of the small steps in the list you wrote down in the upper right part of the matrix. Now write down, in the lower right corner, the reasons that justify this change of attitude. One reason could be respect for your values, but also note the objective reasons why the relationship as it currently is might not deserve such an investment from you. Also write down the ways this relationship moves you away from other things in your life that would be important to you if you didn't have to struggle so much.

➤ ME _____

What you just wrote is consistent with what is really important to you, and it justifies the fact that it's now essential to begin exiting the comfort zone. This will inevitably lead to brief discomfort but also to a real sense of consistency with your values, freedom, and pushing yourself beyond your limits in the longer term.

7. If the step is too big or too difficult to do as it is, what can you do to make it easier? What other life areas can you develop that take care of you and that in the bigger picture enable you to take the step that's important to you later on?

➤ ME _____

8-a. Now choose one or at most two small steps from the list in the upper right part of the matrix. These will be the first small steps for improving the situation. Remember that these tiny steps must be tolerable for you. They will inevitably get you out of the comfort zone and thus bring about unpleasant thoughts and feelings.

➤ ME _____

_____

8-b. When you make this choice, write down in the lower left part of the matrix (along with the number of the small step) the thoughts and feelings that this is likely to bring about and that you are ready to accept. When consciously doing the small step, you will choose to accept these hooks and you will allow them to have the

Fill in the matrix below with the answer that corresponds to each question number.

4. _____

5. _____

8. _____

SENSE-
DRIVEN
EXPERIENCE

Actions Controlled by Hooks

Actions that Move Me toward
Who or What Is Important

AWAY ←—————————————————→ TOWARD

Inner Obstacles/Hooks

Who or What Is Important to Me

2. _____

1. _____

3. _____

6. _____

MENTAL
EXPERIENCE

INNER
EXPERIENCE

7. _____

9. _____

space they take up in order to do your small step anyway. Be aware that these hooks will most likely appear. *(Typically at first, acting on the right side of the matrix works less well, but as a little time goes by you'll feel much better.)*

➤ ME _____

Reread the right-hand side of your matrix.

9. What does it make you feel in your body? Where? How would you describe it?

Are the things written on the right-hand side of the matrix more meaningful than those written on the left-hand side?

If YES, would you agree to leaving a little room for inner obstacles should they arise for you, quit fighting them, and nonetheless take the small step that you've identified in the upper right of your matrix, because it allows you to move forward toward a life that has meaning for you?

For the hours and days to come, watch what you do to take care of yourself in this relationship. What next tiny step will you take to go in the direction outside of your comfort zone but within your self-care zone?

Watch what happens. If you aren't able to take the small step, don't worry. The simple act of having written it down in the matrix is already a way you're moving forward in that direction.

And if you did take the small step, great! In that case, observe the difference in your feelings. Could it be related to pushing yourself beyond your limits and pride?

 ME _____

If you realize that despite the precautions you've taken today, the small steps are still too big and the feelings too scary, then with kindness choose a new small step that's even smaller and that takes even more care of you, but that still continues to move you in the chosen direction.

If at some point you start doing a behavior from the upper left part of the matrix again in attempt to move away from unpleasant thoughts and feelings, identify it and consciously choose with kindness to accept that it was too hard. However, also recognize that it's still possible to take the small step the next time you go back in the direction you initially identified; you're not starting from scratch.

Whenever your small step leads to very high emotional stress but you mindfully choose to do it anyway, look at your secure relationship cards or, even better, reach out to those people. This will reassure you about your interpersonal skills and about the strong and comforting relationships that really exist. This challenging card to play is part of an entire game, and in this game there are other cards that are really amazing! In practicing mindfulness, pick these cards—they're the game-changers when it comes to the big picture.

4.
- Sulk, speak curtly to her
- Distance myself from the relationship
- Criticize her commitment to the relationship
- Think obsessively about the quality of the relationship
- Talk about this relationship for hours with my close friends so they'll reassure or help me
- After sending Olivia a text, stop focusing on what I was doing and obsess over her reply. Check my phone every ten minutes to see if I've received a text without realizing it.
- When I have doubts about the relationship, ask her again to spend time together outside of work.

5.
- Small Step 1: Stop asking her to spend time together, let her ask me herself, and say yes when that happens.
- Small Step 2: As much as possible, speak to her in a pleasant/cordial manner at work, don't sulk or overtly distance myself, even if I'm disappointed by her behavior toward me.
- Small Step 3: Keep doing favors for her at work, but only if she asks me to explicitly and only after finishing what I have to do before going to help her so that I don't put myself in a difficult position.

7. Develop friendships with other colleagues in the department: ask Sophie to do something

8a. To start with, I'm going to move in the direction of small steps 2 and 3.
- Small Step 2: At work on Monday, I'll answer her with a smile without having any expectations.
- Small Step 3: If she doesn't ask me to help her, I won't offer, unlike what I usually do.

SENSE-DRIVEN EXPERIENCE

Actions Controlled by Hooks

Actions that Move Me toward Who or What Is Important

AWAY ←———————————————→ **TOWARD**

Inner Obstacles/Hooks

Who or What Is Important to Me

2. She uses me when she doesn't know how to do certain procedures.
- Anger: "I care more about her than she does about me," "I'm pathetic," "I'm not interesting"
- Shame, sadness
- Fear that the relationship will end
- Doubt: What if I was wrong about her? Maybe she also wants to see me outside of work, but maybe won't ask me out of fear of imposing?

3. Feeling of suffocation in my chest, flushed face, tears in my eyes, clenched jaw

8b. Concerning small step 2: she doesn't want a friendship, disappointment, sadness (weak muscle tone, heavy sighs)
Concerning small step 3: fear, if I don't do favors for her, I'll lose the special relationship I have with her at work (knotted stomach, feeling flushed)

MENTAL EXPERIENCE

INNER EXPERIENCE

1. Candace (Olivia)

6. This relationship doesn't respect my expectations of a friend: a stable relationship, invested (timewise and emotionally), integrity
- Small Step 1: Self-respect and self-esteem. Don't lower my standards for a relationship that doesn't match my expectations.
- Small Step 2: Keep my dignity, pride in my attitude and behavior toward myself and also toward my colleagues. Don't make a fool of myself.
- Small Step 3: Fairness at work, professional awareness (taking the necessary time with my patients as much for technical care as for the patient-nurse relationship).

9. Lightness, freedom, in my stomach

A MESSAGE FROM DÉBORAH AND VÉRONIQUE

The hooks arising for us in the context of a relationship are indicators of needs resulting from how we conceive of ourselves (depending on our personal and socio-cultural background). They're indicators of our expectations for the external reality to make us feel comfortable and/or valued. The therapeutic pathway will always be to change our position relative to others: moving away from craving objects to fulfill our desires for comfort and toward choosing useful objects for practicing valued commitments. It's the only way to attain inner growth and really benefit ourselves and others.

SHAME AND INTERPERSONAL EFFECTIVENESS

SHAME AND BORDERLINE PERSONALITY DISORDER

Shame and guilt are frequently confused. Let's clarify these concepts.

- *Shame* is the feeling of being unworthy, of being unlovable for our personal characteristics. This emotion may be related to certain recurring thoughts such as "I don't have as much worth as other people," "I'm ridiculous," or "I'm pathetic." Shame is the painful feeling of believing oneself unworthy of love, integration, and belonging. Shame is about who we are.

- *Guilt* is the awareness of having acted badly or of acting badly in general. This emotion may be related to certain recurring thoughts such as "I'm responsible for everything that's happening to me," "I'm responsible for what's happening to them," "It's always my fault," or "I never make good decisions." Guilt is about what we do—our behavior—whereas shame is about who we are as a person.

What Scientific Studies Say

Individuals with borderline personality disorder are particularly sensitive to experiences of self-awareness,[1] and they tend to avoid situations that increase the focus on their personal characteristics.[2] In fact, shame—an emotion related to self-awareness—is an emotion that is central to this disorder.[3] The published data shows a greater propensity for shame in individuals with borderline personality disorder than in people with other psychological problems or healthy subjects,[4] with a specific increase in levels of "existential shame."[5] What is "existential shame"?

It's a kind of shame that has to do with oneself as a person, in their entirety ("shame of who I am, of what characterizes me"). It's different from "cognitive shame," which refers to one's intellectual skills.[6]

What's more, shame is the emotion most strongly associated with suicidal and parasuicidal behaviors, anger, and impulsivity in individuals with borderline personality disorder.[7] It has even been suggested that borderline personality disorder could be thought of as a chronic response to shame.[8] That's how central to the disorder this emotion seems to be. Moreover, in comparison with healthy people, the increased emotional reactivity—the highly emotional state—of patients with borderline personality disorder appears to be context-dependent.

> *Guilt is about what we do—our behavior—*
> *whereas shame is about who we are as a person.*

In fact, these individuals are particularly sensitive to other people's negative assessments, which leads to them feeling the emotion of shame.[9] When it's triggered, this emotion takes time to fade.

Interpersonal effectiveness can be understood as the ability to be yourself and to express what you feel, what you want, and what you don't want. Therefore, it's closely related to self-confidence, since it's a matter of not being afraid to openly express your ideas, even if they're different from others', or to show your feelings and reactions. Interpersonal effectiveness will allow you to respect yourself, be in harmony with yourself, and assert your rights while taking those of others into account.

Therefore, it's a willingness to say no when you're thinking no, to make clear demands, to set boundaries, to defend yourself, and to express your point of view.

Thus, being ashamed of yourself and avoiding any situation that can trigger this emotion is an obstacle to interpersonal effectiveness. In fact, shame makes your mind suggest negative thoughts about yourself and about your worth as a person. It's as if your mind is offering you a hook, and when you take the bait, it leads you to act under the control of this hook and makes you struggle. This prevents you from applying effective skills when you act. In fact, this type of hook makes you feel a need to please and conform to the expectations of the important people in your life because your only goal is to behave how the other person expects so you don't disappoint them or risk losing them.

PRACTICAL APPLICATION:
MATRIX FOR OVERCOMING MOMENTS OF SHAME _____

Think back to a situation that triggered shame for you. If you can't decide between several situations, choose the last time it happened. Describe the facts of this situation—what a camera filming it would've seen:

➤ ME _____

_____

1. What are you saying to yourself? What is your mind telling you?

➤ ME _____

_____

2. How does it feel in your body when you're in contact with these obstacles? Where do you feel it in your body? How would you describe it in a few words?

➤ ME _____

_____

Stay in touch with these sensations for a few moments: make space, breathe into them.

3. Write down what you do or tend to do when these obstacles arise for you. These are things that you do more to move away from these obstacles, or under the control of these obstacles, rather than to take care of yourself, respect yourself, or move toward what is important to you.

a. What do you feel like doing in the moment? What is the urgent need?

➤ ME _____

_____

b. What do you tend to do a few hours or days later?

➤ ME _____

_____

4. What would the person you'd really like to be do? What would the YOU who has pride in and kindness for yourself do? In practicing mindfulness, I choose to accept what arises for me because I acknowledge that I'm feeling shame and:

➤ ME _____

Fill in the matrix below with the answer that corresponds to each question number.

3. _____

_____

_____

4. _____

_____

_____

SENSE-DRIVEN EXPERIENCE

Actions Controlled by Hooks

Actions that Move Me toward
Who or What Is Important

AWAY ←——————————————————→ **TOWARD**

Inner Obstacles/Hooks

Who or What Is Important to Me

1. _____

_____

2. _____

_____

5. _____

_____

6. _____

_____

MENTAL EXPERIENCE

INNER EXPERIENCE

_____

5. What is really important to you in all of this?

▶ ME _____

_____

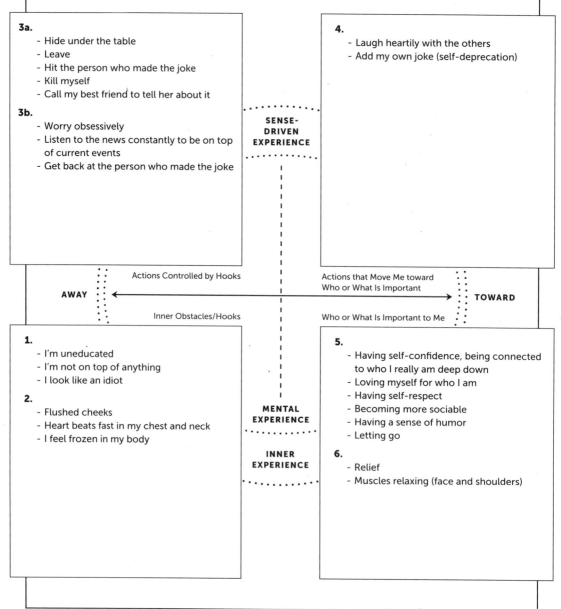

CANDACE'S MATRIX

Situation: *Three days ago, I ate lunch with my co-workers. One of them brought up a current event I wasn't aware of and asked me what I thought. I replied that I didn't know about it. Someone else made a joke about the fact that I didn't know, and the whole table started laughing.*

3a.
- Hide under the table
- Leave
- Hit the person who made the joke
- Kill myself
- Call my best friend to tell her about it

3b.
- Worry obsessively
- Listen to the news constantly to be on top of current events
- Get back at the person who made the joke

4.
- Laugh heartily with the others
- Add my own joke (self-deprecation)

SENSE-DRIVEN EXPERIENCE

Actions Controlled by Hooks

AWAY ← Actions that Move Me toward Who or What Is Important → **TOWARD**

Inner Obstacles/Hooks

Who or What Is Important to Me

MENTAL EXPERIENCE

INNER EXPERIENCE

1.
- I'm uneducated
- I'm not on top of anything
- I look like an idiot

2.
- Flushed cheeks
- Heart beats fast in my chest and neck
- I feel frozen in my body

5.
- Having self-confidence, being connected to who I really am deep down
- Loving myself for who I am
- Having self-respect
- Becoming more sociable
- Having a sense of humor
- Letting go

6.
- Relief
- Muscles relaxing (face and shoulders)

6. What do you feel when you tell yourself that this is important to you?

Where do you feel this in your body?

➤ ME _____

_____

Now, reread the entire right-hand side of the matrix.

Does what is written down make more sense than what is written on the left-hand side of the matrix?

If YES, would you agree to leaving a little room for inner obstacles (written in the lower left part of the matrix) should they arise for you, quit fighting them, and take the small step that you've identified in the upper right of your matrix, because it allows you to move forward toward a life that has meaning for you?

The next time a situation triggers the emotion of shame for you, watch what happens. If it doesn't happen the way you wrote it down in the upper right part of your matrix, don't worry. The simple act of having written it down in the matrix is already a way you're moving forward in that direction.

And if you did take the small step, great! In that case, observe the difference in your feelings. Could it be related to pushing yourself beyond your limits, pride, and consistency with your values?

STRATEGIES FOR REGULATING SHAME

Acceptance

The most effective thing to do is of course to recognize this emotion and accept it for what it is, because in the end we're not responsible for the feelings that arise for us. It's very likely that simply acknowledging shame will make it lose its power to act like a hook. It becomes a "simple mental phenomenon" that can go through me without me letting it have control over me.

The Interpersonal Card

In order to lessen the impact of shame, we'll make a new game card. But this time, it's about yourself. This will allow you to reassure yourself of your own worth as a human being. Have this card with you always, and take it out at times when the feeling of shame is strong and is baiting you. This will bring a bit of rationality to the emotional—with the goal being, of course, to be able to choose our behavior mindfully.

This card is part of your "game," and it's an excellent card!

PRACTICAL APPLICATION

Card Profile

Front

Start by writing your name where indicated on the card in the box below.

Next, complete each item as follows:

- *Your core values:* Write down your core values, what is really important to you. You can refer to chapter 1, pp. 12–18.

- *Your personal strengths:* Refer to chapter 11, p. 122.

- *Your areas of expertise:* Refer to chapter 11, p. 122.

- *Your accomplishments:* Write down the objective accomplishments you've achieved during your life (related to your life events, family, friends, volunteer work, profession, or education).

- *Caring people in your life:* List the people in your life who care for you. These are the people whose cards are in your security card category.

INTERPERSONAL CARD

FRONT	BACK
YOUR NAME	**Letter of Kindness**
- Core values: _____	_____
- Personal strengths: _____	_____
- Areas of expertise: _____	_____
- Accomplishments: _____	_____
- Caring people in your life: _____	

Back: Letter of Kindness

- *Choose,* from among your secure relationships, someone for whom you feel a lot of kindness.
- *Reread* the shame-related thoughts in the lower left part of your matrix, but instead imagine that these thoughts were written by this person about themself.
- *Write* a letter below expressing your kind feelings for them. What do you want to say to them about all these difficult thoughts that make them feel ashamed? Write everything you have in your heart to be truly supportive and caring toward this person who is dear to you.

_____

_____

_____

_____

_____

_____

_____

_____

This letter is actually for you! Write it on the back of your personal card.

The Gratitude Journal Applied to Self-Esteem

We're going to write in *your gratitude journal.*

Every day, in addition to the three things you can be grateful for, write down three things you can be proud of on that day—for example, arriving at an appointment on time, receiving a compliment, or completing a task you had to do.

Describe the source of this pride in a few words: why do each of these three things make you feel proud? Which of your talents, qualities, or skills do they reveal?

At the end of the week, take the time to reread your journal entries, preferably out loud, and pay attention to how you feel.

You can write down some of these sources of pride on your personal card.

FRONT

BACK

CANDACE

- *Core values:* being reliable, loving, helping, attentive, creative and helpful
- *Personal strengths:* honesty, integrity, generosity, kindness, love of learning, ability to love and be loved, creativity
- *Areas of expertise:* care, close relationships, painting, dance
- *Accomplishments:* nursing school entrance exam at age 18; stable relationships with Logan, Mia, and Melanie; painting exhibition last year
- *Caring people in your life:* Chris, Mom, Mia, Melanie, Logan

Letter of Kindness

You're a great person and someone who people can always count on. You invest yourself in each of your relationships with a lot of heart and sincerity. You're ready to push yourself beyond your limits to right an injustice or to defend a cause that seems important and just to you. Your loved ones enjoy your spontaneity and optimism, and they're always there to spend time with you, whether in a group or one-on-one. You nurture relationships, both in your work and in your private life. So, it's true that sometimes you're not up to date on current events or even sometimes on subjects of public opinion, but in the end it's your right not to be interested in that, and in no case does that mean that you don't contribute anything important to the world around you. It's just that the path you're taking to move toward that doesn't involve the media; you prefer to take care of the relationships that cross your path. And along with that, you always take care of your environment, and you remain very true to and consistent with your values. So, continue like this—you're a wonderful person who's very appreciated for what you give and who you are. Simply, you're really great!

A MESSAGE FROM DÉBORAH AND VÉRONIQUE

The more you acknowledge and embody who you really are, the less you'll be afraid of rejection.

Many people wear a mask, pretending to be someone they're not and hoping it will make them more lovable. What happens in this case? If they're loved, it's for being someone they're not, and if they're not loved, again, it's for being someone they're not. Therefore, by playing the role of a person they're not, they're appreciated or rejected for this role (and not for being themselves). But I prefer to be loved for who I am, and not loved for who I am not.

Be yourself!

This helps to attract the people who are like you and to move away from the people who aren't. It's also about accepting and having kindness for your strengths and weaknesses, for your darkness and your lightness.

All human beings are imperfect and fallible.

In situations when you tend to blame yourself for certain aspects of yourself, think about the most important person in your life, for whom you feel the most kindness, and ask yourself the following questions:

– What would I think of them if I saw the same faults in them that I see in myself?
– Would I keep loving them if they had the same flaws as me?

Probably yes.

Then ask yourself: "Am I the only human being who has to be perfect and infallible?"

Behave like a caring friend or parent toward yourself.

CHAPTER 19

INTERPERSONAL EFFECTIVENESS SKILLS

BEING EFFECTIVE IN AN INTERACTION: WHAT DOES THAT MEAN?

It's about learning to assert your desires, goals, needs, and opinions in a way that leads others to take them seriously. This will allow you to respect yourself, be in harmony with yourself, and stand up for your rights while taking into account those of others.

Therefore, it's being willing to say no when you're thinking no, to make clear demands, to set boundaries, to defend yourself, to express your point of view, and so on. But what affects communication? Filters, on both sides . . .

> "Between what I think, what I want to say, what I believe I say, what I say, what you want to hear, what you hear, what you think you understand, what you want to understand and what you understand . . . there are at least ten ways we're not communicating. But let's try anyway."
>
> —BERNARD WERBER

DETERMINING YOUR GOALS AND PRIORITIES IN INTERPERSONAL SITUATIONS

The way in which behavior proves effective or ineffective in a situation depends on the person's priorities in that particular situation.[1]

Three types of priorities (goal, relationship, and self-respect) are an integral part of an interaction and must be taken into consideration in all problematic, contentious interpersonal situations. They determine how the other person should be approached.

Goal

   — What I would like from this interaction.

Pursue a goal with the aim of getting what you want in the interaction and of having your wishes taken into consideration. Among these include:

- Defending your rights
- Allowing yourself to ask for help and having your requests heard
- Knowing how to refuse unwanted requests
- Resolving contentious situations
- Making your opinion heard

Relationship

   — How I would like the relationship to be after this interaction.

   — How will the other person feel?

   — What should I do to build (or maintain) this relationship?

A relationship is effective when it at least maintains its quality and, if possible, is improved while also trying to achieve the goal of the interaction. Therefore, it's a question of:

- Making the other person want to respond favorably to you, and if that doesn't happen, then making them feel free not to agree to your request.
- Remaining aware of what is important to you about this relationship in the long run beyond achieving your immediate goal for the interaction.

Self-Respect

   — How I would like to feel about myself once this interaction is over.

   — What should I do to feel this way? What will work?

Self-respect is effective when it maintains, or even improves, the image and respect you have for yourself. This involves acting in such a way as to:

- be consistent with your values
- feel competent

We suggest that you explore, guided by the questions that follow, what your goals and priorities are in social interactions with high stakes.

- What was the pivotal moment of my problem: who did what to whom?

- What did this lead to? What aspect of the situation is problematic for me?

- My *wishes and desires* in this situation. We suggest that you refer to the three types of priorities to answer this:

  - *Goal:* What specific result would I like to achieve? What change would I like this person to make?
  - *Relationship:* How would I like the other person to feel about me after the interaction?
  - *Self-Respect:* How would I like to feel after the interaction?

Then, rank these three items in their order of priority to you in a given situation, from 1 (the most important) to 3 (the least important). We'll see later on how our priorities play a role in the attitude we need to adopt in an interaction.

PRACTICAL APPLICATION: THREE EXAMPLES

First Example

Your upstairs neighbor wakes you up every morning by dragging furniture across the room.

- How would you define the goal, relationship, and self-respect priorities?

➤ ME _____

- What do you think the order of priority should be in this situation?

➤ ME _____

Here's how we would define each of the three items and the order of priority we would give them.

- *Goal:* not to be awakened by the noise of the furniture

- *Relationship:* maintain a good relationship with my neighbor

- *Self-Respect:* not to lose control during the interaction, protect my sleeping hours

- My order of priorities (Déborah and Véronique would prioritize the goal):

_____

- What conflicts between the priorities hinder success in this situation?

_____

Second Example

Your best friend asks you to pick up her kids from school this afternoon. You've already done this three times this week.

- How would you define the goal, relationship, and self-respect priorities?

➤ ME _____

- What do you think the order of priority should be in this situation?

➤ ME _____

Here's how we would define each of the three items and the order of priority we would give them.

- *Goal:* not to pick up the kids from school
- *Relationship:* maintain a good relationship with my friend
- *Self-Respect:* not to be taken advantage of, to have time for myself

- My order of priorities (Déborah and Véronique would prioritize the relationship):

_____

- What conflicts between the priorities hinder success in this situation?

_____

Third Example

Your mother-in-law regularly stops by your house unannounced.

- How would you define the goal, relationship, and self-respect priorities?

➤ ME _____

- What do you think the order of priority should be in this situation?

➤ ME _____

Here's how we would define each of the three items and the order of priority we would give them.

– *Goal:* that my mother-in-law lets me know before coming over

– *Relationship:* maintain a good relationship with my mother-in-law

– *Self-Respect:* that my privacy and rights are respected

- My order of priorities (Déborah and Véronique would prioritize self-respect):

  _____

- What conflicts between the priorities hinder success in this situation?

  _____

CHAPTER 20

ACTING EFFECTIVELY IN DIFFICULT INTERPERSONAL SITUATIONS

In this chapter, we'll see *three types of interpersonal situations*:

1. Situations in which achieving your goal will be the priority
2. Situations in which the relationship will be the priority
3. Situations in which self-respect will be the priority

Depending on what the priority is (goal, relationship, or self-respect), we'll choose different types of communication tools. However, whatever the final priority order, we'll always use the same process: the matrix.

Start by reading the examples below, then it'll be your turn.

PROBLEMATIC INTERPERSONAL SITUATION: CANDACE'S FIRST EXAMPLE

Candace made the arrangements for a group birthday gift for one of her friends (Paul). She paid for the gift with the understanding that everyone would pay her back. One person (Anthony, also a friend) committed to be part of the group gift but still hasn't paid his share (it's been two weeks since the birthday party).

▷ CANDACE *Here's the problematic situation: Anthony didn't pay me back for Paul's gift. The birthday party was two weeks ago.*

Candace fills in her matrix

Candace answers the following questions and then transfers her answers into her matrix (p. 206) as indicated by the number corresponding to each question number.

1. Describe what this situation brings up for you. What thoughts? What emotions?

2. When you're in touch with these thoughts and emotions, it's unpleasant. Where do you feel this in your body? How would you describe this sensation? *(It's important to describe it precisely so that when we experience this unpleasant sensation, we can recognize that we're reacting physically to these particular thoughts and emotions.)* Get in touch with these feelings for a few moments.

3. When you're in touch with these feelings, what does it make you want to do? If you completely latch onto what is written down in the lower left part of the matrix, what does it push you to do in the moment? *(These may be things you do or don't do [but that you strongly feel like doing in the moment].)*

4. This is a difficult situation because it interferes with something that is important to you. It may be hindering what you want to achieve, putting you in a difficult position in a relationship, or damaging your self-respect.

    Goal: Describe what you want to achieve in this situation. What is really important to you in achieving this goal?

    Relationship: Describe what you want the relationship to be like after you have overcome this situation. What is really important to you in this relationship? Why is this person important to you?

    Self-Respect: Describe how you want to feel after you have overcome this situation.

5. If anything were possible, if there weren't all the stuff that's written in the lower left part of your matrix, what would be the order of the "goal/relationship/self-respect" priorities in this situation? *(Sometimes it's difficult to choose an order. If this is the case, be aware that the order you choose is not set in stone and that your decision will still respect all three aspects [while still prioritizing one a little bit more than the other two].)*

6. Can you identify a behavior—an action or something that you're going to do—to move toward what you just identified as the priority in this situation? *(This behavior should be a little different from what you usually do and should still take care of you.)*

7. If the step is too big or too difficult to do as it is, what can you do to make it easier? What other life areas can you develop that take care of you and that in the bigger picture enable you to take the step that's important to you later on?

8. In the hours and days to come, what might we see you do specifically to move in this direction?

Candace rereads the right-hand side of her matrix

9. What does that make you feel in your body? Where? How would you describe it? Does this make more sense than what is written on the left-hand side of the matrix?

If YES, would you agree to leaving a little room for inner obstacles (written in the lower left part of the matrix) should they arise for you, quit fighting them, and take the small step that you've identified in the upper right of your matrix, because it allows you to move forward toward a life that has meaning for you?

So, for the hours and days ahead, watch what happens. If you aren't able to take the small step, don't worry. The simple act of having written it down in the matrix is already a way you're moving forward in that direction.

And if you did take the small step, great! In that case, observe the difference in your feelings. Could it be related to pushing yourself beyond your limits, pride, and consistency with your values?

Skills to Implement When the Goal Is the Priority

One helpful technique to try is to follow the steps of the DEAR MAN mnemonic, devised by psychologist Marsha Linehan.[1] Using these steps has been found to be effective in helping you communicate your needs in a productive way.

Describe (the situation)

Describe the situation as objectively as possible. Base it on the facts without interpreting them. For example: "I paid for Paul's gift for everyone two weeks ago, and you didn't pay me back."

Express (your feelings or opinions about this situation clearly)

Describe your thoughts, feelings, and emotions related to the situation as honestly as possible. Describe your mo-

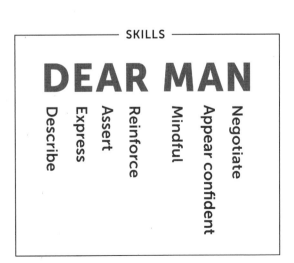

3. Go yell at Anthony and tell him that he's worthless and not trustworthy at all.
- Delete Anthony's number from my phone.
- Call other people who were at the party to tell them about it and ask their opinion.

6. Call Anthony and ask him pleasantly when we can meet so he can pay me back for his share of Paul's gift.

7. To be sure that the relationship isn't negatively affected, suggest to Anthony that we take advantage of meeting up to have a drink together.

8. Call Anthony and ask him pleasantly to meet for a drink in town and suggest that at the same time he can pay me back for Paul's gift.

SENSE-DRIVEN EXPERIENCE

Actions Controlled by Hooks

Actions that Move Me toward Who or What Is Important

AWAY ← → **TOWARD**

Inner Obstacles/Hooks

Who or What Is Important to Me

1. Thoughts: He's not going to pay me back. He's going to let it slide. I've been had again. People are worthless.

Emotion: anger

Thoughts: I can't ask him, it's up to him to give it to me voluntarily. It's awkward. He may be annoyed with me.

Emotion: fear

2. Lump and tension in my throat, flushed face, tension in my neck muscles

MENTAL EXPERIENCE

INNER EXPERIENCE

4. Goal: get paid back by Anthony: it's fair, he committed to be part of the group gift, I counted on everyone contributing to the price of the gift, "short reckonings make long friends," I don't want to let it slide but secretly hold it against him

Relationship: maintain a trusting friendship with Anthony, embody trustworthiness in the relationship

Self-Respect: asserting myself, defending myself, embodying trustworthiness, making a request without changing the image I have of myself

5. 1st: goal; 2nd: relationship; 3rd: self-respect

9. Lightness in my chest

AS YOU KNOW, THE GOAL IS THE PRIORITY IN THIS CASE!

tivations or what is important to you. For example: "I feel embarrassed to ask you, but haven't you forgotten to pay me back?"

Assert (your desires)

Clearly assert what you want or do not want. Don't assume that the other person will guess what it is. For example: "Can you send a transfer or write me a check for $20 today?"

Reinforce

Thank the person in advance for their effort in granting your request. Don't hesitate to motivate them by explaining all the potential benefits for you. For example: "It would be really great if I could wrap this up today, it would clear my mind."

(stay) Mindful

Never lose sight of your goal. Two techniques can be used to do this.

"The broken record" Ask constantly, again and again, without changing the content of your words. Stay determined. Repetition will be your strength. For example: "I would really like you to pay me back today."

Ignoring Don't respond to possible criticism, and don't be fooled if they change the subject. Ignore these attempts to gain control or distract you, and stay focused on your topic as calmly as possible. For example: "I understand that you forgot to pay me back because you had some things to sort out, and I would really like to find a time to talk calmly about that later, but right now I would prefer if we could finish talking about the subject of the birthday gift."

Appear confident

Speak in a confident voice, make direct eye contact, and pay attention to your posture so that it conveys a sense of strength and stability.

Negotiate

While maintaining your position, stay open to alternative solutions. Keep in mind that the other person is more likely to respond favorably if they have something to gain in return. For example: "If it's really difficult for you to go get the money now, you can also bring it to me in a bit and then while we're at it, we can try out this nice new bar that I mentioned to you last time."

Turn the tables Ask the other person to suggest other options since they didn't say yes to yours. For example: "What solution do you propose? How can we find an arrangement that satisfies us both?"

PROBLEMATIC INTERPERSONAL SITUATION: CANDACE'S SECOND EXAMPLE

Candace has an old friend, Mia, who calls her every day for about two hours to tell her about the problems she has with her partner and the pain and suffering that this causes her. Candace feels particularly vulnerable at the moment and would like the calls with Mia to be less frequent.

▷ CANDACE *Here's the problematic situation: Mia calls me every day to talk about the difficult relationship she has with her boyfriend and all the pain and suffering she experiences because of it. We stay on the phone for an average of two hours a day.*

Skills to Implement When the Relationship Is the Priority

Marsha Linehan developed another mnemonic, GIVE, that outlines skills for building and maintaining interpersonal relationships.[2] Using these skills has been found to be effective in helping you navigate difficult situations and conversations with other people.

(be) Gentle

Remain courteous, calm, and respectful regardless of the other person's reaction. Therefore, as much as possible, avoid criticism, threats, and judgments. For example: "Mia, I understand and I feel that you particularly need me right now, and it's also very important for me to support you in this difficult situation. Which, by the way, is how I see our friendship. It's great that we can be there for each other in good times and also when things are more difficult. On the other hand, sometimes I feel a little fragile, and I'd like to be able to tell you when I don't feel capable of supporting you effectively, because sometimes your pain and suffering brings up too many difficult things for me. What do you think? Honestly, my priority is to be able to help you, and I'd even like for this ordeal that you're going through to be an opportunity to improve the quality of our relationship even more, but sometimes it's hard for me, and I'd like to be able to tell you that."

(act) Interested

Be sincerely interested in the other person. What are their motivations, their feelings? How is this situation important to them? Give them time to speak without interrupting. For example: "Tell me exactly how you feel when he says that to you. What does it bring up for you? What are your thoughts and feelings? Do you feel respected, or would there be a way to take better care of yourself, given the current reality of the situation? How? What would be really important to you in that?"

Candace answers the same questions as before (pp. 203–5) and then transfers her answers into her matrix as indicated by the number corresponding to each question.

3.
- Stop answering her calls
- Tell her everything I think about her lousy relationship with her boyfriend and her inability to leave him
- End the relationship

6. Tell Mia that I don't want to only talk about problems she's having when we call each other.

7. Ask Mia about her passion and future plans for painting when I get her on the phone; recommend that Mia see a therapist to help her better deal with her relationship problems.

8. The next time I'm talking with Mia on the phone, listen to her talk about her relationship with her boyfriend for 15 minutes, then tell her that it's a situation that makes me really sad and that we have to help one another get better. I'll recommend a therapist for her.

SENSE-DRIVEN EXPERIENCE

Actions Controlled by Hooks

Actions that Move Me toward Who or What Is Important

AWAY ← → **TOWARD**

Inner Obstacles/Hooks

Who or What Is Important to Me

1. Thoughts: She brings me down. I waste two hours on the phone every day. It makes me feel bad.

Emotion: sadness

Thoughts: She takes advantage of me. I'm not a therapist.

Emotion: anger

Thoughts: She's often been there for me in the past; I'm a lousy friend to think that she's bothering me.

Emotion: guilt

2. Lump and tension in my throat, flushed face, tension in my neck muscles, tears in my eyes, trembling lips

MENTAL EXPERIENCE

INNER EXPERIENCE

4. Goal: limit the amount of time spent on the phone with Mia talking about negative things

Relationship: maintain my friendship with Mia, be present and supportive

Self-Respect: protect myself psychologically

5. 1st: relationship; 2nd: self-respect; 3rd: goal

9. Easing sensation, back muscles relaxing

AS YOU KNOW, THE RELATIONSHIP IS THE PRIORITY IN THIS CASE!

Validate

Acknowledge, then validate without judgment the other person's emotions or feelings. For example: "You know, it's understandable to feel that way. Other people experiencing similar situations are also deeply affected when that happens to them. This touches on something very important for you, and there's no question that there's something to grieve, at least in terms of this relationship that you thought was perfect. There's also a lot of anger in what I'm hearing, because you feel strongly that you're being treated unfairly, and frankly that's understandable. At the same time, I feel conflicted because sometimes you really want to cut him out of your life but at other times that seems impossible to you, too painful to imagine a life without him. So, know that I'm here and that I'm not judging you, even in moments when it seems that you're moving less in the direction that you set for yourself."

SKILLS

GIVE

Gentle
Interested
Validate
Easy Manner

(use an) Easy manner

Be enthusiastic and cheerful; use humor. Remain soothing and caring. For example: "And in moments when you feel a little stronger, when it gets a little easier to move forward, you can also count on me! And if you'd like, we'll go see him together to tell him what you have on your mind. Aside from that, could we join the gym together? It's been a long time since we talked about going. Wouldn't this be a good opportunity?"

PROBLEMATIC INTERPERSONAL SITUATION: CANDACE'S THIRD EXAMPLE

Candace is a conscientious person who's very invested in her work. Since she's efficient in what she does (throwing herself 100% into each task assigned to her), her boss tends to ask her to do even more. However, Candace is currently overwhelmed by everything she has to do. There's too much. And now the head nurse is giving her another task.

▷ CANDACE *Here's the problematic situation: I'm feeling overwhelmed at work right now. My manager just asked me to add an extra patient to my schedule.*

Skills to Implement When
Self-Respect Is the Priority

The third mnemonic developed by Marsha Linehan is known as FAST.[3] These skills have been found to be effective in helping you navigate interpersonal relationships—but not at the expense of your self-respect.

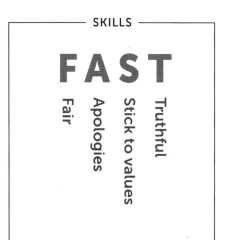

(be) Fair

Choose to remain honest in any situation. For example: "I'll honestly tell you that in this case I'd prefer to say no. I won't be able to see an additional patient because I'm already overwhelmed most of the time, even when I'm not given any extra patients."

(no) Apologies

Only apologize if it's justified, but avoid making multiple or repeated excuses, which reduce your self-esteem and do a disservice to the relationship in the long run. For example: "I don't want to give you excuses to justify saying no. It's just that I want to do my job well, and in order to do that, I need time, and that's a reality I cannot change."

Stick to values

For example: "If I agreed to fit in one more patient, that would mean that I wouldn't have time to build a relationship with that patient, which is one of my most important values. I chose this profession in the first place to be able to embody this value. Working otherwise wouldn't make sense for me, and I wouldn't be respecting myself."

(be) Truthful

Don't make false excuses or offer false explanations. As much as possible remain honest and truthful in the relationship. For example: "I prefer telling you what I really think about things because this is what respects me best, and I sincerely hope that you'll understand my reasons."

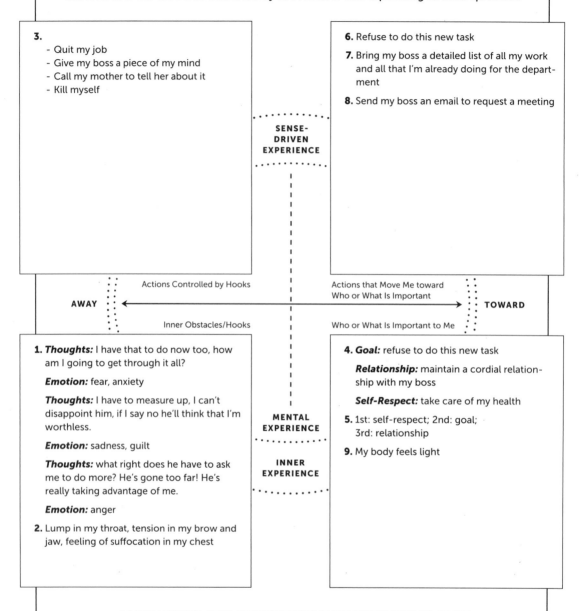

CANDACE'S MATRIX

Candace answers the same questions as before (pp. 203–205) and then transfers her answers into her matrix as indicated by the number corresponding to each question.

3.
- Quit my job
- Give my boss a piece of my mind
- Call my mother to tell her about it
- Kill myself

6. Refuse to do this new task

7. Bring my boss a detailed list of all my work and all that I'm already doing for the department

8. Send my boss an email to request a meeting

SENSE-DRIVEN EXPERIENCE

Actions Controlled by Hooks

Actions that Move Me toward Who or What Is Important

AWAY ←————————————————————→ **TOWARD**

Inner Obstacles/Hooks

Who or What Is Important to Me

MENTAL EXPERIENCE

INNER EXPERIENCE

1. *Thoughts:* I have that to do now too, how am I going to get through it all?

Emotion: fear, anxiety

Thoughts: I have to measure up, I can't disappoint him, if I say no he'll think that I'm worthless.

Emotion: sadness, guilt

Thoughts: what right does he have to ask me to do more? He's gone too far! He's really taking advantage of me.

Emotion: anger

2. Lump in my throat, tension in my brow and jaw, feeling of suffocation in my chest

4. *Goal:* refuse to do this new task

Relationship: maintain a cordial relationship with my boss

Self-Respect: take care of my health

5. 1st: self-respect; 2nd: goal; 3rd: relationship

9. My body feels light

AS YOU KNOW, SELF-RESPECT IS THE PRIORITY IN THIS CASE!

PRACTICAL APPLICATION: LET'S TAKE CARE OF ONE OF YOUR CURRENT DIFFICULT INTERPERSONAL SITUATIONS _____

Describe the interpersonal situation that is currently problematic for you:

➤ ME _____

1. Describe what this situation brings up for you. What thoughts? What emotions?

➤ ME _____

2. When you're in touch with these thoughts and emotions, it's unpleasant. Where do you feel this in your body? How would you describe this sensation? *(It's important to describe it precisely so that when we experience this unpleasant sensation, we can recognize that we're reacting physically to these particular thoughts and emotions.)* Get in touch with these feelings for a few moments.

➤ ME _____

3. When you're in touch with these feelings, what does it make you want to do? If you completely latch onto what is written down in the lower left part of the matrix, what does it push you to do in the moment? *(These may be things you do or don't do [but that you strongly feel like doing in the moment].)*

➤ ME _____

4. This is a difficult situation because it interferes with something that is important to you. It may be hindering what you want to achieve, putting you in a difficult position in a relationship, or damaging your self-respect.

➤ ME _____

Goal: Describe what you want to achieve in this situation. What is really important to you in achieving this goal?

_____

Relationship: Describe what you want the relationship to be like after you have overcome this situation. What is really important to you in this relationship? Why is this person important to you?

_____

Self-Respect: Describe how you want to feel after you have overcome this situation.

_____

5. If anything were possible, if there weren't all the stuff that's written in the lower left part of your matrix, what would be the order of the "goal/relationship/self-respect" priorities in this situation? *(Sometimes it's difficult to choose an order. If this is the case, be aware that the order you choose is not set in stone and that your decision will still respect all three aspects [while still prioritizing one a little bit more than the other two].)*

➤ ME _____

6. Can you identify a behavior—an action or something that you're going to do—to move toward what you just identified as the priority in this situation? *(This behavior should be a little different from what you usually do and should still take care of you.)*

➤ ME _____

7. If the step is too big or too difficult to do as it is, what can you do to make it easier? What other life areas can you develop that take care of you and that in the bigger picture enable you to take the step that's important to you later on?

➤ ME _____

8. In the hours and days to come, what might we see you do specifically to move in this direction?

➤ ME _____

Reread the right-hand side of your matrix.

9. What does that make you feel in your body? Where? How would you describe it?

➤ ME _____

Does this make more sense than what is written on the left-hand side of the matrix?

If YES, would you agree to leaving a little room for inner obstacles (written in the lower left part of the matrix) should they arise for you, quit fighting them, and take the small step that you've identified in the upper right of your matrix, because it allows you to move forward toward a life that has meaning for you?

So, for the hours and days ahead, watch what happens. If you aren't able to take the small step, don't worry. The simple act of having written it down in the matrix is already a way you're moving forward in that direction.

And if you did take the small step, great! In that case, observe the difference in your feelings. Could it be related to pushing yourself beyond your limits, pride, and consistency with your values?

MY MATRIX

Fill in the matrix below with the answer that corresponds to each question number.

3. _____

_____

_____

6. _____

7. _____

8. _____

. . . .
**SENSE-
DRIVEN
EXPERIENCE**
. . . .

Actions Controlled by Hooks

Actions that Move Me toward
Who or What Is Important

AWAY ←————————————————→ **TOWARD**

Inner Obstacles/Hooks

Who or What Is Important to Me

1. *Thoughts:* _____

Emotions: _____

**MENTAL
EXPERIENCE**
. . . .

**INNER
EXPERIENCE**

2. _____

4. *Goal:* _____

Relationship: _____

Self-Respect: _____

5. _____

9. _____

CHAPTER 21

CREATING A POSITIVE INTERPERSONAL ENVIRONMENT AROUND YOU

THE IMPORTANCE OF OUR ENVIRONMENT

> "We are the average of the five people we spend the most time with."
>
> —JIM ROHN

What does Jim Rohn's quote mean? Our environment is made up of the people around us, our loved ones, and all the people we spend time with on a regular basis.

If I spend time with enthusiastic people, I'll become enthusiastic myself. If I spend time with people who share what's on the right side of my matrix with me, I'll develop those areas and values.

— INTERPERSONAL ENVIRONMENT —

WHO WE SHOULD MOVE TOWARD

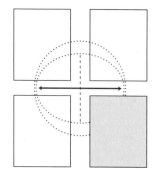

The people who share the same values and important life areas, which are the ones written in the lower right part of your matrix.

WHO WE TEND TO MOVE TOWARD

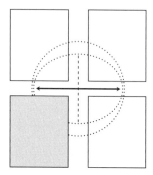

Often it's the people who share the same suffering, which are the things we wrote down in the lower left part of the matrix.

WITH WHOM SHOULD WE SURROUND OURSELVES?

With people who can inspire us. These could be people who have achieved the results we also want. Sometimes these people have experienced the same problems and doubts as us, and they successfully overcame them. They allow us to embrace the belief that *it's possible.*

If we want to grow in an area, we have to spend time with the people who are successful in this area. Not just people who are at the same stage as us, but people who are moving forward and who share the same values and prize the same areas of life.

Do you like creating things? Then surround yourself with creative people. Is sharing important to you? Then surround yourself with people for whom this value is important.

Three circles of people can be identified in your environment:

— the people in your immediate circle: friends, family, colleagues
— the people who are more distant but with whom you spend time: friends of friends, acquaintances, classmates, neighbors
— the special case of people with whom you can't spend time in person but who can inspire you: via the Internet, film, biographies

Be careful! We often tend to spend time with the people who share our pain and suffering ("She understands what I'm going through," "By helping her, I'll be helping myself at the same time").

This strategy is destined to fail. It leads to dwelling on and making our hooks bigger. *Whatever we focus our attention on grows.*

This doesn't mean that we should never talk about what is making us suffer, but rather that *sharing the same hooks should never be the basis of a relationship.*

HOW DO WE FORM HIGH-QUALITY CONNECTIONS?

Imagine . . .
Ellen and Mary meet for the first time.

Ellen: "I just bought myself a new mountain bike. I love this sport. I try to go for a ride every weekend."

Mary: "I hate mountain biking! I fall almost every time I skid on gravel . . . It's far from being enjoyable! I practice the violin on the weekend."

Ellen: "The violin, how awful! Several times a week my downstairs neighbor makes a racket with the squeaky sound of that instrument. It's such torture . . ."

Creating a connection seems to have gotten off to a bad start, right? Why's that? Because we're asking the question: what binds people together? They're called *commonalities*. Does that mean that differences between individuals are a bad thing? Certainly not!

Variety is the spice of life. Imagine a spoonful of curry. Visualize it. Now, imagine yourself delicately putting this spoon in your mouth . . . Unpleasant, right? But in a dish, the curry enhances the flavor.

Similarities make up the *foundation of a relationship* while *differences enhance it*. So then, what strategy should we use to create this high-quality interpersonal foundation?

Listen to what the other person has to tell you by being fully present in this interaction

Does it ever happen that you let the person in front of you do all the talking, and meanwhile you're caught up in your mind thinking about what you can tell them after (that really interests you) or what you'll do after they're done talking? If so, know that this is a common human experience.

During moments like these, do you feel connected to the other person? Do you manage to remember what the other person is telling you? Probably not . . .

Having stray thoughts while the other person is talking to you is not the problem. Remember, we can't control what comes to our minds; it's the human mind's nature. The problem lies in pursuing these thoughts and starting a dialogue with them. In other words, you're not being fully present in that moment. Therefore, the strategy is to be aware, as best you can:

— of what the other person has to say

— of the thoughts that emerge in your mind

And to *make the choice* to bring our attention back to the present moment as soon as it has strayed.

Be sincerely interested in the people you meet

Give the other person time to speak, and be interested in what they're passionate about. Ask questions to bring out what is really meaningful to them in life:

- What are you passionate about?
- What can you spend hours doing without realizing time has passed?
- What makes you . . . (choose to live here, choose this trip, do this job, and so on)?
- What do you like about it the most? What is really important to you in that?

Talking about what is important makes us come to life and creates a very pleasant emotional state. So, when someone is talking about what is important to them and you're in their presence, they associate you with that pleasant emotional state. They feel good when they're with you.

> *One of the things that attracts us to others is the emotional state in which we find ourselves in their presence.*

Find commonalities

As the person in front of you talks about what is important to them, be fully aware of what it reflects in you. To do this, you need to explore, with an open mind, what is underlying each activity or life area that's important to that person. Imagine that you're a curious explorer, trying to fill in the right-hand side of the other person's matrix.

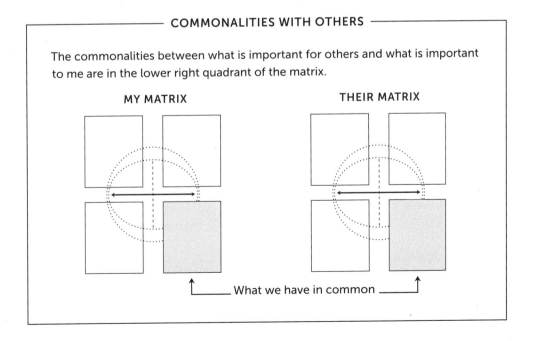

COMMONALITIES WITH OTHERS

The commonalities between what is important for others and what is important to me are in the lower right quadrant of the matrix.

MY MATRIX   THEIR MATRIX

What we have in common

Let's go back to Ellen and Mary.

Ellen: "I just bought myself a new mountain bike. I love this sport. I try to go for a ride every weekend."

In the previous interaction, Mary dwelled on the sport itself, saying categorically that: "That doesn't interest me, I don't like mountain biking." What could Mary have done differently?

Here's an example:

Mary: "Oh, a ride every weekend! That activity seems to be important to you. What do you like most about mountain biking? What is important to you in that?"

Ellen: "I like riding with my family and sharing these moments together. And being close to nature."

Mary: "I love being in nature too! I often go for walks in the forest next to my house, it's so refreshing!"

This time the interaction is very different. In going beyond the stated activity, Mary was able to bring to light a commonality she shares with Ellen. A connection was made!

The next step could be to suggest doing an activity together, embodying what is important that they have in common (in this case, contact with nature).

Do not stop at outer appearances; explore what's underneath. You may discover the gift of connecting with others.

PRACTICAL APPLICATION:
APPLY THE STRATEGIES FOR MAKING A CONNECTION _____

Answer the following questions, then fill in the matrix on p. 222 where specified by each question number.

1. Choose a social activity that's important to you (you can refer to the life areas in your initial matrix). This is an activity that involves a connection with other people.

➤ ME _____

2. What are the inner obstacles that tend to arise for you, make you suffer, and prevent you from doing this social activity in the way you would like to?

➤ ME _____

3. When you're in touch with these thoughts and emotions, it's unpleasant. Where do you feel this in your body? How would you describe this sensation? *(It's important to describe it precisely so that when we experience this unpleasant sensation, we can recognize that we're reacting physically to these particular thoughts and emotions.)*

➤ ME _____

Get in touch with these feelings for a few moments.

4. When you're in touch with these feelings, what does it make you want to do? If you completely latch onto what is written down in the lower left part of the matrix, what does it push you to do in the moment? *(These may be things you do or don't do [but that you strongly feel like doing in the moment].)*

What can we or could we see you do when these obstacles arise for you? *(These are things that you do more to move away from what you don't want to think or feel, or under the control of what you don't want to think or feel, rather than to move toward what is important to you.)*

➤ ME _____

5. What can we or could we see you do to practice or implement this social activity in the way you would like to do it? What would the person you'd like to be do?

➤ ME _____

6. What is really important to you in that? *(Deep things that are important to you underlie it. That's why it's painful.)*

Why is this area important to you? What deep meaning does this area of life have for you? If anything were possible, if there weren't all the stuff that's written in the lower left part of your matrix, what kind of person would you want to be in this area? How would you like to behave, and how would that take care of you?

➤ ME _____

7. If the step is too big or too difficult to do as it is, what can you do to make it easier? What other life areas can you develop that take care of you and that in the bigger picture enable you to take the step that's important to you later on?

➤ ME _____

8. In the hours and days ahead, what might we see you do specifically to move in this direction?

➤ ME _____

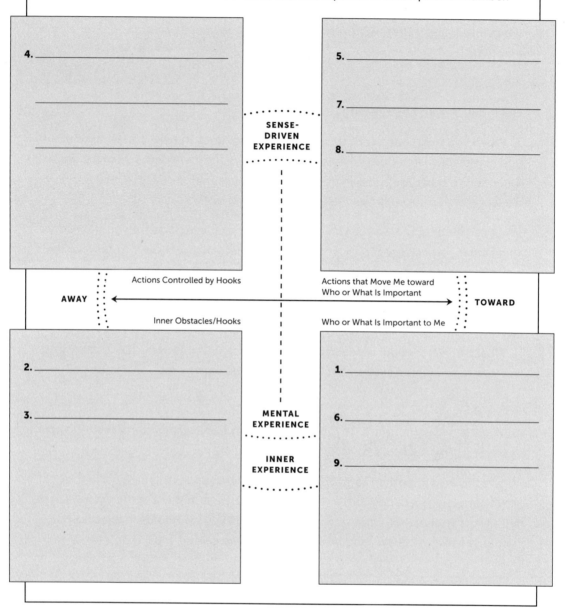

MY MATRIX

Fill in the matrix below with the answer that corresponds to each question number.

4. _____

_____

_____

5. _____

7. _____

8. _____

SENSE-DRIVEN EXPERIENCE

Actions Controlled by Hooks

AWAY ←——————————————————→ **TOWARD**

Actions that Move Me toward Who or What Is Important

Inner Obstacles/Hooks

Who or What Is Important to Me

2. _____

3. _____

1. _____

6. _____

MENTAL EXPERIENCE

INNER EXPERIENCE

9. _____

Reread the right-hand side of your matrix.

9. What does that make you feel in your body? Where? How would you describe it?

➤ ME _____

Does this make more sense than what is written on the left-hand side of the matrix?

If YES, would you agree to leaving a little room for inner obstacles (written in the lower left part of the matrix) should they arise for you, quit fighting them, and take the small step that you've identified in the upper right of your matrix, because it allows you to move forward toward a life that has meaning for you?

So, for the hours and days ahead, watch what happens. If you aren't able to take the small step, don't worry. The simple act of having written it down in the matrix is already a way you're moving forward in that direction.

And if you did take the small step, great! In that case, observe the difference in your feelings. Could it be related to pushing yourself beyond your limits, pride, and consistency with your values?

DEVELOPING HIGH-QUALITY RELATIONSHIPS

HOW TO DEVELOP A HIGH-QUALITY RELATIONSHIP BETWEEN TWO PEOPLE

Sharing What Is Important

Like in any relationship, bonding over *the important things that you have in common* strengthens the connection. But when you get used to spending time with the same person, you're at risk of losing interest in sharing stimulating things in favor of sharing worries of everyday life. This is an ordinary human process. It's normal to tend to experience this. Just notice, with kindness, when this happens in your relationship. Observing is the first step in the process of change.

And then what's next? How do we change it?

Be sincerely interested in your partner as if you had just met them or as if you had just met them again after being gone for years. Be sincerely interested in your relationship. It's a shared endeavor, and the two of you are the co-creators.

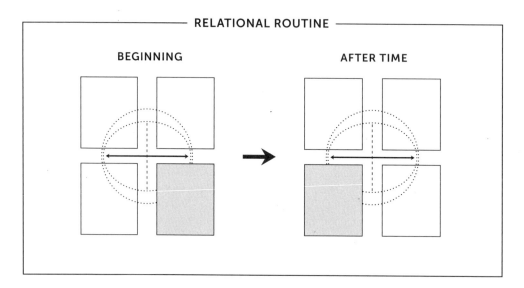

RELATIONAL ROUTINE

BEGINNING   AFTER TIME

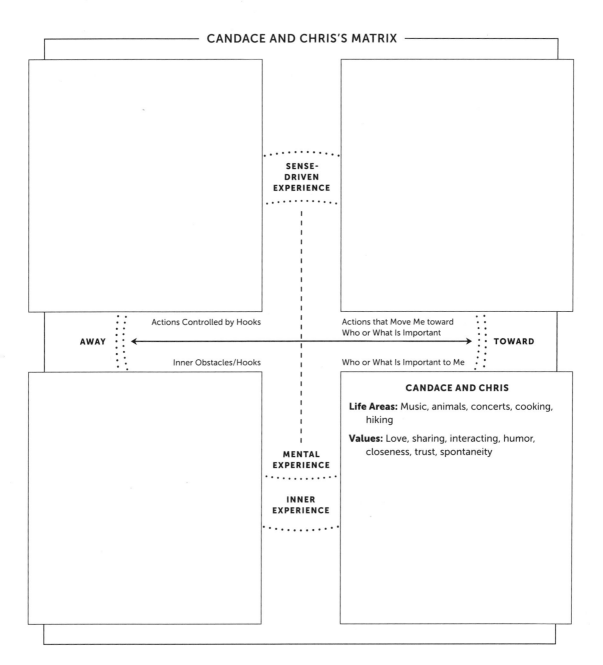

SENSE-
DRIVEN
EXPERIENCE

Actions Controlled by Hooks

AWAY ←——————————————————→ **TOWARD**

Actions that Move Me toward
Who or What Is Important

Inner Obstacles/Hooks

Who or What Is Important to Me

CANDACE AND CHRIS

Life Areas: Music, animals, concerts, cooking,
hiking

Values: Love, sharing, interacting, humor,
closeness, trust, spontaneity

MENTAL
EXPERIENCE

INNER
EXPERIENCE

What life areas and values do you share? What is *really* important to you in this relationship?

At all times, the questions that you ask will define what you bring to light in the relationship. Here are some to ask each other after sharing any amount of time together:

- What are the three things you liked best in the time we spent together?

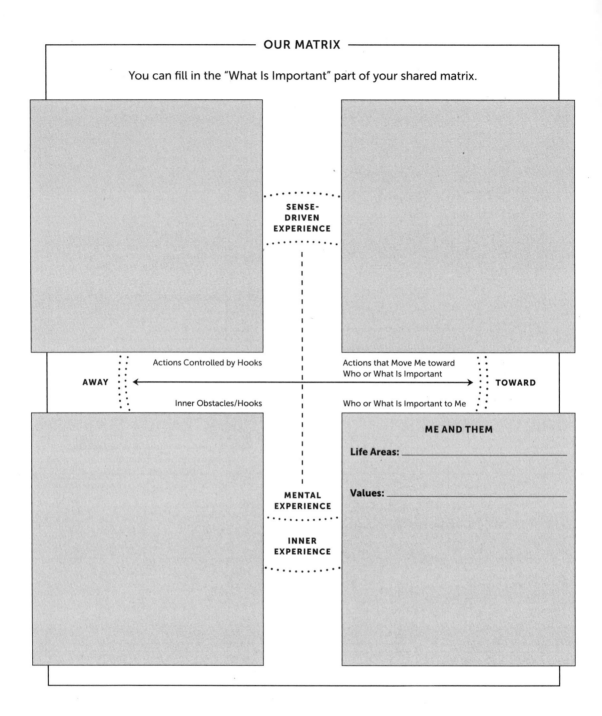

OUR MATRIX

You can fill in the "What Is Important" part of your shared matrix.

SENSE-DRIVEN EXPERIENCE

Actions Controlled by Hooks

AWAY ← → **TOWARD**

Actions that Move Me toward Who or What Is Important

Inner Obstacles/Hooks

Who or What Is Important to Me

ME AND THEM

Life Areas: _____

Values: _____

MENTAL EXPERIENCE

INNER EXPERIENCE

- Why these three things? What was important to you in that?
- What would you like us to do next time that would enable us to go in that direction?

Dialectics

People with borderline personality disorder think in black or white, all or nothing. They think in hyper-absolute terms. This way of perceiving the world can create a major obstacle for the relationship: alternating between *idealization* and *devaluation* of the other person.

> **CANDACE** *Sometimes I tell myself that Chris is the man of my dreams. He's just perfect. But I'm very demanding, and I don't tolerate it when he disappoints me. When that happens, I never see it coming. And then I tell myself that he's not the person I thought he was after all and that our relationship is really pointless. It's a roller coaster.*

All relationships, like all realities, are complex, ever-changing, and transactional.

Complex Relationships

Everybody has strengths and weaknesses, aspects that we like and others that we like less. And these opposing aspects coexist constantly.

In the previous chapters, you created cards for all the people in your life. Each of these cards has two sides:

— front = strong points

— back = limitations

Loving someone is loving them for both their "dark" part and their "light" part, while keeping in mind that the two parts coexist constantly. It's not a question of making gray from the black and the white, but rather *juxtaposing* the black and the white.

When the "dark" part of a person doesn't interfere with our core values and respect for ourselves, then if we choose to develop a relationship

---

IN BLACK *AND* WHITE

What a relationship (or any other element of reality) is not:

■ or □ or ■

What a relationship (or any other element of reality) is:

■ and □

When my partner's behavior *moves away from the relationship that is important to US,* this signals that my partner's behavior is probably being guided by their hooks.

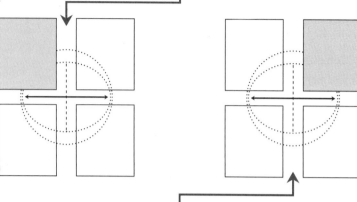

If I act in the direction of what is important in our relationship as a couple, I can hope that my partner will adapt their behavior to be compatible with how I changed.

with that person, we will love them fully. We will love them for who they are, in their entirety.

Ask yourself: in what way is their "dark" part a challenge for me and will make me grow?

Ever-Changing Relationships

The Tibetan Dzogchen lama Sogyal Rinpoche stated, "There is only one law in the universe that never changes—that all things change, and that all things are impermanent."

Transactional Relationships

There are permanent transactions between the constituent elements of reality. Everything is interdependent.

What does this mean in concrete terms? If I change, then the reality around me will change. The elements around me will reorganize to be compatible with how I changed. For example, if I don't know how to say no, a multitude of people will gravitate toward me and make multiple requests of me. From the moment I start saying *no,* the environment around me will change. The people taking advantage of my inability to say no will disappear. The people who love me for who I am will stay. And new people, who correspond to the new version of myself, will enter my life.

In any relationship, I must accept that *I cannot change the other person*. On the other hand, I can influence them to change through my own change (see box on previous page).

Emotional Expression

Imagine . . .

You meet a person who only speaks Chinese. You try to communicate with her by speaking English. She doesn't understand you. What could you do?

1. "I speak English, it's the most widely spoken language in the world! Why can't she understand me?" And then I continue to speak English.

2. "Maybe I should try to find a common language?" Then I change languages.

The second solution, for sure.

So then, why do we act differently when it comes to love languages?[1]

```
──────────── YOUR LOVE LANGUAGES ────────────

What is your primary love language? _____

Do you have another love language? _____

What is your partner's primary love language? _____

Do they have another love language? _____

               Do you have a love language in common?


        YES                               NO

Common love language:        The language I'm willing to develop
                                 to move toward my partner:


_____     _____
```

▷ **CANDACE** Candace expresses her love to Chris by sending him long, affectionate text messages or by giving him long hugs.

Chris expresses his love to Candace through acts of service and thoughtfulness (fixing things in Candace's apartment, taking out the trash, buying her what she likes to eat).

Candace feels dissatisfied, and Chris doesn't understand why ("I do so much for her!").

What's happening?

Chris is speaking his own language, not Candace's. He gives Candace love in his own way, not in Candace's way.

There are different ways to communicate your affection (different love languages):

- acts of service
- words of affirmation
- physical touch (hugging, holding hands, cuddling)
- quality time
- receiving gifts

These are not the same as ways to give love—those aren't the same love languages.

Effective Communication for Preventing Conflicts
How do we communicate our discomfort to other people?

What creates a conflict is not the discomfort we feel, but the way we express it.[2] Do you ever feel uneasy and:

- *blame* the other person for being the cause?
- *attribute* negative intentions toward you to the other person?
- *sulk* and not say a word for hours?

If that's the case, you're far from being the only person to experience this.

Even if this type of behavior can be a relief in the (very) short term, it's never effective in the long run for the relationship or your self-esteem.

Candace's Example

▷ **CANDACE** *I spend the evening with Chris and tell him about an important part of my day. He listens to me while reading and replying to his text messages at the same time.*

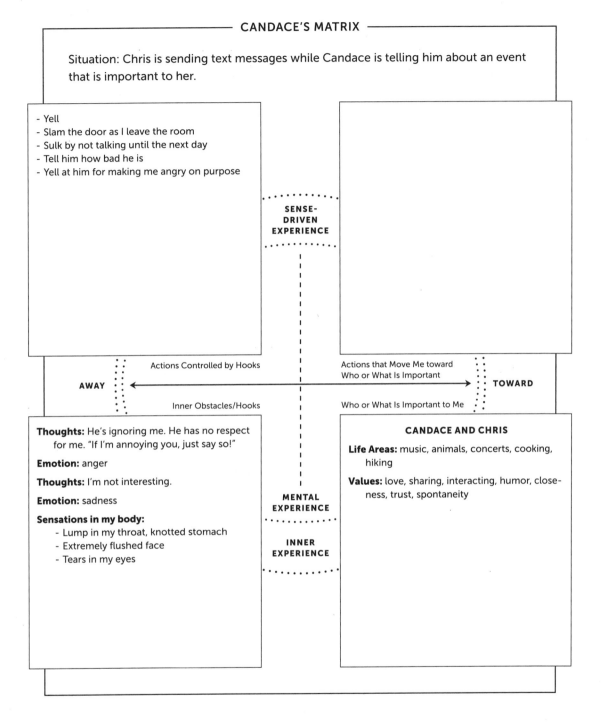

CANDACE'S MATRIX

Situation: Chris is sending text messages while Candace is telling him about an event that is important to her.

- Yell
- Slam the door as I leave the room
- Sulk by not talking until the next day
- Tell him how bad he is
- Yell at him for making me angry on purpose

SENSE-DRIVEN EXPERIENCE

Actions Controlled by Hooks

AWAY ← Actions that Move Me toward Who or What Is Important → TOWARD

Inner Obstacles/Hooks

Who or What Is Important to Me

Thoughts: He's ignoring me. He has no respect for me. "If I'm annoying you, just say so!"

Emotion: anger

Thoughts: I'm not interesting.

Emotion: sadness

Sensations in my body:
- Lump in my throat, knotted stomach
- Extremely flushed face
- Tears in my eyes

MENTAL EXPERIENCE

INNER EXPERIENCE

CANDACE AND CHRIS

Life Areas: music, animals, concerts, cooking, hiking

Values: love, sharing, interacting, humor, closeness, trust, spontaneity

Candace fills in her matrix (above). In this situation, if she communicated above effectively, what could she say?

▷ CANDACE *When you read your text messages while I tell you about my day, I think that what I'm saying to you doesn't interest you and that you're ignoring me. It makes me feel angry and sad. In the heat of the moment, it would even make me yell and leave the room. It hurts me because what is important to me is the interaction and the intimacy between us.*

Put yourself in Chris's shoes. Yes, yes, do it! First, reread the behaviors in the upper left part of Candace's matrix. Have you done that?

Now, reread what Candace just said about how she feels.

- Do you see a difference between these two?

 ME _____

- Which makes you want to take a step toward Candace to fix the relationship?

 ME _____

Which rules of effective communication are highlighted in this example?

1. *Only talk about what's in your own matrix:* your thoughts, your emotions, your needs.
2. *Don't attribute any thoughts or intentions to others.* Only the other person is able to access what's in their own matrix.
3. *Have a positive intention for the relationship:* I express what I feel and what my needs are in a caring way to make the relationship grow.
4. Apply a *technique to express your feelings and needs effectively,* such as the one Candace used, which can be seen in the box below.

HOW TO EXPRESS YOUR FEELINGS AND NEEDS EFFECTIVELY

When . . . = describe the situation objectively: the facts

❶ I have the thought that . . . ; I feel . . .

❷ At first, that would drive me to . . .

❸ It hurts me, because what is important to me is . . .

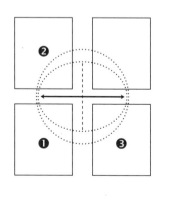

How do we listen effectively to other people's discomfort?

- *Listen sincerely*. Offer a caring and nonjudgmental space for the other person to speak.

- *Validate the other person's emotions*. Recognize that the other person's feelings exist and have a reason to exist. Never judge the other person's emotional experience.[3]

▷ CANDACE

HOW CHRIS SHOULDN'T RESPOND	HOW CHRIS SHOULD RESPOND
You have no reason to be angry! I'm just sending two text messages! The slightest thing makes you angry!	It's hard to feel what you're currently feeling. I'm sorry you're feeling that way.

Notice that it's not about Chris apologizing for his behavior, but simply that he shows empathy for Candace's inner experience.

Be careful never to:

- *Relativize or trivialize the other person's suffering*: "It's useless to feel that!" "It's not that important anyway!" "Get off the couch, you'll feel better." "Be positive!" "Think of all those people who are even unhappier than you, who don't even have anything to eat!"

- *Try to relativize the suffering*: "It will pass." "Tomorrow is another day, it'll be better, you'll see!"

Instead, help the other person find their own answers.

WHAT NOT TO DO	WHAT TO DO

– Give advice when the other person doesn't ask us: "You should . . ."
 	
– Bring the conversation back to yourself: "It reminds me of what I experienced with Sylvia two months ago . . ." or "If I were in your place, I . . ."
 	
– Try to distract the other person: "Come on, let's take our minds off things by . . ." or quickly changing the subject.
	– After having sufficiently acknowledged and validated the other person's suffering:
	
	  - Consider: What does this suffering tell you about what is important to you?
	
	  - Consider: How can you reconnect a little more with what is really important to you?

OVERCOMING A PROBLEM OR A CONTENTIOUS SITUATION (EVEN A LONG-STANDING ONE)

There's nothing better for overcoming a problem than a well-made matrix. And now you're an expert! We're going to guide you in filling out your matrix for two: you and your partner. But first, let us show you the problem Candace and Chris encountered as an example.

▷ **CANDACE** She criticizes Chris for not spending enough time with her and favoring his friends. If it were up to Candace, she'd spend as much time as possible with Chris. When Candace is alone, she misses him terribly, and she has the impression that she's not important enough to Chris.

Chris is a rather independent person. He loves Candace, but he needs to spend time alone or with his friends, without Candace.

This situation gives rise to the couple's frequent arguments. Here is the interpersonal situation that is currently problematic for Candace and Chris (what would a camera filming this situation show us? What would a TV commentator describe?):

▷ **CANDACE** Candace and Chris are in a relationship. Candace regularly asks Chris to spend more time with her and accuses him of not loving her enough. Chris wants to spend time with Candace, but he also wants to spend time alone and with his friends.

Candace and Chris answer the following questions and then transfer their answers into the matrix on p. 236 according to the numbers that correspond to each question:

1. Describe what this situation brings up for you. What thoughts? What emotions?

2. When you're in touch with these thoughts and emotions, it's unpleasant. Where do you feel this in your body? How would you describe this sensation? *(It's important to describe it precisely so that when we experience this unpleasant sensation, we can recognize that we're reacting physically to these particular thoughts and emotions.)*

Get in touch with these feelings for a few moments.

3. When you're in touch with these feelings, what does it make you want to do? If you completely latch onto what is written down in the lower left part of the matrix, what does it push you to do in the moment?

(*These may be things you do or don't do [but that you strongly feel like doing in the moment].)*

4. *Your relationship:* This situation is a difficult one because it concerns an important relationship: yours! It's painful because the relationship is really important to you.

In your relationship, what is really important? If there weren't all the stuff that's written in the lower left part of your matrix, what would your relationship be like? How would you behave toward each other? What would your relationship embody? Write these shared things in the spot indicated ("your relationship").

Other areas: for each of you, does this problematic situation affect another life area that is important to you?

If YES, write down this area and what is important to you in that. If this problematic situation weren't happening, how would you behave?

What would be really important to you?

5. For each of you, can you identify:

(a) A change you would like the other person to make in this situation? A concession you would like the other person to make that would still take care of them and that would take care of what is important to them outside this relationship?

(b) An action to move you toward your relationship? You've identified what is important in these actions in the lower right part of the matrix. An action to move you toward the relationship you really want?

(c) A change you would be willing to make to take care of the problems or hooks the other person identified in the relationship but that will also take care of you and respect your boundaries?

6. If the step is too big or too difficult to do as it is, what can you do to make it easier? What other life areas can you develop that take care of you and that in the bigger picture enable you to take the step that's important to you later on?

7. In the hours and days to come, what might we see you each do specifically to move in this direction?
Candace and Chris reread the right-hand side of their matrix.

8. What does that make you feel in your body? Where? How would you describe it?

Does this make more sense than what is written on the left-hand side of the matrix?

If YES, would you agree to leaving a little room for inner obstacles (written in the lower left part of the matrix) should they arise for you, quit fighting them, and take the small step that you've identified in the

CANDACE AND CHRIS'S MATRIX

3. CANDACE
- Check the texts on Chris's phone
- Call one of his friends to see if he's really with him
- Badger Chris with texts while he's with his friends
- Tell Chris that he's worthless
- Threaten to leave him
- Beg him to stay with me

CHRIS
- Get some distance from Candace

5. CANDACE
a) For Chris to spend at least half the weekend with me, just the two of us
b) Stop checking Chris's phone
c) Let him spend two nights a week with his friends without having to explain himself and for me not to sulk when he tells me that

CHRIS
a) For Candace not to badger me with texts and calls while I'm with my friends. On the other hand, I can send her 2-3 texts each night I'm out to tell her that everything's fine.
b) Plan a romantic getaway once a month (spontaneity/sharing moments)
c) Ask to paint and/or cook with her from time to time (show her that what she does interests me too)

6. CANDACE Ask one of my friends to go out with me when Chris is with his friends.

7. - Saturday: Chris is spending the evening at a friend's, and Candace is spending it with her friend Melanie.
- Sunday: romantic day in the country

· · · · · · · · ·
SENSE-DRIVEN EXPERIENCE
· · · · · · · · · ·

AWAY ← Actions Controlled by Hooks

Inner Obstacles/Hooks

Actions that Move Me toward Who or What Is Important → **TOWARD**

Who or What Is Important to Me

MENTAL EXPERIENCE
· · · · · · · · · ·
INNER EXPERIENCE
· · · · · · · · · ·

1. CANDACE
Thoughts: He doesn't love me as much as I love him. I don't matter to him.
Emotion: sadness
Thoughts: I'm worthless, I don't deserve to be loved. He doesn't want to spend more time with me because I'm not interesting.
Emotion: shame
Thoughts: He's cheating on me. He couldn't care less about me.
Emotion: anger

CHRIS
Thoughts: She doesn't respect the fact that my buddies are important to me. She's suffocating me.
Emotion: anger

2. CANDACE Tears in my eyes, lump in my throat, flushed face, feeling of suffocation in my chest

CHRIS Tension in all my muscles

4.
- Your relationship: love, sharing, interacting, humor, closeness, trust, spontaneity
- Other areas:

CANDACE Having self-respect, having pride in myself

CHRIS Friendship: being present with my friends, sharing, closeness

8.
- My body feels light

upper right of your matrix, because it allows you to move forward toward a life that has meaning for you?

So, for the hours and days ahead, watch what happens. If you aren't able to take the small step, don't worry. The simple act of having written it down in the matrix is already a way you're moving forward in that direction.

And if you did take the small step, great! In that case, observe the difference in your feelings.

PRACTICAL APPLICATION

It's your turn to work on a problem you're currently experiencing with another person. To do this, follow this guide.

Describe the interpersonal situation that is currently problematic for you (What would a camera filming this situation show us? What would a TV commentator describe?):

_____

Now, answer the following questions, and then transfer your answers into the matrix on p. 239 according to the numbers that correspond to each question:

1. Describe what this situation brings up for you. What thoughts? What emotions?

➤ ME _____

➤ THEM _____

2. When you're in touch with these thoughts and emotions, it's unpleasant. Where do you feel this in your body? How would you describe this sensation? *(It's important to describe it precisely so that when we experience this unpleasant sensation, we can recognize that we're reacting physically to these particular thoughts and emotions.)*

Get in touch with these feelings for a few moments.

➤ ME _____

➤ THEM _____

3. When you're in touch with these feelings, what does it make you want to do? If you completely latch onto what is written down in the lower left part of the matrix, what does it push you to do in the moment? *(These may be things you do or don't do [but that you strongly feel like doing in the moment].)*

> ME _____

> THEM _____

4. *Your relationship:* This situation is a difficult one because it concerns an important relationship: yours! It's painful because the relationship is really important to you. In your relationship, what is really important? If there weren't all the stuff that's written in the lower left part of your matrix, what would your relationship be like? How would you behave toward each other? What would your relationship embody?

Write these shared things in the spot indicated ("your relationship").

> ME _____

> THEM _____

Other areas: for each of you, does this problematic situation affect another life area that is important to you?

If YES, write down this area, and what is important to you in that. If this problematic situation weren't happening, how would you behave?

What would be really important to you?

> ME _____

> THEM _____

5. For each of you, can you identify:

(a) A change you would like the other person to make in this situation? A concession you would like the other person to make that would still take care of them and that would take care of what is important to them outside this relationship?

> ME _____

> THEM _____

(b) An action to move you toward your relationship? You've identified what is important in these actions in the lower right part of the matrix. An action to move you toward the relationship you really want?

> ME _____

> THEM _____

(c) A change you would be willing to make to take care of the problems or hooks the other person identified in the relationship but that will also take care of you and respect your boundaries?

OUR MATRIX

Fill in your matrix below with the answer that corresponds to each question number.

3. ME _____

_____

_____

_____

THEM _____

_____

_____

_____

5. ME _____

THEM _____

a)
b)
ME _____

a)
b)
THEM _____

6. ME _____

THEM _____

7.

SENSE-
DRIVEN
EXPERIENCE

Actions Controlled by Hooks

Actions that Move Me toward
Who or What Is Important

AWAY ◄──────────────────────────► **TOWARD**

Inner Obstacles/Hooks

Who or What Is Important to Me

1. ME
Thoughts: _____

Emotion: _____

Thoughts: _____

Emotion: _____

THEM
Thoughts: _____

Emotion: _____

Thoughts: _____

Emotion: _____

2. ME _____

THEM _____

MENTAL
EXPERIENCE

INNER
EXPERIENCE

4.
Your relationship:
Other areas:

ME _____

THEM _____

Self-Respect:

8.

 ME _____

 THEM _____

6. If the step is too big or too difficult to do as it is, what can you do to make it easier? What other life areas can you develop that take care of you and that in the bigger picture enable you to take the step that's important to you later on?

 ME _____

 THEM _____

7. In the hours and days to come, what might we see you each do specifically to move in this direction?

 ME _____

 THEM _____

Reread the right-hand side of your matrix.

8. What does that make you feel in your body? Where? How would you describe it?

 ME _____

 THEM _____

Does this make more sense than what is written on the left-hand side of the matrix?

If YES, would you agree to leaving a little room for inner obstacles (written in the lower left part of the matrix) should they arise for you, quit fighting them, and take the small step that you've identified in the upper right of your matrix, because it allows you to move forward toward a life that has meaning for you?

So, for the hours and days ahead, watch what happens. If you aren't able to take the small step, don't worry. The simple act of having written it down in the matrix is already a way you're moving forward in that direction.

And if you did take the small step, great! In that case, observe the difference in your feelings.

YOUR JOURNEY CONTINUES

Here we are at the end of this book and *at the beginning of your new life*. You have all the tools in your hands. You have all the knowledge you need to live the life you really want to live.

Remember, always keep in mind that it isn't what you know that determines your life, it's what you do. Just keep experimenting!

You can come back to this book at any time to guide you, like a travel companion.

We suggest that you complete the baseline test once again that assesses the intensity of borderline personality traits. You can retake this test at different times in your life if you want to evaluate your own progress. Self-assessment allows you to measure your progress in concrete terms. Applying the strategies offered in this book and objectively measuring your progress will encourage you to continue to implement the strategies over the long term.

PRACTICAL APPLICATION: SELF-ASSESSMENT _____

For each question, write down to what extent the statement corresponds to your usual way of operating—in other words: how much has the described behavior been present over the last few months? *(Rate yourself between 0 = not at all characteristic of me and 10 = completely characteristic of me.)*

1. Over these last few months, has the idea that a person who's very important to you might leave you often made you angry? Is fear of abandonment very present in your life?

| 0 | 1 | 2 | 3 | 4 | 5 | 6 | 7 | 8 | 9 | 10 |

2. Do your relationships with the people who are very important to you regularly have lots of ups and downs?

- Are you a person who is "too absolute," who quickly gives 100% of yourself in a relationship, who idealizes the other person, and then ultimately feels disappointed when that other person doesn't measure up to your expectations?

0	1	2	3	4	5	6	7	8	9	10

- Do you frequently tend to have intense relationships?

0	1	2	3	4	5	6	7	8	9	10

3. Over the last few months, have you, on several occasions, suddenly changed how you think of yourself? In other words, does the image you have of yourself often change radically? Are you different depending on who you're with so much so that sometimes you don't know who you really are?

0	1	2	3	4	5	6	7	8	9	10

- Over the last few months, have there been many sudden changes in your goals, career plans, religious beliefs, or lifestyle?

0	1	2	3	4	5	6	7	8	9	10

- Has what you love or what you believe varied a lot over time?

0	1	2	3	4	5	6	7	8	9	10

4. Over the last few months have you *often* done things impulsively? For example:
- buying things you can't afford
- having sex with people you barely know or having unprotected sex
- drinking too much or taking drugs
- driving recklessly
- eating uncontrollably
- making decisions on a whim that you regret afterward

0	1	2	3	4	5	6	7	8	9	10

5. Over the last few months, have you tried to harm yourself (cutting, burning, hitting the wall with your fists or head), or attempted or threatened to commit suicide?

0	1	2	3	4	5	6	7	8	9	10

6. Over the last few months, have you been very sensitive to everything happening around you, so much so that your emotions changed a lot in the same day and were more intense than those of most other people? Would you define yourself as "an emotional sponge"?

0	1	2	3	4	5	6	7	8	9	10

7. Over the last few months, have you often felt empty inside?

0	1	2	3	4	5	6	7	8	9	10

8. Over the last few months, have you been prone to anger? In other words, did even small things make you feel intense anger?

0	1	2	3	4	5	6	7	8	9	10

- Over the last few months, have you often had angry outbursts or been so angry that you lost control of yourself?

0	1	2	3	4	5	6	7	8	9	10

9. Over the last few months, when you've been very stressed, did you become suspicious of others ("people are mad at me" or "people want to hurt me"), or did you feel especially disconnected (the feeling of not being yourself anymore or like being in a daydream)?

0	1	2	3	4	5	6	7	8	9	10

“We wish you a safe journey, Living In the Full Experience.”
—DÉBORAH AND VÉRONIQUE

ACKNOWLEDGMENTS

To Prof. Philippe Courtet

We are honored to work with you. Thank you for enabling and facilitating the development of our specialized psychotherapeutic work. Thank you for allowing us to bring together continuous scientific research, innovation, and autonomy.

To Dr. Émilie Olié

Thank you for your intellectual curiosity and open-mindedness, which is a source of valuable exchange. We are very grateful for your unwavering support.

To our families and friends

Thank you for the wonderful relationships and shared moments.

To those with whom we've crossed paths in therapy

Thank you for our exchanges, all sources of enrichment. Thank you for the feedback on how your lives have changed, which is often impressive and inspiring. This is the deepest motivation for our work and our passion.

" Perhaps the only limits to the human mind are those we believe in. "

—WILLIS HARMAN

NOTES

Chapter 1. Which Direction Do You Want to Go?

1. R. Harris, *Passez à L'ACT: Pratique de la thérapie d'acceptation et d'engagement* (Brussels: De Boeck, 2012); S. C. Hayes, K. D. Strosahl, and K. G. Wilson, *Acceptance and Commitment Therapy: An Experiential Approach to Behavior Change* (New York: Guilford Press, 1999); B. Schoendorff, J. Grand, and M.-F. Bolduc, *La Thérapie d'acceptation et d'engagement: Guide clinique* (Brussels: De Boeck, 2011).

2. Harris, *Passez à L' ACT.*

Chapter 2. What Is Borderline Personality Disorder?

1. K. L. Polk and B. Schoendorff, *The Act Matrix: A New Approach to Building Psychological Flexibility across Settings and Populations* (Oakland, CA: New Harbinger, 2014). B. Schoendorff, J. Grand, and M.-F. Bolduc, *La Thérapie d'acceptation et d'engagement* (Brussels: De Boeck, 2012).

2. American Psychiatric Association, *Diagnostic and Statistical Manual of Mental Disorders*, 5th edition (*DSM-5*) (Arlington, VA: American Psychiatric Publishing, 2013).

3. S. C. Hayes, K. D. Strosahl, and K. G. Wilson, *Acceptance and Commitment Therapy: An Experiential Approach to Behavior Change* (New York: Guilford Press, 1999).

Chapter 4. The Three States of Mind

1. M. M. Linehan, *DBT Skills Training Manual* (New York: Guilford Press, 2017).

Chapter 11. Becoming Less Hypersensitive to Emotions

1. National Institutes of Health, *Your Guide to Healthy Sleep* (2011), https://www.nhlbi.nih.gov/files/docs/public/sleep/healthy_sleep.pdf.

2. Agence nationale de sécurité sanitaire de l'alimentation de l'environnement et du travail, *Programme national nutrition santé, 2011–2015* (http://inpes.sante-publiquefrance.fr/reperes_nutritionnels/pdf/pnns-2011-2015.pdf) World Health Organization, *Global Action Plan on Physical Activity, 2018–2030: More Active People for a Healthier World* (June 2018), https://www.who.int/publications/i/item/9789241514187.

3. World Health Organization, *The Global Strategy on Diet, Physical Activity and Health (DPAS)* (2016), https://www.who.int/nmh/wha/59/dpas/en/#:~:text=The%20 Global%20Strategy%20emphasizes%20the,and%20levels%20of%20physical%20 activity, D. Perlmutter, *Grain Brain: The Surprising Truth about Wheat, Carbs, and Sugar* (Boston: Little, Brown, 2013).

4. American Psychiatric Association, *Diagnostic and Statistical Manual of Mental Disorders*, 5th edition (*DSM-5*) (Arlington, VA: American Psychiatric Publishing, 2013).

5. S. Y. Lim, E. J. Lim, E. J. Kim, A. Kim, H. J. Lee, H. J. Choi, and S. J. Yang, "Nutritional factors affecting mental health," *Clinical Nutrition Research* 5 (2016): 143–152; Perlmutter, *Grain Brain*.

6. L. Kerti, A. V. Witte, A. Winkler, U. Grittner, D. Rujescu, and A. Floel, "Higher glucose levels associated with lower memory and reduced hippocampal microstructure," *Neurology* 81 (2013): 1746–52.

7. R. O. Roberts, L. A. Roberts, Y. E. Geda, R. H. Cha, V. S. Pankratz, H. M. O'Connor, D. S. Knopman, and R. C. Petersen, "Relative intake of macronutrients impacts risk of mild cognitive impairment or dementia," *Journal of Alzheimer's Disease* 32 (2012): 329–39; S. Wu, Y. Ding, F. Wu, G. Xie, J. Hou, and P. Mao, "Serum lipid levels and suicidality: A meta-analysis of 65 epidemiological studies," *Journal of Psychiatry & Neuroscience* 41 (2016): 56–69.

8. J. R. Hibbeln, T. A. Ferguson, and T. L. Blasbalg, "Omega-3 fatty acid deficiencies in neurodevelopment, aggression and autonomic dysregulation: Opportunities for intervention," *International Review of Psychiatry* 18 (2006): 107–18; M. Lavialle, I. Denis, P. Guesnet, and S. Vancassel, "Involvement of omega-3 fatty acids in emotional responses and hyperactive symptoms," *Journal of Nutritional Biochemistry* 21 (2010): 899–905.

9. F. Ng, M. Berk, O. Dean, and A. I. Bush, "Oxidative stress in psychiatric disorders: Evidence base and therapeutic implications," *International Journal of Neuropsychopharmacology* 11 (2008): 851–76.

10. M. Hadjivassiliou, D. S. Sanders, R. A. Grunewald, N. Woodroofe, S. Boscolo, and D. Aeschlimann, "Gluten sensitivity: From gut to brain," *Lancet Neurology* 9 (2010): 318–30.

11. F. Bourgognon, *La Méditation en 10 questions* (Paris: La Réponse du psy, 2015); B. K. Holzel, S. W. Lazar, T. Gard, Z. Schuman-Olivier, D. R. Vago, and U. Ott, "How does mindfulness meditation work? Proposing mechanisms of action from a conceptual and neural perspective," *Perspectives on Psychological Science* 6 (2011): 537–59; Ng, Berk, Dean, and Bush, "Oxidative stress in psychiatric disorders."

12. G. R. Fox, J. Kaplan, H. Damasio, and A. Damasio, "Neural correlates of gratitude," *Frontiers in Psychology* 6 (2015): 1491; Y. J. Wong, J. Owen, N. T. Gabana, J. W. Brown, S. McInnis, P. Toth, and L. Gilman, "Does gratitude writing improve the mental health of psychotherapy clients? Evidence from a randomized controlled trial," *Psychotherapy Research* (2016): 1–11; A. M. Wood, J. J. Froh, and A. W. Geraghty,

"Gratitude and well-being: A review and theoretical integration," *Clinical Psychology Review* 30 (2010): 890–905.

Chapter 14. What Is Dissociation?

1. E. M. Bernstein, and F. W. Putnam, "Development, reliability, and validity of a dissociation scale," *Journal of Nervous and Mental Disease* 174 (1986): 727–35.

2. S. Boon, K. Steele, and O. Van der Hart, *Coping with Trauma-Related Dissociation* (New York: W. W. Norton & Company, 2011); M. Kedia, J. Vanderlinden, G. Lopez, I. Saillot, and D. Brown, *Dissociation et mémoire traumatique. Psychothérapies* (Paris: Dunod, 2012).

Chapter 18. Shame and Interpersonal Effectiveness

1. M. Crowe, "Never good enough, part 1: Shame or borderline personality disorder?" *Journal of Psychiatric and Mental Health Nursing* 11 (2004): 327–34; K. L. Gratz, M. Z. Rosenthal, M. T. Tull, C. W. Lejuez, and J. G. Gunderson, "An experimental investigation of emotional reactivity and delayed emotional recovery in borderline personality disorder: The role of shame," *Comprehensive Psychiatry* 51 (2010): 275–85; N. Rusch, K. Lieb, I. Gottler, C. Hermann, E. Schramm, H. Richter, G. A. Jacob, P. W. Corrigan, and M. Bohus, "Shame and implicit self-concept in women with borderline personality disorder," *American Journal of Psychiatry* 164 (2007): 500–508.

2. D. Winter, K. Koplin, and S. Lis, "Can't stand the look in the mirror? Self-awareness avoidance in borderline personality disorder," *Borderline Personality Disorder and Emotion Dysregulation* 2 (2015): 13.

3. Crowe, "Never good enough"; Gratz, Rosenthal, Tull, Lejuez, and Gunderson, "An experimental investigation of emotional reactivity and delayed emotional recovery."

4. Gratz, Rosenthal, Tull, Lejuez, and Gunderson, "An experimental investigation of emotional reactivity and delayed emotional recovery"; C. N. Scheel, C. Bender, B. Tuschen-Caffier, A. Brodfuhrer, S. Matthies, C. Hermann, E. K. Geisse, J. Svaldi, E. L. Brakemeier, A. Philipsen, and G. A. Jacob, "Do patients with different mental disorders show specific aspects of shame?" *Psychiatry Research* 220 (2014): 490–95.

5. Scheel et al., "Do patients with different mental disorders show specific aspects of shame?"

6. Scheel et al., "Do patients with different mental disorders show specific aspects of shame?"

7. S. E. Bachtelle, and C. M. Pepper, "The physical results of nonsuicidal self-injury: The meaning behind the scars," *Journal of Nervous and Mental Disease* 203 (2015): 927–33; M. Z. Brown, M. M. Linehan, K. A. Comtois, A. Murray, and A. L. Chapman, "Shame as a prospective predictor of self-inflicted injury in borderline personality disorder: A multi-modal analysis," *Behaviour Research and Therapy* 47 (2009): 815–22; L. N. Scott, S. D. Stepp, M. N. Hallquist, D. J. Whalen, A. G. Wright, and P. A.

Pilkonis, "Daily shame and hostile irritability in adolescent girls with borderline personality disorder symptoms," *Personality Disorders* 6 (2015): 53–63; M. Wiklander, M. Samuelsson, J. Jokinen, A. Nilsonne, A. Wilczek, G. Rylander, and M. Asberg, "Shame-proneness in attempted suicide patients," *BMC Psychiatry* 12 (2012): 50.

8. Crowe, "Never good enough."

9. Gratz, Rosenthal, Tull, Lejuez, and Gunderson, "An experimental investigation of emotional reactivity."

Chapter 19. Interpersonal Effectiveness Skills

1. M. M. Linehan, *DBT Skills Training Manual* (New York: Guilford Press, 2017).

Chapter 20. Acting Effectively in Difficult Interpersonal Situations

1. M. M. Linehan, *DBT Skills Training Manual* (New York: Guilford Press, 2017), 233.

2. Linehan, *DBT Skills Training Manual*, 233

3. Linehan, *DBT Skills Training Manual*, 233.

Chapter 22. Developing High-Quality Relationships

1. G. Chapman, *The Five Love Languages* (Chicago: Moody Press, 2015).

2. M. B. Rosenberg, *Les Mots sont des fenêtres (ou bien ce sont des murs)* (Paris: Hors Collection, 2004).

3. R. Harris, *Le Choc de la réalité* (Québec: Éditions de l'Homme, 2014).

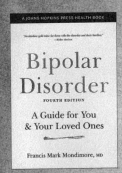   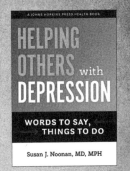